The Louisiana Iris

The Taming of a
Native American Wildflower

Second Edition

The Society for Louisiana Irises

CONTRIBUTING EDITORS
Marie Caillet
J. Farron Campbell
Kevin C. Vaughn
Dennis Vercher

TIMBER PRESS
Portland, Oregon

Material in this volume has been revised, updated, and expanded from *The Louisiana Iris: The History and Culture of Five Native American Species and their Hybrids*, edited by Marie Caillet and Joseph K. Mertzweiller and published in 1988 by Texas Gardener Press of Waco, Texas, and the Society for Louisiana Irises.

Published in 2000 by
Timber Press, Inc.
The Haseltine Building
133 S.W. Second Avenue, Suite 450
Portland, Oregon 97204, U.S.A

ISBN 0-88192-477-6

Printed in Hong Kong

Library of Congress Cataloging-in-Publication Data

The Louisiana iris ; the taming of a native American wildflower / the Society for Louisiana Irises ; contributing editors, Marie Caillet . . . [et al.].—2nd ed.
    p.   cm.
  Includes bibliographical references (p.   ).
  ISBN 0-88192-477-6
  1. Louisiana irises. I. Caillet, Marie. II. Society for Louisiana Irises.

SB413.I8 L68 2000
635.9′3438—dc21
                                      99-057037

To JOSEPH K. MERTZWEILLER, co-editor and main author of the first edition of *The Louisiana Iris* published in 1988. As chairman of the Society for Louisiana Irises Publications Committee, he was responsible for six *Special Publications* produced by the Society for Louisiana Irises. He contributed numerous articles to the *American Iris Society Bulletin*, to national magazines and to the *Quarterly Newsletter of the Society for Louisiana Irises*. He was the first hybridizer to produce tetraploid Louisiana irises and was just beginning to produce interploids and to work with interspecies.

Contributing Editors
(Society for Louisiana Irises Publications Committee)

Marie Caillet   Kevin Vaughn
J. Farron Campbell   Dennis Vercher

Other Contributors

Richard A. Goula   Joseph K. Mertzweiller
Pat Norvell

Paintings and Drawings

Marie Caillet   Georgene Wood

Photographs

Marie Caillet   Charles Mann
J. Farron Campbell   Joseph K. Mertzweiller
Perry Dyer   Pat Norvell
Paul W. Gossett   Earl Olsted
Graeme Grosvenor   Heather Pryor
Ben Hager   Doris Simpson
Carolyn Hawkins   Kevin Vaughn

Contents

Color plates follow page 144

Acknowledgments

Revising, updating, and most writing of this book, including the initial editing and preparing for publishing, have been done by the Society for Louisiana Irises Publication Committee. However, we are indebted to the original contributors to *The Louisiana Iris: The History and Culture of Five Native American Species and their Hybrids* published in 1988. We wish to acknowledge the late Joseph K. Mertzweiller, whose fine writing formed the basis for much of this revised edition, and the other original contributors: Charles W. Arny Jr., Robert L. Bledsoe, Marie Caillet, Mary Dunn, Charles Fritchie Jr., Richard A. Goula, Graeme Grosvenor, Akira Horinaka, Richard L. Johnson, Barbara Nelson, Louise Nichols, Helen Reid, Dorothy M. Riddler, Henry C. Rowlan, Eberhard Schuster, Doris Simpson, Richard Sloan, Kirk Strawn, and Melody Wilhoit. Our thanks to the staff of Texas Gardener Press and its editor, Chris Corby, who helped make the first edition possible and handled the sales for two printings of the book.

We wish to recognize several people besides those on the Publication Committee who have contributed to the preparation of this book. Our thanks to Richard A. Goula for the update and revision of his original chapter on the history of Louisiana irises and the Society for Louisiana Irises. Our thanks to Carolyn Hawkins and Pat Norvell for their photographs and contributions to the chapter on flower arranging. Our thanks to Georgene Wood, for her watercolors and line drawings, and to the photographers who furnished illustrations, especially Graeme Grosvenor and Heather Pryor of New South Wales, Australia, and Charles Mann of New Mexico. And our thanks to J. Farron Campbell and Dennis Vercher for their skill in preparing the manuscript on computer.

Through a questionnaire we were able to collect up-to-date information on culture of Louisiana irises throughout the United States and several foreign countries. We wish to thank those who responded: Oleg A. Amekhin of the Ukraine, Dr. T. J. Betts of Western Australia, Heather and Bernard Pryor of New South Wales, Pat Brooks of South Carolina, William F. Caldwell of Texas, Jill Copeland of Michigan, Doug Davis of California, Albert Detwiler of Arizona, Eugenio Barcelona of the Philippines, Ada Godfrey of Massachusetts, Paul Gossett of Oklahoma, J. D. Hill of Arkansas, Gordon and Jan Hueller of Arizona, Bob Kendall of Connecticut, Marcia Kilpatrick of Connecticut, Everette Lineberger of South Carolina, Walter Moores of Mississippi, Richard Morgan of Arkansas, Samuel N. Norris of Kentucky, Shirley Paquet of South Carolina, Mark Schexnayder of Louisiana, Mrs. Wayne C. Smith Jr. of South Carolina, David and Barbara Schmieder of Massachusetts, Shirlann Strickland of Florida, J. Shumake of South Carolina, Kevin Vaughn of Mississippi, Brian A. Wendel of Indiana, Larry Westfall of Pennsylvania, Jerry and Melody Wilhoit of Illinois, Marlene Wolinski of Minnesota, and C. Earnest Yearwood of Georgia.

And finally, our thanks to Timber Press for their decision to publish this new edition of *The Louisiana Iris* and to Neal Maillet, executive editor, for all his help in making this possible.

Introduction

This book, prepared by members of the Society for Louisiana Irises, is a revised edition of the first complete reference devoted exclusively to Louisiana irises, published in 1988. Much of the original book, written by twenty-one members and edited by Marie Caillet and Joseph K. Mertzweiller, has been retained. The revisions and additions that produced this new edition are intended to tell the Louisiana iris story from its earliest beginning to 1999. Illustrations show the progress these native American irises have made from the species found in their natural habitats to the current hybrids found on the market.

The genus *Iris* is very large and contains more than 200 species in four subgenera and several sections and subsections. The beardless irises, which comprise the subsection *Apogon*, number fifteen series and more than sixty species. One of these series, the *Hexagonae*, includes the five species given the common designation Louisiana irises. Thus, this book is devoted to a very small part of the genus *Iris*. Limited references are made to some species of the series *Laevigatae* because of similarity to the *Hexagonae* and the tendency to mistake them for the *Hexagonae*.

Natural distribution of the *Hexagonae* is greatest in the warm and wet habitat of south and southwest Louisiana. Some species are distributed up the Mississippi Valley and in the southeastern United States. All are native only to the United States. Natural phenomena and growth of these irises, undisturbed for centuries or longer, led to the most extensive population of natural hybrids in the genus *Iris* anywhere in the world. This treasure in horticulture remained virtually unknown until the 1920s when Dr. John K. Small, curator of the New York Botanical Garden, recognized the situation for its true significance. Small provided the incentives and publicity to raise awareness of Louisiana irises on a grand scale.

Possibly due to the fact that the bearded irises are not well adapted to the warm and humid Deep South, the beardless Louisianas made the transition from practically unknown swamp wildflowers to esteemed garden plants in less than four decades. Oddly enough, Small was among very few horticultural professionals associated with these activities. Practically everything was done by amateur gardeners and iris enthusiasts. Beginning in the 1930s, scores of collectors took to the swamps and collected many thousands of species and natural hybrids. Collecting gradually gave way to controlled hybridizing in the 1950s, and the early hybridizing gave way to more advanced and scientific hybridizing in the 1970s. With the first modern hybrids appearing around 1975, the quality of hybrid cultivars has improved accordingly. The transition from diploids, cells with the usual two sets of chromosomes, to tetraploids, cells with four sets of chromosomes, has only recently been achieved, and the Louisiana irises remain decades behind the bearded irises in more advanced developments.

The main objective of this book is to interest people all over the world in growing Louisiana irises and participating in the many activities of the Society for Louisiana Irises and the American Iris Society. These organizations are the primary sources of information, communication, and knowledge about Louisiana irises. To promote this objective, we have emphasized the how-to aspects of adaptability, propagation, culture, and hybridizing. Adaptability of the series *Hexagonae* continues to expand and is far greater than thought even as late as 1980. The limits are unknown and can only be defined by the cooperation of gardening interests. Louisiana irises will grow with moderate to excellent results in most of the United States and in many foreign countries.

Chapter 10, on the culture of Louisiana irises, has been drawn from the fifteen culture articles of the original edition and from questionnaires answered by thirty growers from throughout the continental United States, Hawaii, Australia, Canada, England, Ukraine, and other countries. The wild populations of Louisiana irises are rapidly disappearing, or have died out entirely, in most of what was once their native range. Thus, it is up to private and public gardens to preserve these irises for the future.

We have made every effort to document and distinguish the achievements of the early collectors and hybridizers. They are responsible for the wealth available to us. In view of the shortcomings of early documentation and communication, we have recognized the main contributors to the body of Louisiana irises, but many contributions have been lost and go unrecognized.

CHAPTER 1

History of Louisiana Irises

Louisiana irises comprise a unique group in the iris family. Among all irises Louisianas are perhaps the most distinctive in color and in form. They exhibit an incredibly broad color range and were significant in providing the color red to the iris spectrum. Louisiana irises exhibit an equally wide range of forms, which when combined with the color range, provides specimens of great horticultural interest and variation.

Louisiana irises belong to the subsection *Apogon*, meaning "without beard" or "beardless," of the series *Hexagonae* of the genus *Iris* in the family Iridaceae. They consist of five species most of which are indigenous to a limited area of south-central Louisiana and the Gulf Coast marsh areas from Texas to Florida. Two species, *Iris brevicaulis* and *I. fulva*, extend the range northward up the Mississippi Valley, and *Iris hexagona* inhabits the southeastern states along the Atlantic and Gulf Coasts. By far the greatest concentration is in the State of Louisiana, hence the name Louisiana irises.

The genus *Iris* consists of about 200 species, about half of which are well known today in private and public gardens and contribute to horticultural and hobby interests. The American Iris Society is dedicated to all iris interests and has a national membership of nearly 8000. The Society for Louisiana Irises is the primary organization dedicated solely to the interests of Louisiana irises. By judicious choice of the many species in the genus *Iris* it is possible, in temperate areas, to have garden color from blooming irises for almost twelve months of the year.

The Iridaceae are found growing native in most temperate countries. Although the genus *Iris* is not found natively in the Southern Hemisphere, many Iridaceae do occur in southern Africa. Most genera are hardy flowering plants having perennial rootstocks or bulbs.

The structure of the iris flower differs from most other types. The three outer perianth segments tend to hang downward to some extent and are commonly referred to as falls, while the three inner segments generally stand erect or semi-erect and are known as standards. This condition is modified and somewhat less obvious in some Louisiana iris species, and has been rendered even less apparent through selective hybridization. What is perhaps most apparent is the incredible diversity and beauty of color and form available for landscape and gardening applications.

The Iris Throughout History

Since the dawn of recorded civilization the iris has been a horticultural thread painstakingly woven into the fabric of history. The iris has been the flower of kings, princes, and priests; it has been a symbol of organized religion and of heraldry; it has been used in magic and in the practice of medicine.

Orris root (*Iris germanica*) has been used medicinally for centuries; the peeled rhizome was commonly used as a diuretic and an expectorant. It has also been used in the liquor industry. Indeed, the multiplicity of ailments for which iris preparations were prescribed is truly astonishing. Common among these prescriptions were the removal of freckles, the cure of ulcers, the inducement of sleep, the production of tears, and general gynecological applications. The iris is Gerard's "Floure-de-luce" (fleur-de-lis), which in "two daies at the most take away the blackness or blewness of any bruise."

The earliest extant picture of an iris appears in the *Vienna Codex Dioscorides* which was transcribed and illustrated at the beginning of the sixteenth century AD. In 1576 Carolus Clusius published the first work revealing an intimate knowledge of irises as flowering plants. Louisiana irises were understandably not represented. The first edition of Linnaeus's *Species Plantarum*, published in 1753, described about twenty-four iris species and shows clearly that Louisiana irises were still unknown in Europe. It was not until 1788 that Thomas Walter first described *Iris hexagona* from the southeast coast of the United States. Thus, *I. hexagona* was the first species described of that group of native North American irises which were later to come under the designation of "Louisiana irises." William Rickatson Dykes, the great British naturalist and horticulturist of the early twentieth century, lists three species of Louisiana irises in his epic monograph *The Genus Iris*: *I. fulva*, *I. brevicaulis* (*foliosa*), and *I. hexagona*.

Discovery of Louisiana Irises

So far as is possible to determine, John James Audubon was the first to use the term "Louisiana iris" in referring to this group of swamp dwellers. Audubon painted an iris as part of the background for the parula warbler and, in the text, referred to it as a Louisiana flag. And the October 1812 publication of *Curtis's Botanical Magazine* was among the first to feature a likeness of a Louisiana iris, depicting *Iris fulva* in a beautiful, hand-colored copper plate etching.

But this does not adequately address the issue—when were Louisiana irises discovered? It seems plausible that many a Native American Indian or wandering European explorer would doubtless have stumbled across these beauties and regarded the amazing display of color with awe and admiration. It seems a bit strange that more of these "discoveries" were not reported or documented in some way. Surely in an area noted for its connection with mystical and occult, colorful voodoo rituals, set in the swamp locale, these equally colorful horticultural symbols would have become an integral part of these ceremonies. However, no such evidence is reliably documented. Additional speculation regarding the discovery of Louisiana irises is pointless, but it is important to chronicle significant botanical discoveries, particularly those accompanied by valid descriptions and serious publicity.

Shortly after Walter first described *Iris hexagona* in 1788, *I. fulva* and *I. brevicaulis* were described. John Bellenden Ker-Gawler in 1812 described *I. fulva*, so important for introducing the color red to the genus *Iris*. It was originally recorded as limited to the vicinity of New Orleans, but today, *I. fulva* is known to have a much broader range. Constantine Samuel Rafinesque-Schmaltz described *I. brevicaulis* in 1817 but originally named it *I. foliosa*. It is the most cold hardy and the latest blooming of the species. *Iris giganticaerulea* is the giant blue of the coastal marshes, and perhaps the most spectacular and prolific of all the species. It was not described until 1929, however, by Dr. John K. Small. The final species remained for L. F. Randolph to describe in 1966: *I. nelsonii*. This species had attracted national horticultural attention in the late 1930s and was well known as the "Abbeville reds," "Abbeville yellows," or "Super fulvas."

Equally significant, if not more so, than discovery of the botanical species was their transplantation and adaptation into gardens, plant collections, and landscapes. In only a few decades the swamp wildflowers were transformed into cultivated garden plants. Only by growing and displaying Louisiana irises in public and private gardens was it possible to generate the kind of interest and enthusiasm these irises currently enjoy. Louisiana irises benefited from many early collectors, growers, and ambassadors, particularly in the vicinity of New Orleans. Near New Orleans the irises grew in such profusion, in such close proximity to established civilization, and in so complete a color representation that they were impossible to ignore.

Among the more prominent collectors and growers from the New Orleans area in the early 1900s were Mary Nelson and her sister Ethel Hutson. These two ladies spent a lifetime collecting and growing Louisiana irises, evidenced in the words of Nelson: "As a child I used to go on my uncle's back looking for irises, and was never ready to go home until I found a yellow one. . . . until very recent years we gathered many shades of blue ones from the dump near Broad Street and the new basin canal, but Old Bayou Savage which runs along Gentilly Highway was our favorite place, for all the colors grew there." It is difficult for those of us who are familiar with present-day New Orleans to visualize such an abundance and variety of Louisiana irises growing and blooming near the heart of the city.

Ellsworth Woodward, the first professor of art at Newcomb College in New Orleans, may be credited with bringing these irises to the attention of many during the same period in the early 1900s. Woodward, who was highly enthusiastic about the artistic value of Louisiana irises, sketched and painted them with his students in a field on Frenchmen Street. Many of Woodward's iris paintings now hang in the Delgado Museum in New Orleans and in private collections. His contagious enthusiasm for Louisiana irises was spread by his students, notably Beverly Randolph Stevens who is credited with encouraging Mary Swords DeBaillon. DeBaillon eventually amassed the largest and most varied collection of Louisiana irises in existence.

Other early collectors in the area included George Thomas, superintendent of parks for New Orleans, who discovered the first yellow *Iris fulva*. Mr. and Mrs. Clifford Lyons were avid and discerning collectors and possessed a collection among the finest of the time. O. F. R. Bruce, also an avid collector, had the good fortune to discover the first true bicolor, known as 'Bruce's Bicolor' though it was never officially named.

Perhaps more significant than their own contributions was the contagious enthusiasm that these pioneers inspired in other interested individuals from diverse areas. Notable among these individuals were Mary Swords DeBaillon of Lafayette, Caroline Dormon of Saline, Percy Viosca of New Orleans, Ira S. Nelson of Lafayette, W. B. MacMillan of Abbeville, and perhaps most importantly, John K. Small of New York. These and many others were ultimately responsible for guiding the development of Louisiana irises to their present level of horticultural recognition.

Historical Contributions of John K. Small

While it was noteworthy that Louisiana irises had existed for centuries or longer and had been collected and nurtured in a few gardens, it was not until John K. Small publicized them botanically that they became widely known.

Small's enthusiasm and untiring dedication are unparalleled in the annals of Louisiana iris history and development. Those who work with and appreciate Louisiana irises owe a great debt to Small, for he liberated Louisiana irises from the depths of the swamps and literally introduced them to the world.

John Kunkel Small, curator of the New York Botanical Garden, first saw Louisiana irises from the windows of a train traveling through south Louisiana. He was so impressed by their beauty and great diversity of color that he made many trips back to south Louisiana in the mid- to late 1920s and early 1930s collecting, identifying, photographing, and describing some seventy-seven species. Many of these he himself suspected would turn out to be species variants or natural hybrids, once sufficient study and taxonomic evaluation had been completed. It was Small who termed Louisiana the "Iris Center of the Universe." During his many and varied collecting trips to south Louisiana and the broader area covered by those trips, strangely enough, he never encountered the "big reds and yellows" of the Abbeville area, the *Iris nelsonii* that has been so prominent in the development of many outstanding hybrids.

Accompanying Small on many of his field trips into the swamps was Randolph Bazet of Houma, Louisiana, an amateur botanist and avid collector of Louisiana irises. Bazet has documented a number of amusing stories concerning these collecting trips, some involving Thomas Edison, a close personal friend of Small. These stories are documented in past publications of the Society for Louisiana Irises.

Although *Iris giganticaerulea* is the only species named by Small to have withstood the test of time, his efforts cannot be overestimated. Perhaps more significant than his naming and describing species was the publication of their descriptions, along with color plates, in the prestigious botanical publication *Addisonia*, a regular publication of the New York Botanical Garden. The publicity given in *Addisonia*, together with material by Small in other publications, brought Louisiana irises to the forefront of the horticultural community, a position they have maintained through the ensuing years.

Following Small, Percy Viosca, a south Louisiana herpetologist and taxonomist, spent a great deal of time studying Louisiana irises from the standpoints of type, location, and ecological requirements. In view of the narrow limits of distribution of some of the species, Viosca came to the conclusion that there were only four species including *Iris virginica*, but excluding *I. nelsonii* which was yet to be named. *Iris virginica* is not considered a species of the *Hexagonae* today, although it has been successfully used in hybrid development involving tetraploid Louisiana irises.

Founding of the Society for Louisiana Irises

Prior to Small's first expedition to Louisiana to study the irises, plant enthusiasts of the area, such as Mary Swords DeBaillon, had done limited collecting of "les glais de marais" (the gladiolii of the marsh), as Louisiana irises were then known to the trappers and fishermen who traversed the swamps in pursuit of their livelihood. With the impetus of the publicity provided by Small, collecting in the wild increased enormously in the 1930s. The time had arrived for the organization of these efforts.

By 1941, Ira S. Nelson had become established as professor of horticulture at Southwestern Louisiana Institute (now the University of Louisiana, Lafayette). During the course of his many horticultural forays into south Louisiana, "Ike" Nelson met W. B. MacMillan of Abbeville who shared his information and enthusiasm for Louisiana irises. "Mr. Mac" had been collecting for years and in 1939 had discovered the remarkable Abbeville irises of *Iris nelsonii*. Nelson convinced MacMillan of the need for organization and the dissemination of information about these irises, and in the spring of 1941 approximately twenty iris collectors met and founded the Mary Swords DeBaillon Iris Society, named to honor a leading collector and grower from 1920 to 1940. Among the founding members were Caroline Dormon, to whom DeBaillon later willed her extensive collection, and other such botanical luminaries as Percy Viosca, Clair Brown, Joe and Jackie Richard, Mrs. Rufus McIlhenny, George Arceneaux, Eddie Arceneaux, Randolph Bazet, Lillian Trichel, Minnie Colquitt, Marie Caillet, and Katherine L. and Ray Cornay. The objectives first outlined for this new society are still valid today for the Society for Louisiana Irises (see Appendix A).

MacMillan was elected first president of the fledgling organization, with Joe G. Richard as vice president and Nelson as the first secretary-treasurer. Within a few years membership had skyrocketed to more than 200. In 1942 the society staged its first show for members, and in 1943 it invited the public to view the show. The policy of opening the show to the public has continued each year since. Under Nelson's management, many spectacular shows were presented, generating a tremendous amount of interest in and public awareness of Louisiana irises.

In the years since that first meeting of what is now the Society for Louisiana Irises, the organization, with the aid of a large number of talented and diverse volunteers, has done much toward achieving the goals of its founding members. The society and its members have published countless articles in various journals and magazines. The society began producing bulletins of interest to members in the very first year, evolving into a quarterly newsletter devoted to the culture and development of Louisiana irises in addition to news about the organization and its members. The year 1951 saw the beginning of annual yearbooks, organizational handbooks, bibliographies, and registration checklists. *Special Publications* financed by a separate fund were begun in 1966 and were the society's first use of full-color photographic reproductions. *Special Publications* are bulletins on new developments in Louisiana irises with pictures of the newer introductions. *The Louisiana Iris: The History and Culture of Five Native American Species and their Hybrids* published in 1988 by the society was its most ambitious project until this second edition. The book was the first published in the United States devoted to one type of iris, and it spurred other specialty iris groups to follow suit with books of their own.

In 1978 the Society for Louisiana Irises was aided greatly by the organization of the Louisiana Iris Society of America (LISA) which was a section of the American Iris Society. In 1993, in an effort to provide focus and eliminate confusion and duplication, LISA was dissolved and the Society for Louisiana Irises became a cooperating society of the American Iris Society, completely devoted to the cause of Louisiana irises. Under the dynamic leadership and guidance of their respective leaders, these organizations have succeeded in creating enthusiasm for their goals and objectives as well as strong relationships among growers and hybridizers. The benefits provided by the various organizations are not limited to the United States, but apply to such diverse areas of the world as Australia, New Zealand, South Africa, and Europe.

Modern Hybrid Development

The great milestones that contributed most to the development and popularity of Louisiana irises were the activities and publications of John K. Small; the collecting activities which his work stimulated, particularly W. B. MacMillan's discovery of the Abbeville irises; and the founding of the Society for Louisiana Irises. The stage was now set for an intensive effort of controlled hybridizing.

Long before the discovery of *Iris nelsonii* in 1939, some hybridizing had been done by William Rickatson Dykes of Great Britain, whose 'Fulvala' (1910 and 'Fulvala Violacea' (1910) were seedlings from *I. fulva* × *I. brevicaulis*. E. B. Williamson, also of Great Britain, produced 'Dorothea K. Williamson' from the same parents and registered it with the British Iris Society in 1918. This iris has an interesting history of use in hybridizing (see the beginning of Chapter 6) and is still used today. Undoubtedly a direct result of Small's work, J. C. Nicholls Jr. of Camillus, New York, collected, hybridized, and registered twenty-six Louisiana irises with the American Iris Society in the 1930s. His 1933 catalogue *The Royal Iris Gardens* introduced twenty-two Louisiana irises, most collected. During about the same period Percy Viosca of New

Orleans registered fourteen and Thomas Washington of Nashville registered fifty-three. In the 1930s and 1940s Eric Nies and C. S. Milliken of California also were involved in hybridizing with the species *I. fulva* and *I. hexagona*. Unfortunately, none of these irises can be linked directly to today's modern hybrids.

Growers and collectors living in Louisiana in the early to mid-1940s were interested in hybridizing, but for the most part they had little or no scientific background or curiosity. They were merely looking for pretty new colors and further improvements, but this group had a far-reaching effect in revolutionizing the development of Louisiana irises. The experiments of these early amateurs were the first great step forward in hybridizing.

Once W. B. MacMillan discovered *Iris nelsonii*, he developed a number of important hybrids involving this species. He produced the immensely popular 'Black Widow' which is still very much grown and sought after. His most notable efforts involve bolder and brighter colors, varied color patterns, bigger flowers and more varied forms. These characteristics are the legacy of *I. nelsonii*. Two of MacMillan's hybrids, 'Harland K. Riley' and 'Margaret Hunter', attract as much attention today as any modern hybrid, and both cultivars remain in widespread commercial circulation.

Caroline Dormon was an outstanding early hybridizer as well as an accomplished naturalist, writer, and artist. She inherited the vast Louisiana iris collection of Mary Swords DeBaillon, who was primarily a collector and grower and not a hybridizer. Through the efforts of Dormon, many DeBaillon irises realized their potential in hybridizing. Many of Dormon's irises can be seen today at the magnificent wildlife refuge and botanical preserve, Briarwood, in Saline, Louisiana, her hometown. She is probably best remembered for her breakthrough cultivar 'Wheelhorse' and for others equally popular, such as 'The Khan', 'Saucy Minx', and 'Violet Ray'.

Professor Ira S. Nelson, known for his leadership in forming the Society for Louisiana Irises, accomplished most of his collecting, hybridizing, and other scientific work during the 1940s and 1950s. Nelson registered a number of irises, most notably 'King's Gold' and 'Cherry Bounce', and provided great inspiration through his teaching.

Other collectors, growers, and hybridizers of this period from Louisiana were George Arceneaux of Houma; Eddie Arceneaux and Ray and Katherine Cornay of Lafayette; Edmond Riggs of St. Martinville; Hamilton Robertson and Blyth Rand of Alexandria; Mrs. J. C. Roberts of Baton Rouge; Cammie Henry of Nachitoches; and a large group from the Shreveport area, including Ruth Dormon, Sally Smith, Lenora Mathews, Hattie Clark, Claire Gorton, Minnie Colquitt, Lillian Trichel, Ruth Shehee, and William Fitzhugh. Growers and collectors from neighboring Texas also contributed to the effort, including Ila and Stayton Nunn, Dean Lee, F. A. C. McCulla, and Laurel Bridgman, all from the Houston area.

Claude Davis of Baton Rouge, a Louisiana pioneer in hybridizing, was devoted to development of better blues and also to the development of highly vigorous varieties which would perform in any garden. Davis is still represented by varieties such as 'Blue Shield', 'New Offering', and 'Flat Top'.

Sidney Conger of Arcadia, Louisiana, specialized in new and better red varieties and pioneered in the development of the flaring, overlapping form which has become so popular. Some of Conger's irises still grown today are 'Acadian', 'Captain Bill', 'Royal Velour', 'Dr. Dormon', and 'Marie Caillet'.

Marvin Granger of Lake Charles, Louisiana, began hybridizing in the 1940s and remains active in it. Much of Granger's work involves the production of double Louisiana irises in striking colors. This work is based on the semi-double 'Creole Can-Can', an *Iris giganticaerulea* variant, which Granger collected in the marshes. Granger's work with doubles is a fine example of what hybridizers can do with a closely defined objective.

The Lake Charles area was also home to two other hybridizers and collectors of note during this early period, G. W. Holleyman and Bill Levingston. Holleyman produced many outstanding hybrids. The best known is 'G. W. Holleyman', the first large yellow, having what is considered the modern form of wide, overlapping petals. Other notable Holleyman irises include 'Queen O' Queens' and 'King Calcasieu'. Levingston was noted for collecting and introducing white variants of *I. giganticaerulea*, principally 'Her Highness'.

The name Frank Chowning of Little Rock, Arkansas, is legend among hybridizers of Louisiana irises. His hybridizing spans more than four decades. Only with his passing in 1981 at the age of 87 did his production of Louisiana iris hybrids end. His 'Dixie Deb' (1950) is an all-time garden favorite and still captures awards in today's shows. Chowning's early efforts involved *Iris hexagona*, *I. fulva*, and *I. brevicaulis* and were directed to the development of irises that were more cold hardy in less temperate regions than their native habitat. He was eminently successful and produced many beautiful, serviceable garden irises still grown today. Many good blue irises emerged from these efforts, such as 'Little Rock Skies', but among the most distinctive was the copper-colored 'Gold Reserve', with a purple picotee edge. 'Little Miss Leighley', an offspring of 'Gold Reserve', is noteworthy for its intense freesia fragrance. Chowning's 'Ann Chowning' (1977), a stunning red iris, is a more recent contribution and first winner of the new DeBaillon Medal, the highest award bestowed on an iris by the Society for Louisiana Irises. Chowning was diligent about distributing his irises in gardens across the country and consequently has contributed greatly to the spread of their popularity.

It is gratifying that most of Frank's work and hybridizing objectives are being continued by two other Little Rock hybridizers, Henry Rowlan and Richard Morgan. Henry Rowlan is known for having produced many good irises in a variety of colors—all remarkably good growers. Special among these are 'News Brief', 'Red Echo', and some of the Voodoo Series. Richard Morgan's creations have typically resulted in hybrids of smaller stature but all with very beautifully formed flowers, such as 'Cherry Cup', 'Heavenly Glow', and 'Noble Moment'.

Charles W. Arny Jr. of Lafayette, Louisiana, began hybridizing in the 1950s and was the most prolific producer of good modern garden hybrids. He remained active in hybridizing until his passing in 1993. Arny registered and introduced more than 120 cultivars, always demanded distinctive beauty and garden performance in his hybrids, and produced many landmark specimens. 'Charlie's Michele' was among the first Louisiana irises to show distinctive ruffling, a trait which climaxed in its offspring, the superbly ruffled and beautiful 'Clara Goula'. Bicolors and unusual color combinations were also a specialty with Arny, resulting in 'Eastertide', the immensely popular yellow and lavender bicolor, and more recently, 'Cajundome'. Attractive browns and a wide variety of signal shapes and colors are trademarks of Arny irises.

The advent of the 1960s ushered in a new era of scientific hybridizing. Joseph K. Mertzweiller of Baton Rouge, Louisiana, began efforts to produce tetraploid Louisiana irises in 1964, culminating in the first stable and fertile tetraploid hybrids, 'Professor Ike' and 'Professor Claude', both registered in 1973 and both still popular garden irises. Mertzweiller produced tetraploid hybrids in a variety of colors in the Professor Series, culminating in 'Professor Barbara', 'Professor Neil', 'Professor Marta Marie', and 'Professor Fritchie'. In addition to tetraploids, Joe will certainly be remembered for the development of outstanding garden diploid hybrids such as 'Colorific', 'Cajun Sunrise', 'Aunt Shirley', 'Just Helene', and 'Bera'.

Kenneth Durio of Opelousas, Louisiana, was also a pioneer in the production of tetraploid Louisiana iris hybrids. Among his landmark tetraploid introductions are 'Sauterne', 'Welcome Change', which was a significant bicolor break, and the immensely popular 'Godzilla'. Durio's most recent contribution is the first registered hybrid involving tetraploid Louisiana iris hybrids and *Iris virginica*. This introduction is blue flowered and is named 'Little Caillet'. Sam Norris of Kentucky has likewise been a serious developer of tetraploid Louisiana iris hybrids. Norris's 'Kentucky Cajun' is a highly regarded and desirable addition to any Louisiana iris collection.

Following in the tradition of Charles Arny and others, and using 'Clara Goula' as the primary basis for a hybridizing program, Richard Goula of Lafayette, Louisiana, is known for such irises as 'Joel Fletcher', 'Alabaster Moon', and 'Lavender Ruffles'. Pre-eminent among Goula's hybridizing goals is the production of good garden irises in pastel colors with intense green centers and usually having significant ruffling. More recently, his focus has shifted toward the production of smaller flowered garden irises having smaller stature and interesting markings, such as 'Pat Martin' and 'Gatewood Sapphire Star'.

Dorman Haymon is another Lafayette area hybridizer who has become a top United States producer of good Louisiana iris hybrids. Haymon's efforts have provided such outstanding yellows as 'Rokki Rockwell' and 'Camille Durand Foret' and interesting and very beautiful color variants such as 'Praline Festival'. Haymon's 'Marie Dolores' is among the best white irises available today.

Neil Bertinot of Opelousas, Louisiana, has developed many outstanding Louisiana iris hybrids over the years, but the most outstanding have 'Clara Goula' or 'Ann Chowning' or both in their parentage. Bertinot's hybrid 'Jeri' is a gorgeous dark velvety purple and is a fine garden variety. Other outstanding Bertinot irises are 'Bellevue's Mike' and 'Bellevue Coquette'.

Patrick O'Connor of Baton Rouge, Louisiana, began by following in Frank Chowning's footsteps, using mostly Chowning irises in his hybridizing work. O'Connor is known for the beautiful 'Feliciana Hills' and 'Bayou Fountain', among others.

Rusty Ostheimer of Houma, Louisiana, and Charles Fritchie of New Orleans have also made significant contributions to the hybrid development of Louisiana irises. Jim Leonard of Lafayette, Louisiana, maintains a private collection of Louisiana irises among the largest anywhere and has recently begun to hybridize in earnest.

Those people described above are but a few of the many who contributed to the development of modern Louisiana iris hybrids. This effort has by no means been confined to Louisiana. Kevin Vaughn of Mississippi is involved in an intensive hybridizing program, and Texas has a number of prominent hybridizers. Albert Faggard of Beaumont, Texas, is responsible for a number of fine introductions over the years, notably specimens such as 'Ice Angel' and 'Neches Royalty'. J. Farron Campbell of Dallas is currently introducing the first hybrids from his extensive hybridizing program. Campbell also has a collection of Louisiana irises among the most complete available today. Kirk Strawn of College Station, Texas, a prominent grower and hybridizer of water lilies, has begun a hybridizing program with Louisiana irises. Strawn has registered a number of hybrids which are now showing up in commercial production.

This hybridizing effort is continued in California by Eleanor McCown, Valera Chenoweth, Ben Hager, Joe Ghio, and others. Mary Dunn was perhaps the pre-eminent California breeder of Louisiana irises until her death in 1997. Mary produced an amazing number of hybrids which are widely grown today. Outstanding and award-winning among Mary's introductions are 'Bajazzo',

'Bayou Mystique', 'Crisp Lime', and 'Gulf Shores'. Richard Sloan and Joe Ghio have produced many good hybrids. Ghio's 'Elusive Butterfly' has been an award winner. Archie Owen's 'Exquisite Lady' is renowned for its prominent white edging. And Ben Hager will certainly be remembered for 'Cajun Cookery', an exceptional and serviceable red iris.

Significant hybridizing programs have expanded to Australia, New Zealand, and other parts of the world. Prominent Southern Hemisphere hybridizers include Bob Raabe, T. J. Betts, Graeme Grosvenor, Myrtle Murray, John C. Taylor, Jo Tunny, and Sam Rix, and the list is growing rapidly.

John C. Taylor of Sydney, Australia, has been the prime producer of modern Louisiana iris hybrids from "down under." Taylor's hybridizing began with 'Clara Goula', sent by Charles Arny before the iris was named, and its influence shows in his latest hybrids. His irises are all beautifully formed, usually heavily ruffled, and quite rounded flowers of great merit and beauty—typically in pastel colors. Probably Taylor's three landmark irises to date are the incredibly branched 'Koorawatha'; 'Dural White Butterfly', which was the first Louisiana iris to win the Australasian Dykes medal; and 'Margaret Lee', which has been a parent of virtually all of Taylor's hybrids since its creation. 'Desert Jewel' should also be singled out for special recognition because of its unusual coloring. 'Desert Jewel' has contributed a whole new look to subsequent hybrid development with its blend of two or three colors on a cream background. Taylor irises are widely grown throughout the United States and indeed the world. They are universally highly desirable and sought after.

Janet Hutchinson is another hybridizer from Sydney who has made significant contributions to the development of Louisiana iris hybridizing. As early as 1990, Hutchinson's 'Soft Laughter' and 'Our Mister Bailey' were important offerings from Australia. Her more recent 'Honey Star' is enjoying widespread circulation and is proving to be an outstanding garden iris. Craig Carroll, also from Sydney, has given us a number of good hybrids, most notably 'Our Parris'. Heather Pryor of Sydney, a protege of John Taylor, continues the tradition of quality set by the Taylor irises. Taylor's 'Desert Jewel' figures prominently in Pryor's hybridizing, which has greatly broadened the color base for her beauties. Notable among Pryor's introductions are 'La Stupenda', 'Bushfire Moon', and the award-winning 'Garnet Storm Dancer'. Bernard Pryor, Heather's husband, is just beginning to release his own introductions with an emphasis on low-growing and small-flowered irises. Myrtle Murray is another noted hybridizer from the area. She is perhaps best known for her Brookvale Series. Louisiana irises thrive in the Sydney area—indeed, cultural conditions there somewhat duplicate those of the Louisiana Gulf Coast.

Bob Raabe and T. J. Betts are prominent Louisiana iris growers and hybridizers from other parts of Australia. Raabe enjoyed early success with the beautiful 'La Perouse' and 'Sinfonietta', which is in wholesale nursery production in the United States. Raabe's work with tetraploids has given us one of the most beautiful of all tetraploid introductions, 'Coorabell'. Neighboring New Zealand is the home of Sam Rix who has done a great deal of hybridizing. Rix's most heralded introduction, 'Frances Elizabeth', was the 1965 winner of the DeBaillon Award.

France has provided at least three hybridizers of note. They are Eric Besse, best known for the stunningly beautiful 'Berenice', and Pierre and Laure Anfosso, whose introductions are grown throughout the world.

It is not difficult to recognize how much hybridizing and the distribution of constantly improving hybrids have contributed to the widespread popularity of Louisiana irises. But hybridizers cannot take full credit for this popularity. It is often said that if you want to sell Louisiana irises, all you have to do is introduce them—they sell themselves. This truth has been demonstrated through introductions and promotions by scores of volunteer activists. These volunteers are not hybridizers, but active growers and promoters of these native beauties. They recognize the value and the need to inform and educate by attending conventions, giving talks and slide shows, organizing meetings, entering irises in flower shows, writing letters, and doing many other mundane chores, all for the unselfish love of Louisiana irises. These ambassadors of iris goodwill are too numerous to mention, but Marie Caillet of Little Elm, Texas, is the undisputed leader of these activities. These volunteers have the undying gratitude of all iris growers and they can certainly take pride in the accomplishments of their efforts.

Future of Louisiana Irises

Today Louisiana irises are growing successfully in every country in the temperate world, thriving on every continent except Antarctica. Louisiana irises come in every conceivable color, shape, and size. They are large, small, tall, short. They have ruffles, no ruffles, prominent signals, no signals, pronounced veining, colored edging, fragrance, no fragrance—the list of attributes is endless.

Due to the untiring efforts of hybridizers, volunteer activists, and the mutual cooperation of kindred plant societies, Louisiana irises are known and loved the world over and respected as the horticultural aristocrats they are. Louisiana irises have finally achieved a position of prominence in the landscape and in the arsenals of garden designers and landscape architects.

The future of Louisiana irises depends on the continued interest of the memberships of various fraternal organizations dedicated to these irises, their efforts to disseminate necessary information to the public and the willingness and ability of hybridizers to produce suitable landscape specimens of various kinds, which perform well with few maintenance requirements. The Louisiana iris could never have been a star in French and Italian Renaissance gardens which depended for effect on large, discrete areas of pure color, but they certainly could have starred in naturalistic English landscapes and, of course, in Japanese gardens. The artistic grace and beauty of these irises with their adaptability to water and bog conditions is the key element to their landscape suitability.

Fortunately, a new generation of active hybridizers, growers, and promoters is now showing great promise, and it is to them that we entrust the future. Hopefully, they will not proceed so far with their hybridizing programs that Louisiana irises lose their identity and begin to bear too little resemblance to their ancestors, which for centuries have been protected in the deep recesses of south Louisiana swamps.

CHAPTER 2

Classification and Species

Classification of the genus *Iris* is constantly changing as additional information arises. Continuing changes will occur with discovery, naming, and classification of previously unknown irises. Taxonomy involves identification, nomenclature, and classification of living organisms and cannot be an exact science in the same sense that mathematics is a pure science.

Naming of Iris Species and Cultivars

The naming of irises, as well as other plants, is regulated by international rules. Two types of names are often used in plant publications, one in Latin and the other in the native language, a common name.

The Latin or scientific name refers to classification of species and conforms to rules of the *International Code of Botanical Nomenclature*. Louisiana irises are classified into the beardless iris series *Hexagonae*, for which *Iris hexagona* is the type species. The type species is the plant used by taxonomists to characterize that series, including all other species in the series. Most series contain more than one species.

Iris is the common name that refers to the genus *Iris*, which is the principal classification of these plants. The term *giganticaerulea*, literally meaning "giant blue," is called a specific epithet, just as is *hexagona*, above. This binomial (two-name) system of nomenclature involving the names of genus and species gives the scientific name of the plant. The species discovered, described, and named by John K. Small in 1929 is designated as *Iris giganticaerulea*. According to the international rules of nomenclature, the discoverer of a new species has the right to name that species. Of all species described by Small, only *I. giganticaerulea* has withstood the test of time and maintained species status. Other iris species proposed by Small are now considered variants or natural hybrids.

Most popular iris cultivars are of hybrid origin, many of these being advanced generation hybrids. Although cultivars are generally named after a person, place, or thing ('Professor Fritchie', 'Dural White Butterfly', 'Willow Mint', etc.), coined words ('Colorific') are also valid. Rules for naming these varieties or cultivars are established by the *International Code of Nomenclature for Cultivated Plants*. Cultivar names are given by the hybridizer or collector and are registered with the American Iris Society (AIS), which is the officially recognized registry for all rhizomatous irises. The AIS rules for registration follow the *International Code of Nomenclature for Cultivated Plants*.

Although hybrids account for the greatest number of iris cultivars, some are cultivar selections from a species, for example, 'Barbara Elaine Taylor' from *Iris giganticaerulea*, which would be written *I. giganticaerulea* 'Barbara Elaine Taylor' according to the *International Code of Nomenclature for Cultivated Plants*. The correct English common name for the group of irises discussed in this book is Louisiana iris. The proper scientific name for this group is the series *Hexagonae*. Group names include both species and hybrids. In keeping with international rules of nomenclature, correct and established names cannot be changed or altered. Any other name would be both incorrect and confusing. When ordering or referring to these irises, the terminology Louisiana iris and an appropriate cultivar name are used.

Classification of Louisianas and Related Irises

Iris is the generic, general name and represents the broadest classification of these plants. It is beyond the scope of this publication to consider the detailed classification for all members of this genus.

One of the most famous plant books of all time, *The Genus Iris* was written by William Rickatson Dykes, a taxonomist, collector, grower, and breeder of all kinds of irises. Many iris enthusiasts consider Dykes to be the world's foremost authority on irises from the first half of the twentieth century. Cambridge University Press originally published *The Genus Iris* in 1913, and in 1974 Dover Publications produced an unabridged reprint. More recent publications of the American Iris Society dealing with the entire genus *Iris* include *Garden Irises* (L. F. Randolph, editor) and *The World of Irises* (B. Warburton and M. Hamblen, editors).

The following simplified classification of *Iris* is an attempt to show the positions and relationships of Louisiana irises and other garden irises.

Abbreviated Classification of the Genus *Iris*

I. Subgenus *Iris*
    A. Section *Iris*   (Rhizomatous irises)
        1. Subsection *Iris*   (Bearded irises)
        2. Other Subsections (3)   (Bearded irises)
    B. Section *Spathula*   (Rhizomatous irises)
        1. Subsection *Apogon*   (Beardless irises)
            a. Series *Hexagonae*   (Louisiana irises)
            b. Series *Laevigatae*   (Japanese and other moisture-loving
                                        irises)
            c. Series *Sibiricae*   (Siberian irises)
            d. Series *Spuriae*   (Spuria irises)
            e. Series *Californicae*   (Pacific Coast irises)
            f. Other Series (10)   (Lesser known irises)
        2. Other Subsections (3)   (Lesser known irises)
II. Subgenus *Xiphium*
    A. Section *Xiphium*   (Bulbous irises)
    B. Other Sections (1)   (Lesser known irises)
III. Other Subgenera (2)   (Lesser known irises)

The genus *Iris* is divided into four subgenera, based primarily upon underground plant features (roots, rhizomes, bulbs, and so on). Louisiana irises are rhizomatous irises. The rhizome is an underground stem rather than a root. The bloom stalk is continuous with the rhizome. Roots grow from the rhizome, which serves as a storage organ for plant foods.

Rhizomatous irises are grouped into sections and subsections based upon the presence or absence of beards. The beard consists of conspicuous upstanding hairs along the center line of the haft, the constricted portion of the falls. Some irises do not have a beard and are called beardless. Some beardless irises, particularly Louisianas, may have a brightly colored signal where the beard is located in bearded types. The signal, in bright yellow or orange, may also have a background color, typically white. Different types of signal markings may occur in other beardless iris series.

The subsection *Apogon* is of greatest interest. This subsection contains fifteen series of beardless irises, one of which, the *Hexagonae*, includes all Louisiana irises. The series *Laevigatae* consists of other moisture-loving irises and is considered most closely related to the *Hexagonae*. Other well-known series of the subsection *Apogon* include *Sibiricae*, *Spuriae*, and *Californicae*.

Irises that grow from bulbs include the Dutch, English, and Spanish forms. These irises, being quite different from Louisianas, belong to the subgenus *Xiphium*.

Bearded irises are among the most popular and widely grown members of the genus and are represented in four different subsections. They are widely separated from the Louisianas and no success has been reported in hybridizing bearded irises with Louisianas. Hybridization among bearded irises spans more than two centuries and represents the most extensive state of development of all irises. In contrast, hybridizing Louisiana irises has been underway little more than sixty years. The history of bearded irises and growers' experience with them can greatly benefit Louisiana irises.

The Series *Hexagonae*

All species and hybrids of Louisiana irises are included in the series *Hexagonae*. Most species grow extensively in Louisiana, which is why they are called Louisiana irises. Some of the species grow in Florida, Georgia, the Carolinas, Texas, and up the Mississippi Valley into Arkansas, Missouri, Ohio, and Indiana. The natural occurrence of Louisiana species in states north of Arkansas is believed to be restricted by adverse environmental conditions.

The most current description of the species of Louisiana irises is in the book of the Species Group of the British Iris Society, *A Guide to the Species Iris: Their Identification and Cultivation* (1997, Cambridge University Press). This publication uses the same species as described in the first edition of *The Louisiana Iris* and as accepted by the board of the Society for Louisiana Irises: *Iris fulva*, *I. brevicaulis*, *I. giganticaerulea*, *I. hexagona*, and *I. nelsonii*. Some questions have arisen as to the validity of the names of several of these species. The name of *I. brevicaulis* may return to its former designation as *I. foliosa* because of some breach in taxonomic rules concerning the first publication of this species. Because this question represents a return to a formerly accepted name for this species, too much confusion is unlikely, if indeed this contention can be proven. Some authorities feel that the species *I. hexagona* and *I. giganticaerulea* are single-species variations that are more or less geographically isolated. However, those of us who grow these two plants find remarkable differences in bloom season, blossom substance, and hybridizing results, indicating that they are distinct species, as we and the British Iris Society have published.

Iris hexagona Walter

Flowers 4 to 4¾ inches (10.2–12.1 cm) across, in lilac, medium blue, to deep violet-purple, rarely white. Flowers generally flaring, with somewhat erect standards, 2¾ to 3¼ inches (7.0–8.3 cm), ¾ inch (1.9 cm) wide. Falls 3½ to 4 inches (8.9–10.2 cm), 1½ inches (3.8 cm) wide, obovate-elliptic with conspicuous medial ridge. Terminal cluster is two flowered, other positions single flowered; generally four flower positions. Spathes green, herbaceous, sometimes unequal in length with outer valve the longer. Style arms narrower than haft, convex laterally with well-marked reddish lilac ridge; style crests lilac to purple with coarsely serrated edge. Stalks range in height from 12 to 36 inches (30.5–91.4 cm), generally straight or slightly zigzag. Leaves sword-like, yellowish green, 24 to 35 inches (61.0–88.9 cm) long and up to 1 inch (2.5 cm) wide. Rhizomes stout, greenish, and wide, creeping up to 12 inches (30.5 cm) or longer. Habitat is southeastern United States, adjacent to Atlantic Coast and Gulf of Mexico, specifically South Carolina, Georgia, and Florida. Reported to flower in June-July in these locations. Also reported from Louisiana (New Orleans area) although the latter is more likely the very similar species, *I. giganticaerulea*.

Iris fulva Ker-Gawler

Flowers 4 to 4½ inches (10.2–11.4 cm) across in brick red, rust red, or coppery red, varying to cardinal red at one extreme to chrome yellow at the other. Yellow is rare. Flowers generally drooping, occasionally with slight flare, falls 1 to 1¼ inches (2.5–3.2 cm) wide, 2¼ to 2½ inches (5.7–6.4 cm) long. Cauline leaf 18 to 24 inches (45.7–61.0 cm) long, ¾ to 1 inch (1.9–2.5 cm) wide. Rhizomes 4 to 5 inches (10.2–12.7 cm) long, not exceeding ¾ inch (1.9 cm) diameter. Flower stalks erect, almost straight, 24 to 36 inches (61.0–91.4 cm) tall. Stalk branching is rare. Lower bud positions are usually single flowered, terminal position two flowered. Upper flowers borne well above leaf level. The signal is small or absent. Style arms narrow and anthers may protrude slightly beyond ends of style arms. Found in partial shade to full sun in open swamps sometimes in water up to 6 inches (15.2 cm) deep after flooding by heavy rains. Found also in well-lighted areas of cypress and hardwood swamps, along streams and canals, and in roadside ditches. Occurs most abundantly in south Louisiana, but has been found in Arkansas, Missouri, and Ohio. Does not tolerate dense shade or intrusion of brackish (somewhat salty) water. Grows in acidic, alluvial soils, rich in organic matter and very fertile.

   Iris fulva may be readily distinguished from *I. giganticaerulea* and *I. brevicaulis* because of its color range. When shipped to England in 1814, this species created quite a sensation because of the red color. At that time, red was unknown among bearded irises grown in Europe. Only *I. nelsonii* is close to *I. fulva* in color, but the two are easily distinguished by location in which they are found. The habitat of *I. nelsonii* is very limited. Natural hybridization of *I. fulva* with *I. giganticaerulea* and *I. brevicaulis* has occurred extensively but these hybrids are distinguishable from *I. fulva* and *I. nelsonii*.

Iris brevicaulis Rafinesque

(Note: *Iris brevicaulis* was for some time called *I. foliosa*, and in some older publications you will see it listed as such.) Flowers 3½ to 4½ inches (8.9–11.4 cm) across in pale blue, medium blue, and blue-violet, rarely pure white. Form is flaring. *Iris brevicaulis* is the dwarf species of the *Hexagonae*, with stalk and leaves much shorter than other species. Stalks are thick and short, typically 10 to 14 inches (25.4–35.6 cm), sometimes prostrate and with a pronounced zigzag pattern. Cauline leaves are also short, 16 to 19 inches (40.6–48.3 cm), strap shaped, ¾ to 1 inch (1.9–2.5 cm) wide. Lateral branches may occur at leaf nodes. Rhizomes 3 to 6 inches (7.6–15.2 cm) long, ½ to 1 inch (1.3–2.5 cm) in diameter. Terminal bud positions are two flowered, other bud positions often two flowered. Falls 1 to 1¼ inches (2.5–3.2 cm) wide, 3 to 3¼ inches (7.6–8.3 cm) long. Flowers borne from near the base and always amid the foliage, never above the foliage. Signal inconspicuous, often on a white background. Found in upland locations, pastures, prairies, and bluff areas in partial to full sunlight where moisture is generally high during the growing season (fall, winter, and early spring). Found most extensively in south Louisiana but also found in Arkansas, Missouri, Ohio, and Indiana.

There is no problem in identifying *Iris brevicaulis*. It is probably the most consistently blue flowered of all the Louisiana iris species. The flowers bear a resemblance to *I. giganticaerulea* but stalk and leaf characteristics are strongly different. *Iris brevicaulis* is the latest blooming of all species in the *Hexagonae*, generally early to mid-May in Louisiana, while *I. giganticaerulea* normally blooms in early April. *Iris brevicaulis* is quite hardy and offers the greatest adaptability to low temperatures. Hybridizers probably have not made as extensive use of *I. brevicaulis* as would seem warranted by its many outstanding features.

Iris giganticaerulea Small

Flowers 5¼ to 6 inches (13.3–15.2 cm) across, predominantly blue to blue-purple (from lobelia through shades of wisteria and lavender) to pure white. Albino whites are more common than in any other species. Flower form typically flaring. The largest species in the *Hexagonae*. Cauline leaf 20 to 26 inches (50.8–66.0 cm) long, ¾ to 1 inch (1.9–2.5 cm) wide. Rhizomes large to very large, 5 to 12 inches (12.7–30.5 cm) long, ¾ to 1½ inches (1.9–3.8 cm) in diameter. Stalks tall, virtually straight and unbranched, normally 38 to 46 inches (96.5–116.8 cm) but are known to reach 66 inches (167.6 cm) or more with superior locations in the marsh. Double flowered at terminal position, single flowered at all other positions. Most flowers are borne above the foliage. Falls 1½ inches (3.8 cm) wide, 3½ inches (8.9 cm) long, signal slight to conspicuous, may be superimposed on a white zone. Found only in Louisiana coastal areas, possibly to about 100 miles (160 km) inland. May occur to a limited extent in southeast Texas near the Louisiana line. Grows in full sun or partial sun in open swamps. Thrives under flooded conditions and tolerates brackish water to some extent.

Iris giganticaerulea is truly a distinctive giant and very showy. It varies in size, both stalk height and bloom size, and in color and color pattern. Variations are more prevalent in some areas of Louisiana than others. Natural hybridization within the species and other environmental influences probably account for such variations. It is easy to understand how Small could have described as separate species such variations within the species *I. giganticaerulea*.

Iris nelsonii Randolph

Flowers are 4½ to 5 inches (11.4–12.7 cm) across, generally drooping to very slightly flaring, bright red to purple, rarely in beige brown or yellow brown. Color is more intense than in *Iris fulva*. Rhizomes 4 to 6 inches (10.2–15.2 cm) long, ¾ to 1 inch (1.9–2.5 cm) in diameter. Cauline leaf 20 to 30 inches (50.8–76.2 cm) long, ¾ to 1¼ inches (1.9–3.2 cm) wide, drooping at ends. Stalks are 32 to 42 inches (81.3–106.7 cm), and often branched. Two buds at terminal position and may have two buds at other positions. Falls are 2½ to 3 inches (6.4–7.6 cm) long, 1¼ to 1¾ inches (3.2–4.4 cm) wide. A signal is generally present, though sometimes inconspicuous. Occasionally the anthers may protrude slightly beyond tips of style arms as in *I. fulva*. *Iris nelsonii* is found only in Louisiana in a very limited location south of Abbeville. This species is of hybrid origin, mainly from *I. fulva* and *I. giganticaerulea*.

These irises were discovered by W. B. MacMillan about 1938. Earlier collectors including Small, Percy Viosca, and Mary DeBaillon failed to find these plants. These distinctive plants were given such names as "Abbeville Irises," "Abbeville Reds," or "Abbeville Yellows." Since they were larger, more vigorous, and more brilliantly colored than *Iris fulva*, they were also referred to as "Super Fulvas." Their close relationship to *I. fulva* is evident. Only limited information regarding origin and taxonomy of this group was available until 1989. They were used extensively in early hybridizing by MacMillan, Caroline Dormon, Ira Nelson and many others. *Iris nelsonii* probably contributed as much or more than any of the other species to the quality of present-day hybrids.

The unique evolution of the *Iris nelsonii* species has been studied and well documented by L. F. Randolph in collaboration with Ira Nelson and others. This case is among the few established in which a new species evolved from natural hybrids over a period of time. Morphological and cytological studies established *I. nelsonii* as a stable species differing significantly from allopatric (isolated) populations of *I. fulva* and *I. giganticaerulea*. A relatively large number of plants in the limited *I. nelsonii* habitat were studied from 1953 to 1963. Most morphological characteristics of *I. nelsonii* were either intermediate between *I. fulva* and *I. giganticaerulea* or were closer to *I. giganticaerulea*. Unique and different "marker" chromosomes are present in the three species *I. fulva*, *I. giganticaerulea*, and *I. brevicaulis*. These constitute effective "fingerprints" for the respective species. Cytological studies showed *I. nelsonii* to contain the marker chromosomes of *I. fulva* and *I. giganticaerulea* but not those of *I. brevicaulis*. This is considered the strongest evidence for the hybrid background of *I. nelsonii*. The number of generations required for the stability and true-breeding features of *I. nelsonii* to develop is a matter of conjecture, but could be measured in centuries.

Much recent scientific progress has been made ascertaining the species that might be involved in the formation of the stable species hybrid *Iris nelsonii*. Work in classical taxonomy by Randolph and Nelson established that morphological characteristics of *I. fulva*, *I. giganticaerulea*, and *I. brevicaulis* were all contained within *I. nelsonii* and suggested that the so-called Abbeville reds or super fulvas were a stabilized hybrid of these three species. Each of the three alleged parental species occurs in different environmental niches and the hybrid occupies a fourth, unlike any of the parents. In the days when *I. nelsonii* was described, no satisfactory method could prove such a supposition unequivocally. With the advent of modern methods of molecular biology, however, such theories on the origins of hybrids can be tested directly by determining whether DNA from the proposed parents was indeed present in the hybrid. Mike Arnold and his colleagues, chiefly Bobby Bennett, set out to determine whether the theory of Randolph and Nelson was correct on the origin of *I. nelsonii*. These workers found DNA from all three species in *I. nelsonii*, although there was a preponderance of DNA from *I. fulva*, indicating that species was the source of much of the genetic material in the hybrid. It is possible that *I. fulva* pollen might be more competitive than the other species so that the chances for crosses of an initial hybrid back to *I. fulva* were greater than for other species. All of these data were determined using DNA present in the nucleus, but another sort of DNA is present in the green organelles in the cell called the chloroplast. Unlike nuclear DNA, which is inherited from both parents in a hybrid, all the chloroplast DNA comes from the female (pod) parent only. By knowing this, Arnold and colleagues were able to determine that *I. fulva* was the pod parent for the first cross eventually resulting in the trispecies hybrid complex known as *I. nelsonii*. Thus, using the techniques of molecular biology, these workers were able to confirm the theories of Randolph and Nelson and add new information on the relative contributions of the three species and the pod parent for the original cross.

Relationships existing between *Iris nelsonii* and *I. fulva* prior to 1966 appear somewhat similar to relationships that exist today between *I. hexagona* and *I. giganticaerulea*. Some of the methods and techniques used by Randolph in resolving the *I. nelsonii-I. fulva* problem may also be applicable to the *I. hexagona–I. giganticaerulea* problem.

The above descriptions and other comments are for the five species of the *Hexagonae*. Growth habits and location preferences should allow identification in the field and differentiation between the species and interspecific hybrids.

These species, along with the natural hybrids, are the foundation stock for the Louisiana hybrids of today. Unfortunately, the species continue to grow scarcer in native habitats. Natural interspecific hybrids are even more rare. This scarcity can be attributed to human intrusion through expansion of cities and development of once wild areas. Drainage of natural wet areas is the foremost problem. Water is essential for growth and distribution of Louisiana irises. The species *Iris nelsonii* is most endangered because of its very restricted habitat. Native stands are nearly absent now and saving *I. nelsonii* in its habitat will be difficult. *Iris fulva* is also in danger and natural populations have decreased drastically over the past 70 years. The species *I. giganticaerulea* is in the least danger at this time. Fortunately, all five Louisiana iris species continue to thrive in personal and public display gardens. Distribution of plants or seeds to many areas where these irises are not now grown is an important conservation practice.

The Series *Laevigatae*

The series *Laevigatae* represents some of the closest relatives of the Louisiana irises and is another of the fifteen series of beardless irises of the subsection *Apogon*. We will consider only the three member species, or hybrids thereof, commonly grown in Louisiana. These include *Iris virginica* (Linneus), *I. pseudacorus* (Linneus), and *I. ensata* (Thunberg). These species, or hybrids involving these species, are often mistaken for Louisiana irises. They are bold and vigorous plants with large and stout rhizomes. The series *Laevigatae* is widely distributed throughout the world and is not nearly as homogeneous as the series *Hexagonae*.

Iris virginica is of greatest interest. It is indigenous to south Louisiana and is widely distributed throughout the South and up the East Coast of the United States. Culture and habitat requirements are the same as for the Louisiana irises. It is grown in many gardens in Louisiana and is very frequently mistaken for a Louisiana iris. The color range includes all the blues, a white form, and extends toward the pinks. *Iris virginica* and the series *Laevigatae* do not hybridize with the *Hexagonae* (except in very limited circumstances) and are not in the parentage of Louisiana hybrids. The foliage is a strong distinguishing feature of *I. virginica*. The foliage remains green after Louisiana iris foliage has discolored, and there is a pronounced mid-rib in the center of the leaf. *Iris virginica* is a very vigorous grower.

Iris pseudacorus is another member of the series *Laevigatae* often mistaken for a Louisiana iris. This European species was imported into the United States long ago. It is not native to this country and several forms are known in Europe and the British Isles. It is grown extensively in Louisiana, very often among Louisiana species and hybrids. *Iris pseudacorus* exists only in cream to yellow and has a low ratio of flowers to foliage. The plant is vigorous, makes a large clump, and will crowd out other irises. The foliage remains green in Louisiana, but is deciduous in more severe climates. A distinct, easily felt mid-rib extends up the length of the leaf.

Iris ensata is also known as *I. kaempferi* and is the parent species of the Japanese or kaempferi irises. The species is not well known in Louisiana, but Japanese hybrids are common. This species is of Asiatic origin, and these irises have been cultivated in Japan for almost five centuries. Forms of Japanese and Louisiana hybrids are similar and can lead to confusion.

Other Beardless Series

Other series of subsection *Apogon*, including the series *Sibiricae*, *Spuriae*, and *Californicae*, are important. These beardless, rhizomatous irises are more distant relatives of the series *Hexagonae*. Siberian and spuria irises are commonly grown in Louisiana. The Siberians number at least ten species in two subseries, all of European and Asiatic origin. The color range is not as broad as the Louisianas. Spurias number at least fourteen species from Europe, the Near East, Middle East, North Africa, and Russia. The color range includes yellows, browns, and blends. The series *Sibiricae* and *Spuriae* have many modern hybrids.

The series *Californicae* are North American taxa and another important beardless series. At least eleven species and a number of subspecies are native to California, Oregon, and Washington. A wide variety of colors and color patterns is represented by the species, and natural hybrids have occurred between some species. Many hybrids are known. The *Californicae* are related to some species of series *Sibiricae*, and garden hybrids between the two series are well known. Good drainage is essential for culture of the *Californicae*, and they do not perform well in Louisiana.

CHAPTER 3

Description of the Louisiana Iris

Appearance and growth of Louisiana irises bear similarities to most other irises. When the plant is sufficiently mature to bloom, a stalk emerges at the growing tip of the rhizome. The stalk then develops to its full height. A few leaves, usually three to four, called sheath leaves are attached directly to the stalk. Most bloom buds emerge at the junctions of the sheath leaves with the stalk. Lower sheath-leaf positions may have a secondary stalk, thinner than the main stalk and 6 to 16 inches (15.2–40.6 cm) high. This secondary stalk is called a branch or stalk branch and will have one or even two bloom buds at the terminal end. Stalk branching is very desirable since it adds to the beauty of the iris and represents increased bud count. Such branching is variable, occurring at times but not at other times on the same variety. Culture, weather, and other factors play a role.

A typical hybrid Louisiana iris will have six to eight blooms and sometimes ten, but rarely more than ten. Louisiana irises do not always open the terminal bloom first, and this is not considered a fault. Blooms tend to open sequentially, and each bloom will last two or three days depending on temperature and other weather conditions. The blooms last longer in cooler weather. Two blooms (rarely three) are always at the terminal or uppermost position on the stalk. At least one and often two blooms appear sequentially at the sheath leaf positions. Generally, two blooms will be open simultaneously, sometimes three, but rarely more than three. The number of days a stalk will remain in bloom depends on weather conditions and the number of buds.

Blooms of Louisiana irises, like all irises, have six floral segments in two sets, the standards and the falls. The standards are the narrower segments named for their tendency to stand upright. Falls are the broader segments named for their tendency to droop. In some publications standards are referred to as petals and falls as sepals. The names standards and falls are used here. It is the intensely colored standards and falls which give all irises their beauty. These parts have no direct sexual function, serving only to attract insects to assure pollination in nature's way of preserving the species.

Looking down at the top of the bloom, you see three style arms radiating out from the center of the flower, about 120 degrees apart. The style arms extend about one-third to one-half the length of the falls. Style arms are extensions of the ovaries. The ovaries contain the egg cells, the female sex cells or female gametes. If the bloom is pollinated, the ovary later expands and forms the seed pod. Though not visible from above, the ovaries, stigmas, and anthers along with the style arms constitute the sexual or seed-forming parts of the iris.

Diversity of Color

The name *Iris* is derived from a Greek word meaning "rainbow," a fitting name for this beautiful family of flowers. In Greek mythology the goddess Iris was the personal attendant and messenger of Juno, and she is referred to as the "goddess of the rainbow." The poet Virgil wrote, "Iris of saffron wing displaying against the sun her robe of a thousand hues"—truly descriptive of the color of Louisiana irises.

Color Pigments

The brilliant colors of irises and indeed all flowers are due to specific chemical substances called pigments. In their simplest forms these are very complex organic chemicals. They are rendered even more complex by combinations with themselves and other chemicals, such as sugars. Pigments are merely one example showing living plants as remarkable chemical factories. Pigments contain carbon, hydrogen, and oxygen and are synthesized by the plants from the basic building blocks of carbon dioxide and water. Individual colors result from many different pigments interacting and finding orders of dominance among each other, and from the genetic effects that inhibit formation or action of certain pigments.

Color Range

Color is among the most noted features of Louisiana irises, which have a range as broad or broader than any group in the genus, including the bearded irises. It has been said that a complete color chart could be constructed from the colors and shades among these irises. Their extremely broad color range may have been the most significant factor influencing Small to publicize these irises in the 1930s. At that time the color range was that of the species and natural hybrids. Since then, the color range has been augmented by more than fifty years of controlled hybridizing.

Evolution of Color

The species of the *Hexagonae* represent colors from pure white through dark purple, including all shades of blue, lavender, pale to medium yellow, rust, and red. Whites, blues, and some lavenders and purples are typical of *Iris hexagona, I. giganticaerulea,* and *I. brevicaulis*. Darker purples, yellows, pinks, and reds are associated with the species *I. fulva* and *I. nelsonii*. The color range of the species represents the first stage of color evolution.

When Louisiana irises came to greater public attention in the 1930s, the color range had been evolving for centuries or longer. A broad range of color was found among the species and natural hybrids as they existed at the time of Small. Small's era represents the second stage of color evolution, the combined colors of the species and natural hybrids. Many broader shades, blends, pastels, and bitones—including a wide range of pinks, lavenders, orange-reds, rust-reds, orange-yellows, creamy yellows, creamy whites, and a whole spectrum of blues and purples—were now available to the collector. The colors collected during this period became the foundation stock for controlled hybridizing which began in the 1940s and 1950s.

The third stage of color evolution began with controlled hybridizing, when the few remaining blanks in the Louisiana "color chart" began to fill. Today they are all filled, except for the green spectrum which is restricted to the style arms, signals, and texture veins. Greenish yellows and greenish whites are becoming more numerous. (There are questions as to the appeal of a truly green iris, or any green flower.) Red Louisianas are the most intensely colored reds found in any iris classification. Blends of two or more colors are becoming more common. These are mostly blends of yellow with brown, blue, or red. Such blends are not common among the natural hybrids. Very dark purples, near black, are also the result of selective hybridizing.

Color evolution is by no means complete. Much enhancement in color and color pattern are still to be had at the diploid level. Then, there are the new tetraploids for which color evolution has not really begun. Greater expansion of the color range should be possible with the tetraploids since they represent greater genetic variability. Among future expectations for both diploids and tetraploids are patterns comparable to the amoenas, variegatas, and plicatas found in bearded irises. Amoenas and variegatas are types of bicolors. Amoenas have white standards and colored falls while variegatas have yellow standards and red to brown falls. Plicatas have edging of contrasting colors on other colored segments. All these color patterns have been known for years among the bearded irises, but are now just beginning among the Louisianas. Bicolors are definite bicolors, not bitones. Clarity and contrast in the bicolor pattern in Louisianas needs to be improved. The plicata pattern is becoming more common but the edging is narrow in existing hybrids.

Colors should be clean, clear, and colorfast. Exceptions to the rule of colorfastness can result in pleasing effects, such as a flower that opens a light yellow then fades to creamy white. Blended colors should produce a bright, pleasing color or color combination, one that is not dull or drab. Bicolors should have a good, harmonic color contrast. A new and different color or color combination must not overshadow the other characteristics of a cultivar. New color patterns, such as pronounced veining, spray pattern, plicata pattern, or a halo, should be evaluated along with other good characteristics. Streaking and blotching of color on floral segments is acceptable, but should be consistent. If the streaking or blotches of color are present on one standard, the pattern should be repeated on the other standards and on every bloom to be considered a desirable pattern.

Diversity in Form

Diversity in form among Louisiana irises is even more significant than diversity in color. Here the Louisiana irises stand alone, and the many unique forms are possibly their greatest asset. The various forms are genetically related to the forms of the species. Through hybridization the number of forms have been increased, along with color, size, and other features. Hybridizers must take care that form does not become stereotyped and a "preferred form" dominant. This would, in effect, destroy a great asset and most distinctive feature of Louisiana irises.

Many terms have been used in describing the various forms of Louisiana irises. All the forms are related to the size and geometry of the standards, falls, and style arms. Bloom size is not of great significance provided proportionality exists. Placement of buds along the stalk is not directly related to form but does influence how the iris form affects the observer. The following descriptions and terminology are commonly applied to Louisiana irises. Falls, being larger and more noticeable than standards, contribute more to iris form. Form is also dependent on the age of the bloom, there being some evolution in form as a flower ages.

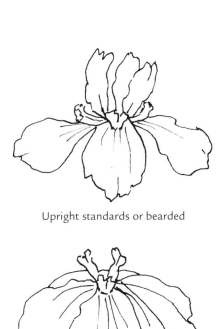

Upright standards or bearded

Flaring or butterfly

Pendent or hanging

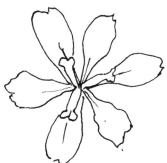

Open or archaic

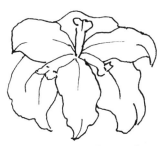

Ruffled and overlapping

Semi-double
with petaloids

Recurved

Cartwheel and flat

Flower Forms

Flaring Form

The segments, particularly the falls, spread outward when the flower first opens. The outward spread may vary from completely horizontal to slightly downward arching. Standards are near vertical when the bloom first opens and may also develop a downward arch. In some cases the falls may touch and support the standards because of overlapping edges.

Semi-Flaring or Arching Form

This is a small difference in the degree of flare. Instead of near-horizontal form, semi-flaring or arching falls describe a downward arch in their outward spread. The downward arch will seldom exceed 45 degrees from the horizontal. Again, flower age makes a difference. Some irises maintain pleasing angular separations between standards and falls during most of their life. A most pleasing and artistic form involves a slight upward arch to the standards and a slight downward arch to the falls.

Pendent Form

In pendent form the falls hang downward in a vertical or almost vertical position. A completely pendent form results when the standards maintain a similar position. Many variations are within pendent form. In some cases the falls have a rather elongated, elliptical shape, which contributes to the graceful effect of the flower, particularly when a slight breeze causes bird-like motion.

Recurved Form

In recurved form, the outermost edges of the falls curve beyond the vertical, giving a "rolled back" effect. This form is relatively new and not common. It is more prevalent among the newer hybrids and it remains to be seen how popular it will be. Some other features may be necessary, such as smaller, more circular falls of heavier substance, for an iris to show the recurved form.

Open Form

Open form and overlapping form depend on the bloom's dimensions, particularly the width of the segments. The open form requires fairly narrow segments. This term is generally used in combination with the above terms to more precisely describe a form, for example, "flaring, open form" or "pendent, open form." Sometimes, the open form is referred to as "spidery," as in the cultivar 'Black Widow'.

Overlapping Form

Overlapping is the opposite of open form. The standards and falls are sufficiently wide to have considerable segment overlap. Essentially no space can be
detected between the segments. Blooms actually hold water, as you can observe
after a light rain. The overlapping form, particularly the flaring, overlapping
form, has become the most popular form of the modern hybrids. The collected
iris 'Peggy Mac', believed to be a variant of *Iris nelsonii*, was most responsible for
development of the flaring, overlapping form. It is here that hybridizers must
exert caution so that the flaring, overlapping form does not become the dominant and only form of the future.

Doubles and Semi-Doubles

Most are derived from 'Creole Can-Can', a collected variant of *Iris giganti-*
caerulea. Marvin Granger collected this unique form of the species in the
marshes near Cameron, Louisiana. This blue self is really a semi-double, having six or more falls, no standards, and varying amounts of petaloids which
replace the anthers normally found on irises. A number of John Taylor's recent
introductions are known to bloom as doubles and are totally unrelated to the
Granger line. However, the doubling in the Taylor irises is not a fixed feature
and does not constitute a true example of the double form. The Taylor double
forms do produce anthers.

No two blooms are identical in the double and semi-double form, which is
considered normal and not a fault. Persistent hybridizing by Granger over
many years has paid off with many unique irises in a wide range of colors and
forms. The hybrids represent two main forms: the "cartwheel" form with six
falls, generally with signals and a minimum of petaloids; and double or semi-
double forms with many more petaloids.

No attempts have been made to recommend or endorse certain colors or
forms. Within each form there may be certain features such as ruffled or tailored segments, lighter colored edgings on the floral segments, or even a mixture of two forms. It is a matter of beauty being in the eye of the beholder.

Placement of buds and blooms along the stalk enhances the effects of
color and form. Buds should be distributed proportionally over the upper two-
thirds of the stalk to achieve a well-balanced appearance. Undesirable bud
placement can mar an otherwise pleasing appearance. Blooms should not cluster in a group, but should be sufficiently separated so that color and form can
be appreciated. Another fault involves emergence of the buds from the bud
sockets. Buds may not emerge properly and blooms may not open properly, or
even at all, which prevents observing the full beauty of the iris.

Other Diverse Features

Other diverse features not only enhance the garden picture but contribute much to the distinctive variability of Louisiana irises. These other features include size, floriferousness, substance, texture, style arms, signal, stalk, foliage, and certain newer features.

Size of Blooms

The size of Louisiana iris blooms have shown a steady increase. Today, they range from about 3 inches (7.6 cm) across to more than 7 inches (17.8 cm). Irises 6 to 7 inches (15.2–17.8 cm) across are typical of current introductions. Very few introductions are in the smaller size. Since the larger flowers are preferred by most show judges, they are also preferred by most hybridizers and growers. Most awards in shows and exhibitions seem to go to the larger irises. In the garden the larger flowers, particularly in the brighter colors, do make a better show, but for most flower arrangements the smaller sizes are desirable. The shorter growing and smaller flowered cultivars are perfect for use in mixed borders and edging in front of taller cultivars.

Most iris lovers feel that Louisiana irises are now large enough. Although new introductions will probably continue in the large size range, we need good irises of 3- to 5-inch size (7.6–12.7 cm). We do not need or desire monstrosities larger than 6 to 7 inches (15.2–17.8 cm). Further increases in size are likely to decrease their utility and the substance of the blooms. A limited trend toward smaller, low-growing flowers began many years ago with the work of Frank Chowning, and other hybridizers are now following this trend. Their work could lead to Louisiana irises of a size comparable to the medians and dwarfs among the bearded irises, a most welcome development.

Floriferousness

Floriferousness is very important in the garden and in iris shows. Total bud count, number of blooms open at one time, and length of time a stalk remains in bloom all contribute to floriferousness. Bud count depends on the number of bloom points including stalk branches and the number of buds in each bud socket. The time a stalk remains in bloom depends on all these factors and also on culture, weather, and the genetics of that particular iris. Some irises are naturally more floriferous than others. Occasionally an iris can be too floriferous. In a certain few irises "suicidal" tendencies may be noted. These irises bloom excessively, generally without making sufficient new growth, and may bloom themselves out of existence.

New cultivars under consideration for introduction or awards should carry a minimum of six buds per stalk. An exception to this rule may be made for cultivars that are very vigorous and produce a large number of stalks per clump, with enough offsets to ensure good bloom the next season. Most newer cultivars carry two buds at each position, and occasionally the terminal position has three buds. Shorter growing cultivars may only have three blooming positions. Floriferousness should always be a foremost hybridizing objective, but culture is an important influence. By providing excellent culture over average culture, growers can realize an increase of at least one, possibly two, flowers per stalk.

Substance and Texture

Substance and texture are important in any flower. Substance is the physical tissue makeup of the flower segments. It directly affects the flower's ability to maintain form and color. Most growers and hybridizers have been concerned with the substance of Louisiana irises for decades. The new irises being introduced tend to show remarkable improvements in substance. Tetraploids, by virtue of larger cell size, show better substance than most diploids. However, hybridizers are now achieving substance in diploid irises once thought only to be possible with tetraploids. The better the substance the better the lasting qualities and resistance to heat, wind, and rain. Flowers, under normal weather conditions, should last two to three days maintaining their color and form without becoming floppy.

Substance may also be related to flower form and color. Today, blooms with flaring or arching form have thicker segments and better substance, but this is very likely due to the fact that these forms have had the most hybridizing attention. The pendent form cultivars still tend to have thinner segments and less substance, but they should also improve with increased work by hybridizers. Lighter colored irises do not absorb as much heat and have more resistance to higher temperatures, but this may or may not translate to better substance and lasting qualities.

Texture is the surface appearance of the floral parts and is described by such terms as leathery, satiny, silky, velvety, rough, or smooth. Any texture is acceptable if the underlying substance is good—it adds to the beauty and distinctiveness of the flower. Certain colors are enhanced by texture, such as crepe-like pastels, satiny reds, and velvety purples. Velvety texture is particularly attractive and seems to be associated with darker colors, mainly dark purples and dark reds. These effects are related to the cellular structure on the surface of the segments. Some irises have protruding cells called papillae on the surface and the velvety texture appears to be associated with these cells.

Style Arms

The style arms are essential sexual parts of all irises. They also have a profound influence on the beauty of the blooms. The style arms are far more visible in Louisiana irises than in the bearded irises, because of the more open form of the Louisianas. It is generally difficult to observe style arm characteristics of a bearded iris because the size and domed shape of the standards hide the style arms from view. The color, size, and other features of the style arms are readily apparent in Louisiana irises. Color may be the same as other segments, or may be completely contrasting. Style arm color varies from dark to almost pure white. The white style arms of 'Mac's Blue Heaven' or 'Katherine L. Cornay' against the violet segments provide a very distinctive contrast.

The style arms vary greatly in length and width. *Iris fulva* and closely related hybrids have narrow and short style arms. *Iris giganticaerulea, I. brevicaulis*, and close hybrids have longer and wider style arms. Most recently introduced diploid hybrids show a wide range of style arm size. A few diploids and most tetraploids have very broad style arms. Some irises have lacy tips at the ends of the style arms called style crests or claws. These are virtually absent in *I. fulva* and *I. nelsonii* and present in *I. giganticaerulea* and *I. brevicaulis*. Style crests are another point of distinction, and may serve a practical function as a sort of umbrella to protect newly pollinated blooms from rain.

Signals

The signal is a marking usually in yellow or orange and typically located on the middle of the base of the falls, where the beards are located in bearded irises. By the diversity of their presence or absence, these markings enhance the beauty of the blooms. From an aesthetic standpoint the most important feature of the signal is its variability. It varies from almost completely absent to most pronounced and contrasting. Dark colored irises with large signals are attractive because of the high contrast. 'Ann Chowning' and 'Professor Ike' are outstanding in this category. Many of the newer cultivars have signals on both the standards and falls. Some very beautiful and popular irises such as 'Black Widow', 'New Offering', and 'Full Eclipse' are almost devoid of signal markings. Line signals are a raised pubescent area sometimes referred to as a crest. Some irises display the signal on a white, cream, or light yellow background that spreads out into the flower in what is known as a spray pattern, such as shown by 'C'est Si Bon' or 'Violet Ray'. A most unusual color combination appears in 'Lockett's Luck' and 'Twirling Ballerina', which have signals outlined in maroon. In some cases long style arms can obscure signal markings.

Nature generally has practical reasons for most features of flowers and plants. It is interesting to speculate as to the practical significance of the signal in Louisiana irises or the beard in bearded irises. Although the significance is uncertain, the signals or beards provide strong color contrast, and they are located at the exact point where insects enter under the style arms in search of nectar. A bumblebee or other insect rubs pollen from its back onto the stigmas on the underside of the style arms and pollinates the bloom. The signal might serve as a target for the bumblebee to land on the iris.

Stalk and Foliage

The stalk and foliage contribute to practical matters and to the garden picture. In garden culture the stalk, which serves as a framework and support for the blooms, varies from about 10 to 50 inches (25.5–127.0 cm) or more. Stalk height should be relatively consistent within a clump. The height and thickness of the stalk should be in proportion to the size of the flowers. Louisiana iris stalks may be straight, gracefully curved, or zigzag. This variability in stalk structure makes Louisiana irises distinct from most other irises. All the variants are acceptable provided they have sufficient strength to remain upright without staking except when seed pods are maturing. To be considered a good garden iris, any new introduction must have stalks that display blooms above the foliage. The zigzag stalk is attributable to *Iris brevicaulis* and should not be confused with stalks that develop a bend or curve before straightening out. *Iris brevicaulis* stalks tend to lie down on the ground with flowers facing upward, or down in the foliage and should not be faulted for doing so, but this courtesy does not extend to hybrid cultivars with *I. brevicaulis* in their lineage.

Good foliage is essential to the health of the plant. Every effort should be made to take advantage of the foliage as a thing of beauty. The irises are in foliage much longer than they are in bloom. The foliage should be attractive except possibly during very hot weather. Foliage color varies from light green to darker blue-green. Most tetraploids have dark blue-green foliage. Heights and widths of foliage and leaf postures vary. Some have leaves near vertical while others gently arch. Normal garden hygiene should suffice to keep the foliage in good condition. Special care may be needed after bloom and during hot weather. Extra moisture supply and mulch may stave off complete dormancy. Remove deteriorated leaves carefully and do any necessary hand weeding. Most importantly, do not disturb or cut back foliage during hot weather.

Newer Features

Any iris being considered for introduction should possess both beauty and distinctiveness. Newer features which add to distinctiveness and diversity of

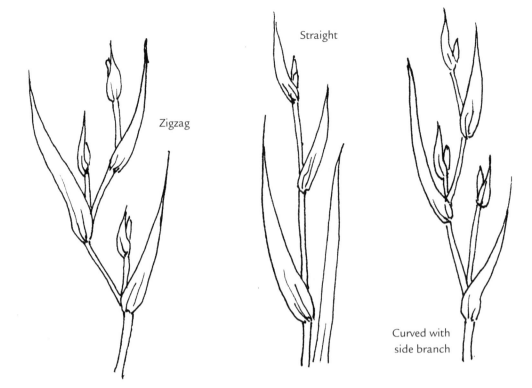

Zigzag

Straight

Curved with side branch

Types of stalks

Louisiana irises include laciness, ruffling, and unusual and exotic color combinations. The latest hybrids show lace or ruffling on the segments, particularly on the falls. This very attractive and artistic feature has been known for a long time among bearded irises but is comparatively new among Louisianas. An early ruffled hybrid was 'Clara Goula'. Younger ruffled progeny include 'Koorawatha', 'Jazz Ballet', 'Garnet Storm Dancer', 'New Vogue', and 'Bayou Mystique', to mention only a few. Today's introductions tend to be heavily ruffled in comparison to those of just ten years ago.

Exotic colors include true bicolors, style arms of contrasting color, a limited plicata pattern, and halos of white or yellow on floral segments. Until

(Facing page) *Above left:* Straight scape development typical of *Iris giganticaerulea*. *Above right:* Zigzag scape structure which allows for proper bud and flower development. *Below left:* Good scape structure with one branch. *Below right:* Improper scape development causing difficulty for buds to properly emerge from sockets.

about the mid-1960s, bitones but no true bicolors were in the Louisiana group. Bicolors introduced since then include 'Creole Rhapsody', 'Just Helene', 'Glow-light', and 'Kitchen Music'.

Adaptability

The great adaptability of Louisiana irises is a relatively new discovery. As recently as the 1950s these irises were grown in Louisiana, California, Arkansas, and very few other states. Growing activities in foreign countries were very limited. Growers thought that the irises required the warm and wet conditions of Louisiana. Due to the dedicated efforts of many people, this misconception has faded. Their adaptability is now recognized as far greater than had been suspected, not only in the United States but also in many international locations. Species and hybrids are now grown in almost every part of the United States. Australia and New Zealand are outstanding in growth and promotion of Louisiana irises. Japan, South Africa, and countries in Europe are becoming increasingly active. Louisianas are not only acceptable in areas where bearded irises do not perform, but they are now recognized as worthy companions for the bearded and other iris types. No one has found strong indications as to where the limits of adaptability lie. It is a matter for interested growers to "get their hands dirty" and try them. More often than not gowers will be amazed with the results. The more that is learned the more the limits of adaptability seem to shrink. Another fifty years of effort may see Louisianas accepted as the most adaptable group in the genus.

Do not neglect the great potential of growing these irises from seed. Seed propagation is a quick and cheap way to get an extensive collection of Louisiana irises. Hand-pollinated seed from hybrids is apt to produce better quality irises than were available among the registered cultivars a few decades ago. Growing from seed should be most useful in more remote locations where it is difficult to procure or import the registered cultivars. Seed from nurseries, iris societies, and growers can be sent almost anywhere. Detailed methods of growing from seed are described in Chapter 5.

A word of caution is in order. Like any plant Louisiana irises will not perform well under conditions of neglect. The would-be grower should not expect good results with a philosophy of "plant and forget." Only in swamps and wetlands where nature provides all cultural requirements do they seem to grow to perfection without attention. Cultural requirements will vary some with the growing area and are discussed in detail in Chapter 10.

Domestic Adaptability

Louisiana iris activities are ever increasing in the Southwest, specifically Texas, Oklahoma, and Arizona. This region offers highly variable climates, from Louisiana-like conditions in the Houston area, to dry and arid but not excessively cold in Dallas, to typical midwestern winter conditions in the Texas-Oklahoma panhandle. High to very high summer temperatures are the rule, often with only slight rainfall. The irises demand special efforts of growers, but such efforts are well worth the trouble. Growers continue to increase in number as do the exhibits of Louisianas at iris shows. They are far more visible than just a few years ago. The plants and blooms produced in some difficult areas are of excellent quality.

California is probably the prime location in the United States for growing Louisiana irises, surpassing even south Louisiana. Much of California is frost-free and many coastal areas have moderate summer temperatures. Rainfall is variable and irrigation is often necessary. The result is a very extended growing season, ten to twelve months duration, compared to about seven months in south Louisiana. Although some special care may be necessary, almost the entire state of California is adapted to Louisiana iris culture. California is probably the center for small and medium nursery activities offering these irises. In recent years California Louisiana irises have been second only to tall bearded varieties in "Queen of the Show" awards.

The Pacific Northwest is usually considered a lush growing area but its climate is less than ideal for growing Louisiana irises. The irises are evergreen in this area and their development seems to proceed too fast. A somewhat similar situation can occur in Louisiana due to late winter cold and results in lost bloom for the early varieties. A partial solution would be to utilize the later blooming cultivars. A still better solution would be for hybridizers to develop still later blooming and cold resistant varieties by extensive use of the species *Iris brevicaulis*.

In the coldest midwestern states a picture of adaptability is beginning to emerge which is nothing short of sensational. As late as the 1980s growing Louisianas in South Dakota and Minnesota would have been unthinkable. Today they grow and bloom in such locations by the hundreds. Cultural methods are very important and much is still to be learned. Two items regarding efforts in these colder areas are noteworthy: success has been achieved for the most part with the currently available varieties developed in warm locations, and complete winter dormancy and the insulating effect of heavy snow cover seem to be essential. Increasing numbers of growers and small nurseries are active in the Midwest.

Adaptability in the south-central states, particularly Arkansas, Missouri,

Tennessee, and Kentucky, has progressed well due mainly to the efforts of Frank Chowning of Little Rock. He was possibly the first to realize that many varieties developed in south Louisiana, while performing reasonably in Arkansas, were not the most satisfactory. His hybridizing was based mostly on *Iris fulva* and *I. brevicaulis* which are found in Arkansas and adjacent states, though to a lesser extent than in Louisiana. These species are more adaptable and better performers in colder locations. In almost five decades of hybridizing, Chowning produced and registered many excellent cultivars. Many of these not only perform better in colder locations but do exceptionally well in Louisiana and other warm areas. His work has inspired several other hybridizers and growers to continue and expand upon his contributions.

The Atlantic coastal states from Maine to Florida present a variety of climates and great opportunities for growing Louisianas. Although activities in the New England area have been limited, they are expanding. The coastal regions of New England are milder, while the interior portions are more like the Midwest. The middle Atlantic states, Maryland, Virginia, and North Carolina, are more comparable to the south-central states. Outstanding success has been reported for the Baltimore area. The southern Atlantic states should be very hospitable to Louisiana irises. They are known to perform very well in Florida although growing and hybridizing activity is lacking in many areas. The southern areas of Alabama and Mississippi are comparable to Louisiana.

Overall adaptability of Louisiana irises to various parts of the continental United States can be summarized as follows:

1. Many areas still show no significant attempts to grow series *Hexagonae*. Where attempts have been made, most have been moderately to highly successful. It does not seem to be an exaggeration that Louisiana irises can be grown in at least 80 percent of the United States.
2. The most adaptable areas are California, Louisiana, the Gulf states, and the southern Atlantic states.
3. Areas of reasonable to good adaptability include the Southwest, the south-central states, most of the upper Midwest, and the middle Atlantic states.
4. Later blooming cultivars tend to perform better in the Northeast.
5. Later blooming cultivars also fare better in the Pacific Northwest.
6. These conclusions are based on currently available cultivars, most of which were developed in warm locations. Cultivars developed in Arkansas seem more adaptable to colder areas.
7. Incentive is great for hybridizers to develop varieties more adaptable to bloom time and cold intensity.

8. Adaptability to all regions is greatly enhanced by following good cultural practices for the respective area.

International Adaptability

Information on international adaptability of Louisiana irises is limited. Only in Australia and New Zealand is activity great. South Africa, Japan, and European countries show limited activity. Most places generally show great interest in ornamental plants. Two items seem important for increasing growing of Louisiana irises in these areas: providing information about and plants and seeds of the *Hexagonae*, and publicizing the activities of the most adaptable areas.

The exact time when Louisiana irises first appeared in Australia is clouded. An early grower was Royce Spinkston of Adelaide in South Australia. He grew Louisianas from seed received from Caroline Dormon and others in the 1940s. Because of the great distances and lack of air transportation, it was virtually impossible to get plants to Australia. The irises from seed grew and performed well, according to accounts by growers. At Cairns in the northern Australia tropical belt, "Louisianas would thrive and increase rapidly while tall bearded types rotted away," one grower reported.

Beginning in the 1960s enthusiasm greatly increased based on much improved irises, which were also grown from seed from Frank Chowning, Claude Davis, and Charles Arny. Seeds were widely distributed in through New South Wales and resulted in exciting new colors. These were the first of the modern hybrids grown in Australia. Greater visibility in iris shows in Sydney and Melbourne vastly increased their popularity.

Commercial nurseries in the Unites States now regularly offer newly introduced Australian Louisiana cultivars. Outstanding new Australian hybrids are now being developed by John Taylor, Bernard and Heather Pryor, Janet Hutchinson, and others. These hybrids are entirely competitive with the best new cultivars from Louisiana, Arkansas, Texas, Mississippi, and California. The popularity of Louisiana irises in Australia is increasing at about the same rate as in the United States, while hybridizers and growers seem to be increasing even faster. Fortunately communication and exchange of both information and irises are good between hybridizers and growers.

The situation in New Zealand may not be quite as advanced as in Australia but indicates very significant activity. Sam Rix of Mt. Maunganui has been growing and hybridizing Louisianas for many years, probably starting with seed from Caroline Dormon. As an example of persistence he grows his irises in specially prepared soils in boxes to overcome the problem of almost pure sand at his beach-side garden. The Rix hybrid 'Frances Elizabeth' won the DeBaillon Award in 1965. Phylliss Kokich grew Louisiana irises for more than thirty years in three gardening areas of widely different soil and climatic conditions. Her experience emphasizes the adaptability of Louisiana irises from northern New Zealand to the Auckland area. Varieties include the species *Iris fulva* and *I. giganticaerulea*, some very early hybrids, and many modern hybrids. The increase is excellent and "each spring produces a more magnificent display than the last."

True irises do not occur naturally in the Southern Hemisphere. Most of southern Australia and New Zealand fall between 25 to 45 degrees latitude south, which corresponds approximately to the northern latitude of most of the United States. Although the two hemispheres are approximately symmetrical in climate distribution, great variations exist in altitude, rainfall, and other factors. It is no great surprise that Louisiana irises perform so well in many areas of Australia and New Zealand. Seasons, of course, are reversed and the irises bloom from September into November.

South Africa is of favorable latitude in the Southern Hemisphere at 20 to 35 degrees south. Audrey Wessels has grown and distributed Louisiana iris for several years. Recently she has been importing newer cultivars from the United States and introducing them to new growers in South Africa. Eugene Scheepers, another South African Louisiana iris grower, has successfully introduced the irises to the cut-flower market.

Much of Japan is between 30 and 40 degrees latitude north and is climatically suitable for Louisiana irises. Akira Horinaka has been growing, distributing, and hybridizing near Osaka and Kyoto for several years. He considers them highly desirable garden plants especially suitable for ornamental plantings around the edges of ponds or streams. Flower arranging is a fine art in Japan and cut blooms of Louisiana irises are very useful for arranging. Horinaka has been importing new cultivars and distributing the increase among members of the Japan Iris Society. He has launched a personal campaign to popularize Louisiana irises in Japan, and the number of gardeners growing them is increasing steadily.

Climates in Europe cover a wide range of conditions. Most of southern Europe falls between 40 and 45 degrees north latitude, and northern Europe is between 45 and 55 degrees. Northern Europe is therefore equivalent to the most northern United States and southern Canada. Except for Spain, parts of France, Italy, and Greece, European cultural requirements are probably similar to those now being developed for the upper midwestern United States. It is not unusual that they have not made great inroads in Europe. It would seem that the time is right for hybridizers to stress development of cultivars more adaptable to the colder climates of Europe.

Louisiana irises are now being grown in more and more public and private gardens around the world. As time passes much valuable information will become available. Eberhard Schuster contends it is possible to grow some of the modern hybrids in eastern Germany where winter temperatures get to −5°F (−20°C). Some cultivars perform better than others and he hopes to stock the more hardy ones in his nursery in the future. Eckard Berlin has been growing Louisiana irises in Germany for several years in a climate "similar to southern Canada at an altitude of 2000 feet (600 meters) above sea level." Many of the sixty cultivars he grows do not perform very well under these conditions. Even borderline results are significant. Improved hardiness by hybridizing and improved cultural methods should improve performance in severe climates.

Many other areas roughly between 25 and 45 degrees latitude in the Northern and Southern Hemispheres should allow Louisiana irises to thrive. Essentially nothing is known about the growth and performance of Louisiana irises in these undocumented locations.

CHAPTER 4

Collecting of the Species and Natural Hybrids

I n no other area on earth but southern and southwestern Louisiana has natural hybridization within the genus *Iris* been so extensive. Both species and
natural hybrids are found in the same geographic locations, from roughly the
Mississippi River Delta westward to near the Texas-Louisiana line and up to
almost 100 miles (160 km) inland. The principal area comprises about 15,000
square miles (38,900 square km) and has been referred to as the "golden rectangle" of Louisiana irises. So extensive were these populations in the 1920s
that Small used the term "the iris center of the universe" to describe the area.
And Small's explorations were limited to only about the eastern third of the
total area. The species *Iris hexagona*, *I. brevicaulis*, and *I. fulva* do grow in other
areas and in other states but with very little evidence of natural hybridization.

The species and particularly the natural hybrids became the foundation
stock for later hybridizing. Natural hybrids offered great advantages. Bumblebees had provided a few, sometimes many, generations of hybrids, greatly
advancing the progress through hundreds of years. Collecting began as a result
of Small's publicity work on Louisiana irises. It was the main activity from
1930 to 1950. This same period marked the beginning of controlled hybridizing, although some hybridizing of historical interest occurred prior to 1930.

Conditions Favoring Natural Hybridization

The principal area of natural hybridization is low land near or below sea level,
and in no instance more than slightly, 10 to 15 feet (3.0–4.6 m), above sea level.
The land is very wet, having many small streams called bayous, also lagoons,
lakes, and rivers. Here, large areas of swamps or sloughs are usually covered
with shallow water up to perhaps 12 inches (30.5 cm) deep. During very rainy

periods the water may be deeper. Many of these swamp areas are wooded with deciduous trees and shrubs, but some low areas, particularly on the western Louisiana coast, are in complete sun. These sunlit areas are almost always flooded. In the deciduous wooded areas considerable sunlight will penetrate in late fall, winter, and early spring, roughly the growing season in the area. During the summer when there may be little or no water the trees are in leaf and the shade protects the rhizomes.

Water served a dual purpose in natural hybridization in the series *Hexagonae*. First, it met a basic requirement for growth of these moisture-loving irises. Second, it met a more sophisticated requirement for distribution of the species to facilitate natural hybridization. It is most probable that the natural hybrids resulted from the different species becoming distributed within the pollination range of the bumblebee. The exact range of pollination is unknown, but it is certainly not very great. This distribution by water was the result of widespread dispersal of seeds. *Hexagonae* seeds have a corky outer layer or seedcoat and can float on the surface of water for prolonged periods in a dormant condition. Seeds were carried by the water and winds for considerable distances in open ponds, swamps, and marshes. They were probably carried even greater distances by the flowing waters of bayous and rivers and by winds and tides moving in from the open waters of the Gulf of Mexico. All this was further facilitated by periodic flooding due to very heavy rains. The annual rainfall in this area is near 60 inches (152.4 cm). The species *Iris giganticaerulea* is native to marsh areas very close to the gulf. Good records document the spread of this species from the gulf marshes northward to the vicinity of Lafayette, Louisiana, a distance of approximately 30 miles (48 km). Similarly, seeds of the more inland species, *I. fulva* and *I. brevicaulis*, were water-borne southward to the same locations.

Near Abbeville, Louisiana, all three species are found in close proximity near a converging point of several small streams. It was here that enormous populations of natural hybrids developed as a result of random pollination by bumblebees over decades or centuries. This is the general area where the species *Iris nelsonii* evolved, an area referred to locally as "Iris Heaven." Natural hybrids are not limited to borderline areas between the species but are dispersed and scattered throughout the population. This allowed persistence of the more vigorous, vegetatively propagated clones for many years and provided excellent opportunity for advanced generation hybrid progenies to be produced in large numbers.

The area around Lafayette and Abbeville was not the only area where large numbers of natural hybrids evolved, but it was probably the most important. Another such environment was along Bayou Savage, a deltaic slough east-northeast of New Orleans. In this general area Small and Edgar J. Alexander, an associate of Small at the New York Botanical Garden, found many of the forms they described in the 1920s and 1930s. These hybrids were mostly types of *Iris fulva* and *I. giganticaerulea*. At that time the number of species and natural hybrids in this area probably exceeded those found in any other part of Louisiana. Today this area is well within the city limits of New Orleans and no irises remain.

About 10 miles (16 km) southeast of Baton Rouge near Prairieville, Louisiana, large stands of *Iris fulva* and *I. brevicaulis* grew in close proximity. These were extensive in the 1940s and even into the 1950s. Natural hybrids of the two species were common in the area. The land has since been drained and all the irises have disappeared. Other important sites for natural hybrids were the vicinities around Thibodaux, Houma, and Morgan City. All that remains today are a few stands of *I. giganticaerulea* in the most remote locations.

Period of Collecting

Following the work of Small, some twenty years passed before hybridizing really came of age, but this was not a static period. It was the most important period of collecting. Prior to about 1920 the only Louisiana irises grown in gardens were through the efforts of explorers, trappers, hunters, and a few horticultural enthusiasts who brought the irises out of the wild. All such activities were limited due to the relatively short bloom season. The available irises often passed from family to family and generation to generation, as far back as the 1800s. It is virtually impossible to determine anything about the origin of such irises. About 1930 collecting came into vogue as a result of Small's pioneering efforts, and with it came at least some documentation of collected varieties. Some hybridizing did take place during the period of collecting, but it was limited, and documentation as to parentage was not kept.

During the 1930s and 1940s thousands of species and natural hybrids were collected. Plant enthusiasts took to the swamps in droves to find the many species named and described by Small. But these efforts were far from successful. They found many irises, but few if any met the recorded descriptions. Instead, the collectors found many different "species." Few of these collections were documented so there is only limited background to emphasize the importance of the period. It was during this period that the vast extent of natural hybridization came to be realized, mainly through the efforts of Percy Viosca Jr. who was to clarify which of Small's many species were true species and which were natural hybrids or variants. (Only Small's *I. giganticaerulea* is considered a true species today.) Thus the modern taxonomical relationships among Louisiana irises began to evolve.

The Society for Louisiana Irises was organized in 1941 and almost immediately provided incentives, communications, and organizational activities related to collecting. Foremost were guided collecting trips to the native iris stands near Lafayette and Abbeville. These were a scheduled part of the annual meeting of the society for the first ten to fifteen years. This was of great interest to members from north Louisiana, Texas, and a few other states. Many people came earlier and went into the swamps on their own. Everyone was collecting.

Very few of these collected irises were registered. They were often given garden names and distributed among the society members, many of whom grew acres of the collected specimens. Lenora Mathews of Shreveport was reported to have over five acres planted in Louisiana irises, most having been collected on her trips to Lafayette. Many others from north Louisiana were instrumental in growing and in early hybridizing. William Fitzhugh of Shreveport was growing and selling them as early as 1939–1940. Some of Frank Chowning's early stock came from Fitzhugh. Also in the north Louisiana group were Hattie Clark, Inez Conger, Minnie Colquitt, Sidney Conger, Lillian Hall Trichel, Claire Gorton, Ruth Dormon, Caroline Dormon, and others.

Another group came from Houston to collect during the early years. Activities due to early members, including Hazel Parks, Mrs. J. Willis Slaughter, Marjorie Cashman, and Ila Nunn, established interest in Louisiana irises in that part of Texas. These women grew great numbers of Louisiana irises, promoted them through their garden clubs and created an interest that continues today.

Many American Iris Society (AIS) officials came during the "collecting period" to see, photograph, and collect. What they collected was not of importance, but the publicity they provided formed a link to the rest of the iris world. Past *AIS Bulletin* editors Geddes Douglas and Sam Caldwell from Nashville were early participants in these swamp tours and collecting trips. Through their writings for iris publications they became some of the best promoters for Louisiana irises.

By the mid to late 1940s controlled hybridizing began to supplant collecting as the preferred method of obtaining superior irises. The foundation stock for the increasing hybridizing effort had been collected. Fortunately so, because the natural populations began to succumb to the advance of progress. Many of the best natural hybrids were collected, but it will never be known how many were lost. By 1950 the period of collecting was all but over and controlled hybridizing was strongly underway. No hard and fast demarcation separates these periods. In the past fifty years or so hybridizing has achieved many milestones, and many milestones are still to be achieved.

Foundation Stock

Many individuals were responsible for collecting the foundation stock, as it is often called. Were it not for these collecting efforts the quality of Louisiana irises would not be what we know today. Many of the best natural hybrids would not have been collected and would likely have been lost forever. Due to limited records it is not possible to describe all these collections or even a major part. Only a few of the best documented collections can be described, but there were many, many more.

Collecting contributions by Percy Viosca Jr., Mary DeBaillon, Caroline Dormon, Ira Nelson, and W. B. MacMillan stand out for their profound effect on hybridizing through their quantity and quality. These people were either contemporaries of Small or close followers. For all his influence Small did not do significant collecting, at least not in terms of registrations with the American Iris Society. Records indicate only two collected irises that were registered by Small. Possibly twenty or more collectors also worked with only a few irises of outstanding quality. Then there were others who accumulated extensive collections, but due to location or other reasons the dispositions and hybridizing impact of these collections remain clouded.

All the collections included species and natural hybrids. Most information presented here was obtained from registrations of the American Iris Society. Generally the registrations do not distinguish between species and natural hybrids, and the irises are designated simply as "collected." In some cases descriptions are sufficient to make the distinction, in some cases not. This does not seem highly important, because no information is available as to what parents the bumblebees used to produce the natural hybrids. Valid registrations are not available in some cases. Others refer to originations by the persons indicated, and still others are descriptions used locally for years. Relatively few of the collected irises are available today. Some go back seventy years or more and are of much historical importance. But the emphasis has long since been on hybridizing and many hundreds of improved and beautiful cultivars have been produced.

Percy Viosca Jr. was a professional biologist who made two great contributions to Louisiana irises. First, he clarified the taxonomy of the group. Prior to his work the *Hexagonae* consisted mainly of the many species named by Small. Except for the species *Iris nelsonii*, which was to be designated later, Viosca revised the taxonomy to essentially what we use today. He accumulated an important collection of *I. fulva*, *I. giganticaerulea*, and hybrids of these two species. His collecting was mostly in the New Orleans area and the Mississippi River Delta and did not include the habitat of *I. nelsonii*. No evidence indicates that Viosca undertook serious hybridizing, but many of his collected irises were probably used by other early hybridizers. Viosca named and registered fourteen irises with the AIS from 1932 to 1938. Table 1 gives some idea of the range of irises in the Viosca collection.

Table 1. Irises collected by Percy Viosca Jr.

Cultivar	Introduction	Color	Probable Identity
'Angel Wings'	1935	pure white	*I. giganticaerulea*
'Choctaw Tribe'	1935	red-brown	*I. fulva*
'Dandywine'	1935	wine purple	natural hybrid
'Encarnado'	1935	cardinal red	*I. fulva*
'Imperialis'	1932	imperial purple	natural hybrid
'Isle Bonne'	1935	clematis purple	*I. giganticaerulea*
'Lafitte'	1932	lobelia blue	*I. giganticaerulea*

The name of Mary Swords DeBaillon ranks with that of J. K. Small in the early history of Louisiana irises. She is most noted for collecting, and her name is most prominent in the early records of the Society for Louisiana Irises. When the society was first founded it was called the Mary Swords DeBaillon Iris Society. The Mary Swords DeBaillon Award, now the DeBaillon Medal, is the highest award exclusively for Louisiana irises. It is presented by the Society for Louisiana Irises through the American Iris Society and sits only one step below the Dykes Medal, the highest award any American iris can receive.

DeBaillon collected in the areas around Lafayette for many years, including the habitat of *Iris nelsonii*. Although she made a very large collection and shared her irises with many, DeBaillon registered no irises herself. Upon her death a part of her collection passed to Caroline Dormon. From 1943 to 1949 Caroline Dormon registered nineteen collected cultivars by Debaillon under the name DeBaillon-Dormon. A cross section of this important collection includes the irises in Table 2.

These are but a few irises in the extensive DeBaillon collection. Most were probably collected in the 1930s and likely found some hybridizing use before the registration dates. DeBaillon did not do extensive hybridizing herself but distributed irises to others for use in hybridizing. Toward the end of her life she also distributed seed, whether planned or bee crosses. Some of these seeds were given to W. B. MacMillan, and from these came the beautiful 'Bayou Sunset', an outstanding early garden hybrid and the second Louisiana iris to win the DeBaillon Award (1949).

Closely related to the activities of Mary DeBaillon were those of Caroline

Table 2. Irises collected by Mary Swords DeBaillon and introduced by Caroline Dormon

Cultivar	Introduction	Color	Probable Identity
'Contrast'	1943	orchid-violet bicolor	natural hybrid
'Homachitto'	1942	dark red	*I. nelsonii*
'Jeune Fille'	1942	frilly white	*I. giganticaerulea*
'Magnolia Petal'	1942	deep cream	natural hybrid
'New Orleans'	1942	pink	natural hybrid
'Royal Highness'	1946	dark blue	*I. giganticaerulea*
'Ruth Marsalis'	1943	wisteria blue	*I. giganticaerulea*

Dormon of Saline, in north Louisiana. Though she did not reside in the golden rectangle, Caroline Dormon did much collecting and later hybridizing. She was also a naturalist, conservationist, author, and artist. Her home in Saline is today a nature preserve for many wildflowers besides Louisiana irises. Her two books, *Flowers Native to the Deep South* and *Natives Preferred*, are outstanding references. In the 1940s and 1950s Caroline Dormon registered and introduced fourteen of her own collected irises and many hybrids. The collected irises included a variety of *I. giganticaerulea*, *I. nelsonii*, and natural hybrids. Table 3 lists a few of the better known irises introduced by Caroline Dormon.

Table 3. Better known collected irises introduced by Caroline Dormon

Cultivar	Introduction	Color	Probable Identity
'Cathedral Blue'	1944	blue	*I. giganticaerulea*
'Forsythia'	1946	yellow	*I. nelsonii*
'Foxglove Bells'	1953	red-violet bitone	natural hybrid
'Golden Glow'	1952	yellow bitone	*I. nelsonii*
'June Clouds'	1945	white	*I. giganticaerulea*
'Lillian Trichel'	1943	rose-pink	natural hybrid
'Old Coral'	1949	coral-pink	*I. nelsonii*

'Cathedral Blue' has an interesting history. According to the checklist this iris was collected in the wild near New Orleans by Mary DeBaillon and later shared with Caroline Dormon. Undoubtedly it was collected considerably prior to 1944. Frank Chowning contends it or an almost identical iris was grown in Little Rock gardens in the 1920s. He also contends it was grown by

T. A. Washington of Nashville in the 1930s. Washington referred to it at times as 'Miss Priscilla' and at other times as *Iris hexagona*. (Today 'Cathedral Blue' is considered to be a hybrid of *I. giganticaerulea* and *I. brevicaulis*, a theory resulting from test crosses of these two species carried out by Joe Mertzweiller and Farron Campbell.) The source of the Washington iris is unknown, but it could be very old, dating even before 1850. This confusion is typical of the information regarding old irises.

The collected 'Mary S. Debaillon' was the first DeBaillon Award winner in 1948. 'Old Coral' was to become a very important parent. Caroline Dormon collected many yellow and pink variants of *Iris nelsonii*. She became extensively involved in hybridizing many of her collected varieties and produced many excellent garden hybrids including several DeBaillon Award winners. Among these winners were 'Violet Ray' (1953), 'The Khan' (1955), 'Saucy Minx' (1954), and 'Wheelhorse' (1958). 'Wheelhorse' turned out to be one of the two great Louisiana iris parents of all time, along with 'Peggy Mac', becoming a parent or grandparent of many great irises and award winners.

W. B. MacMillan was a businessman from Abbeville who had a lifetime interest in plants and was a contemporary of Mary DeBaillon and Caroline Dormon. His interest in Louisiana irises started in the 1930s and led him to develop an extensive collection. He is best known for his discovery of the *Iris nelsonii* habitat; this may be the single most important discovery during the period of collecting. Later, "Mr. Mac" turned his efforts to hybridizing and gave us many fine irises. It is understandable that many of his collected irises were *I. nelsonii* or closely related hybrids. Table 4 lists some irises collected by MacMillan.

Many of these beautiful irises represented breaks in form or color, and foremost among them was 'Peggy Mac'. This was the most important of the MacMillan collection and very possibly the most important of all collected Louisiana irises. 'Peggy Mac' was the first to show the flaring, overlapping form

Table 4. Irises collected by W. B. MacMillan

Cultivar	Introduction	Color
'Bayou Vermilion'	1943	crimson
'Cardinalis'	1943	cardinal red
'Haile Selassie'	1943	royal purple
'Homahoula'	1943	scarlet copper
'Mei Ling'	1943	yellow
'Peggy Mac'	1943	magenta rose
'Reflected Light'	1943	soft yellow

and was unsurpassed in transmitting this form to its progeny. In later hybridizing MacMillan produced the DeBaillon winner 'Black Widow' (1968), which
is among the darkest irises.

Ira S. "Ike" Nelson was a professor of horticulture at the University of
Louisiana, Lafayette. His contributions to Louisiana irises are too numerous to
mention. When he first came to ULL he was instrumental in founding the
Society for Louisiana Irises. He made many scientific contributions and for
many years was the show manager for the society. Many of these early iris
shows were most outstanding. Ike had an abounding interest in all plants and
flowers, but particularly in Louisiana irises. He recognized the great potential
of these irises and was to exert a profound influence on many collectors and
hybridizers.

Nelson collected and introduced a number of Louisiana irises and was
involved in hybridizing as well. But his greatest assets were his knowledge and
his ability to motivate others, particularly his students. Most of his collected
varieties were *Iris nelsonii*. He collaborated with Lowell Fitz Randolph, professor of botany at Cornell University, in identifying this species, which Randolph
later named in his honor. Nelson's collected irises include the metallic red
'Breeders Red' (1949), the yellow-brown 'Jaune-Brun' (1944), the autumn-
yellow 'King's Gold' (1946), and the white *I. giganticaerulea* variant 'Larose
White' (1945). The Nelson hybrid 'Cherry Bounce', a cherry-red self, won the
DeBaillon Award in 1951.

From 1943 to 1957 the species and natural hybrids were becoming scarce
in the wild and collecting was on the wane, but many important irises were
collected, named, and registered with the American Iris Society. Many registered in this period were probably collected earlier than their registration dates.
Table 5 lists only some of the many irises registered in the mid-twentieth century. Twenty collectors are represented below and no collector contributed
more than two irises to this group.

The backgrounds of these irises still hold many blanks and approxima-
tions. 'Pink Joy Roberts', a pink variant of *Iris brevicaulis*, is reported to have
been collected by J. C. Roberts's great-grandfather when the Acadians first
landed in Louisiana. If such is the case, this may well be the oldest known Louisiana iris, over 150 years old. Other irises may have been registered by individuals other than the collector. In another twist, 'Bazeti' is recorded as a registration by Small, but the date is after his death. 'Bazeti' was probably named
by Small in honor of Randolph Bazet, who may have registered the iris. Bazet
assisted Small in many collecting expeditions.

The quality of these irises was exceptional and unusual. Three of this group
became DeBaillon Award winners: 'Wood Violet' in 1956, 'Blue Chip' in 1957,
and 'Her Highness' in 1959. The unique semi-double 'Creole Can-Can' became

Table 5. Some irises collected and registered by others between 1940 and 1960

Cultivar	Intro-duction	Collector	Color	Probable Identity
'Easter Surprise'	1955	Mrs. E. P. Arceneaux	orchid	*I. giganticaerulea*
'Cameron White'	1946	Katherine Cornay	white	*I. giganticaerulea*
'Bette Lee'	1953	Vernon Davis	white	*I. giganticaerulea*
'Wood Violet'	1943	Ruth Dormon	dark blue	natural hybrid
'David Fischer'	1943	D. Fischer	blend	natural hybrid
'Skyfleck'	1945	Hazel Gosslin	plicata	*I. giganticaerulea*
'Creole Can-Can'	1958	M. A. Granger	blue	*I. giganticaerulea* (semi-double)
'Ruth Holleyman'	1954	G. W. Holleyman	blue	*I. giganticaerulea* (triploid)
'Storm Signal'	1957	G. W. Holleyman	blue	*I. giganticaerulea*
'Mrs. Robert Lee Randolph'	1949	Mrs. J. F. Kerper	pink	natural hybrid
'Holleyblu'	1952	Ruth Holleyman	violet	*I. giganticaerulea*
'Kraemer Yellow'	1943	Victorine Kraemer	yellow	natural hybrid
'Her Highness'	1957	W. L. Levingston	white	*I. giganticaerulea*
'All Falls'	1957	Mrs. J. G. Richard	blue	*I. brevicaulis*
'Pink Joy Roberts'	1954	J. C. Roberts	pink	natural hybrid
'Bazeti'	1945	J. K. Small	red	natural hybrid
'Maringouin Fulva'	1943	Mrs. Smith	yellow	*I. fulva*
'Blue Chip'	1950	Sally Smith	blue	*I. giganticaerulea*
'Barbara Elaine Taylor'	1954	J. A. Taylor	white	*I. giganticaerulea*
'Lockett's Luck'	1947	Elmina Thibault	pink	natural hybrid
'Cajan Joyeuse'	1942	G. Thomas	rose	natural hybrid

the basis for all other semi-doubles, doubles, and most cartwheel irises in the *Hexagonae*. One of two known triploids, 'Ruth Holleyman' does not seem to have been given the hybridizing attention it deserves. However, 'Cajan Joyeuse', 'Maringouin Fulva', 'Cameron White', 'Lockett's Luck', 'Holleyblu', 'Barbara Elaine Taylor', and many of the others found extensive use in hybridizing.

Questions and confusion accompanied the collected irises, for clonal distributions in the wild habitat were often extensive and growers did much sharing and interchanging of the collected irises. Many people were involved, and many collected irises were duplicates originating from the same clone. To help clarify some of the confusion the Society for Louisiana Irises set up a test garden at the Horticulture Department of the University of Louisiana, Lafayette.

Most varieties from the DeBaillon collection formed the nucleus for this test garden. Collected varieties had to be grown and bloomed in the test garden to establish eligibility for registration and eventually awards. When the DeBaillon Award was set up, the Society for Louisiana Irises gave the American Iris Society a list of irises that had bloomed in the test garden and that were determined to be new registrations. After 1950 so few irises were being collected and registered that the test garden was eliminated.

Other Contributions to Collecting

Other individuals made contributions to collecting despite having, due to location, only limited access to the golden rectangle. The most influential of these were Frank Chowning of Little Rock, Arkansas, J. C. Nicholls Jr. of Camillus, New York, and Thomas A. Washington of Nashville, Tennessee. Nicholls and Washington were very active in the 1930s before the founding of the Society for Louisiana Irises. They did not have the advantage of contact and communication with the southern Louisiana group.

The efforts of Frank Chowning touched practically every phase of Louisiana irises. Although his main contributions were as a hybridizer, he collected many varieties for use in his hybridizing programs. He collected a yellow *Iris fulva* near DeValls Bluff, Arkansas, and probably other species from outside Louisiana. He also acquired species and natural hybrids from Louisiana including 'Maringouin Fulva', 'Kraemer Yellow', and 'Lockett's Luck', all of which were used in his very successful efforts in developing more hardy hybrids for colder locations.

Other collected species, particularly *Iris hexagona* and *I. giganticaerulea*, played an important role in Chowning's hybridizing activities. He refers to 'Cathedral Blue' and 'Catahoula Blue' (unregistered) as variants of *I. hexagona*. Both these irises are considered to have been collected in Louisiana, but the identity as *I. hexagona* is uncertain—they look like hybrids of *I. giganticaerulea* and *I. brevicaulis* based on controlled hybridizing of *I. giganticaerulea* and *I. brevicaulis* carried out by Mertzweiller and Campbell. Chowning probably obtained and used collected *I. hexagona* from the southeastern states. Many of his hybrids were sold or exchanged with Louisiana growers, and he is the most plausible link, if one exists, between *I. hexagona* and the present-day Louisiana hybrids. At this time it is believed that *I. hexagona* has little or no influence within the Louisiana irises. Only scientific studies of DNA can determine the presence of *I. hexagona* with any degree of certainty.

J. C. Nicholls Jr. amassed a collection among the largest and earliest documented. It included twenty-six registrations made mostly in 1932 and 1933.

He apparently collected his irises from areas in and around New Orleans, the same locations covered and studied by Small. His variety 'Sazerac', a bright red collected *Iris fulva*, was named after a cocktail originated and popularized in New Orleans lounges at that time. The Nicholls collection included many *I. fulva*, some of which must have been spectacular according to such registration descriptions as "red with black velvet streaks" and "red, velvety-black color." He also had *I. giganticaerulea* and certainly natural hybrids bearing such identifications as "I. radicristatae" and "vinicolor," names attributable to Small and no longer recognized as *Hexagonae* species. Nicholls may have done limited hybridizing, but no records indicate use of these irises by later hybridizers. Many of the Nicholls collected varieties were offered commercially by Royal Iris Gardens of Camillus, New York.

T. A. Washington was an early grower and hybridizer. Most of his work was done in the 1920s and 1930s, and more than fifty cultivars were registered from 1931 to 1935. It is not clear how many collected varieties were involved, and most appear to be F_1 hybrids. Washington also used identifications such as "vinicolor" that indicate both Small's influence and possible Louisiana origin. He made many references to *I. fulva* × *I. hexagona* parentage but few references to *I. brevicaulis*. But these references to *I. hexagona* cannot be documented, and as with many of the early irises, Washington's work did not play any role in the development of today's hybrids.

A less-known early collector was Edmond Riggs of St. Martinville, Louisiana, who collected extensively in the 1930s and early 1940s. He registered twenty-two collected varieties from southwestern Louisiana in 1944. Documentation is limited, but his collection included the species *Iris giganticaerulea* and *I. fulva* and many natural hybrids. It is uncertain whether *I. nelsonii* was represented, but many of Riggs's collected varieties are undoubtedly in the ancestry of the modern hybrids.

In Retrospect

It was the opinion of Small in 1931 that the wild iris fields of southeastern Louisiana were being wrecked by man-made factors and that many "species" were being destroyed. This was only too true where civilization encroached upon the wild populations. Small was a very early conservationist.

Shortly later, in 1935, Viosca presented a somewhat different case. First, he considered the great variations in color and form not as distinct species but as natural hybrids of four widespread species. Even if garden enthusiasts collected most natural hybrids, there was nothing to prevent new hybrid seedlings from developing in places where the parental stock remained numerous.

Then Viosca predicted a bright future for Louisiana irises. Even in the 1930s he recognized them to be highly sought after by flower lovers and horticulturists because of their striking beauty. Viosca stated, "With the assistance nature has already given them, hybridizers, within a few years, will be able to produce many hardy garden varieties with undreamed of horticultural qualities."

Now, after seventy years of hindsight, both men appear to have been correct. The wild iris fields of the golden rectangle have been wrecked due to encroachment by civilization more than removal by collectors. Natural hybrids would have replenished themselves had the parent stock not also been a victim of the advance of progress. The most serious destruction appears in the vicinity of medium to large metropolitan areas. Very few species and essentially no natural hybrids remain around New Orleans and Baton Rouge. A few species remain around Houma, Morgan City, and Abbeville, all smaller metropolitan areas. Stands of *Iris giganticaerulea* in the coastal marshes remote from metropolitan centers are surviving fairly well. Colonies of I. *brevicaulis* in moist, bluff areas also do reasonably well. But I. *fulva* is seriously depleted, I. *nelsonii* is almost gone, and natural hybrids are virtually extinct. But Viosca's predictions about the achievements of hybridizing have more than come true. These achievements, along with greatly increasing popularity and adaptability, are outstanding highlights of the past seventy years. Collecting Louisiana irises was an interesting and amazing part of American horticulture, but it is a part of the past.

CHAPTER 5

Propagation of Louisiana Irises

Louisiana irises, as most plants, are propagated by two distinct methods: vegetative or asexual reproduction, and seed or sexual reproduction. Vegetative methods involve shoots or offsets formed on the main rhizome or bloom stalk. These methods virtually always produce offspring identical in every respect to the plant from which they were derived. Seed or sexual methods involve pollination, formation of seed, and growth of seedlings. They are responsible for new and different plants. Both methods have occurred naturally with Louisiana irises for hundreds, possibly thousands, of years. In more recent times growers have aided nature in propagation. Successful application of both methods, particularly the seed method, has contributed greatly to the enormous improvement of these irises.

Vegetative (Asexual) Reproduction

Before blooming, most Louisiana irises form long rhizomes, typically 4 to 8 inches (10.2–20.3 cm) or longer, and at least two offsets or side plants. Some varieties form three, four, or even more offsets. A few irises propagate poorly and may not form any offsets until after blooming. Producing offsets is typical vegetative reproduction in the wild or in the garden. If the plants remain undisturbed for several years they will form a thick clump growing from a tangled mass of rhizomes.

A rhizome blooms only once and then deteriorates, but not before producing tiny offsets. In the following years the offsets bloom. In order to have good bloom every year it is important to have good vegetative reproduction. On the average there will be two non-blooming offsets for every blooming rhizome. It is important to understand and plan for this reproductive cycle, or massive bloom one season may result in sparse bloom the next.

It is almost certain that the blooms of the offsets will be identical in every way to the original plant. However, "sports" or mutations may appear. These strange irises are usually rogue seedlings resulting from seed propagation through pollinated "bee" pods. Such seedlings are generally inferior and undesirable, but they may be much more vigorous, tending to crowd out the superior original irises. Avoid rogue seedlings by taking care to remove the bloom stalks on completion of bloom so that bee pods will not mature and spill seeds on the ground. Of course this does not apply to the controlled pollination of hybridizing.

Vegetative propagation has been remarkably stable for uncounted generations through hundreds or thousands of years. True mutations do occur, but only very rarely. No scientific information indicates how rare a true mutation is, but it is unlikely to occur more than once in tens or even hundreds of thousands of reproductions. True mutations result in significant and unusual changes in the blooms (often color, form, or other features) and involve genetic or chromosomal changes. Changes in ploidy level, the multiplication of chromosome sets, are not mutations. Mechanisms responsible for true mutations are believed to be associated with radiation, such as cosmic rays which continually bombard the earth from space. Plant mutations have been produced artificially by the radiation of X-rays or atomic reactors or by specific chemicals. Very few artificially produced mutations are desirable; however, they have their use in plant breeding just as new natural mutations do.

Maximizing Vegetative Reproduction

Most iris cultivars offered for sale by dealers or otherwise produced by growers are a result of vegetative reproduction from one plant originally grown from seed. However, a few Louisiana growers have been experimenting with propagation by tissue culture, though the high cost of producing plants by tissue culture makes this method less desirable. Many factors limit the rate of vegetative reproduction and hence the rate of distribution and the cost of new varieties. It is always the objective of the grower to maximize the rate and amount of vegetative reproduction. Factors controlling vegetative reproduction of Louisiana irises, as well as other irises, are not completely understood and offer much opportunity for research. It is probable that genetics control the main factors, which will always put a cap on the natural rate and amount of vegetative reproduction. Some varieties will always increase better than others, prompting most hybridizers to consider reproduction rate an important hybridizing objective.

Growers can aid nature in maximizing the rate of vegetative reproduction. Among such aids are: good general culture, frequent division and replanting, culture of the old rhizomes that have bloomed the previous spring, and tissue culture. Laboratory tissue culture of Louisiana irises could one day revolutionalize the way new cultivars are introduced to commerce, or allow for increased supply of classic cultivars. With time and the advancement of tissue culture the consumer should also see a savings in the cost of both new and classic cultivars.

The most important and reliable factor for maximizing vegetative offsets is to follow good cultural practices. Despite genetic limitations, healthy large rhizomes are much more likely to reproduce abundantly than small, undeveloped, and undernourished rhizomes. Since production of offsets occurs during the growing season, it is important that the plants go into the growing season in top condition and under the best cultural influences. If rhizomes go completely dormant during the summer the most favorable conditions cannot be met. Extensive evidence shows that ample moisture, even water culture or semi-water culture, is most important for maximizing vegetative reproduction.

Some growers divide and replant their irises every season. Though this can have an unfavorable effect on the bloom of some cultivars, it generally has a favorable effect on vegetative reproduction. Working the soil, adding humus and fertilizers, and watering frequently appear to stimulate growth and initiate vegetative reproduction. Frequent watering is particularly important after dividing and replanting.

Old rhizomes that have bloomed the previous spring can be a source of additional reproduction. If these rhizomes are left in the ground they remain dormant, generally make no further offsets, and gradually deteriorate. Cut away the old rhizomes from the new growth and carefully remove them. This is best done in late summer with the usual digging and replanting, but the rhizomes can be removed without disturbing the entire bed. Set the old rhizomes in a pot and cover them with about ½ inch (1.3 cm) of soil mix similar to that used for planting seeds, such as a fine milled peat with vermiculite and fine bark chips. Label the pots carefully, place them in a location that receives bright light but not direct sunlight, and keep them moist. New plants should sprout along the length of the rhizomes. Some will form quickly, but others may take several weeks or even months. No rules govern how much reproduction to expect; some varieties give many more plants than others. A few may not give any. Remember that any reproduction gained from these old rhizomes would not be achieved normally.

Let the plants grow in the pots until they are about 12 inches (30.5 cm) tall. It is important to protect the pots from severe cold—small plants in pots are much more sensitive to cold than the same size plants in the ground. The rate of growth is fast, much faster than that of seedlings, because of the nourishment provided by the old rhizomes. The new plants will quickly develop an extensive root system. By late winter or early spring, approximately five months after potting the rhizomes, the plants can be removed from the pot, separated, and set in the growing beds. Do not retain the plants in the pots over a hot summer. If the old rhizomes are still sound they can be replanted in the pots and may produce additional plants. Once in the ground the rate of growth of the offsets is rapid because of their already developed root system. Continue to water generously.

The old rhizomes eventually rot and may develop bacterial or fungal diseases. For this reason it is better to isolate them in pots. Also, probably due to better environmental control, reproduction seems to be better in pots than if the rhizomes were planted directly in the ground.

The methods described here are useful but not necessarily the best. Other growers have developed their own techniques for multiplying old rhizomes. Some use a water culture method and others use plant hormone treatments.

Closely related to reproduction from old rhizomes is the formation of flower stalk offshoots. This is a vegetative method and gives plants identical to the original. Louisiana irises can form bloom stalk offshoots, called proliferations, similar to the daylily (*Hemerocallis*). Flower stalk buds form at the leaf nodes and must be stimulated into growth. Cut the stalks after blooming but while still green and before developing seed pods. Place the stalk in a container of water with the water line slightly above the leaf node and keep shaded. Another method is to place the flower stalk almost horizontal in moist sand or vermiculite. When an offshoot and its roots have developed, remove it from the stalk and transplant to a growing medium. The flower stalk offshoot method is much less effective than growing from old rhizomes.

Tissue Culture

Louisiana irises and many other plants are reproduced vegetatively by tissue culture methods. These methods involve the culture of meristem tissue or small inflorescences in nutrient media in the laboratory. A single meristem or inflorescence can produce a great many small plants. Sterile conditions and special equipment and techniques are required. Tissue culture may never be practical for the average iris grower. Large nurseries may turn over the propagation of superior seedlings to specialized laboratories for tissue culture, thus getting them into commerce much sooner than possible with conventional methods. However, plants should be grown and bloomed before marketing since atypical plants can result from tissue culture.

Seed (Sexual) Reproduction

Outstanding improvements in Louisiana irises are a direct result of growing these irises from seeds. This is the only sure method of producing the variability which gives new and desirable cultivars. Hybrid parents normally give progeny that are all different. The genetic combinations are virtually limitless. Progress has increased almost exponentially since 1940 and the end is nowhere in sight. Many more advances can be expected at the diploid level. The tetraploid Louisianas—those with four sets of chromosomes in their cells, twice the usual diploid number—are still too few to allow reasonable speculation about their future. If the future of tetraploid Louisianas parallels the bearded irises, their future is bright indeed.

Preliminaries to Hybridizing

Here we are concerned with the mechanics of seed propagation of Louisiana irises. Irises in general, and Louisiana irises in particular, are very adaptable to being grown from seed. This process is intimately related to hybridizing, which is covered in detail below. Seed propagation really had its beginning with the natural hybrids. Gardeners then followed up by using the best collected natural hybrids as the parent stock for new and superior varieties. Although the procedures are not difficult, a good deal of effort and "dirt gardening" are required, depending on how extensively you desire to get into these matters. The prospective grower and hybridizer should be warned that marketing irises is not likely to be a lucrative financial operation, but hybridizing is likely to be most challenging and fascinating to those interested in growing things.

Almost all progress in hybridizing Louisianas over the past fifty years has been made by amateur breeders. Most breeders grow only a few hundred seedlings a year in backyard or small nursery plots. Very few large nurseries are active in hybridizing and growing Louisianas from seed.

Seed pods will form on most Louisiana irises due to activities of the bumblebee, nature's main pollinating agent for these flowers. Bee pollination is the basic method by which large fields of species were propagated and natural hybrids produced. Bee pods and the resulting seeds are random and are much less likely to give superior progeny than hybridizing done with specific objectives in mind and with select parent stock. Bee pods should not be used as a source of seed, and the stalks containing such pods should be removed and discarded.

Mechanics of Pollination

Most people who hand pollinate Louisiana irises have their own preferred methods of pollination and related matters and also of the growth of seedlings. The following description represents only one of many possible methods. You should always use the methods most successful for yourself.

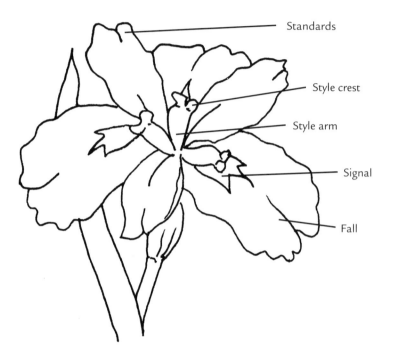

Flower Parts

First, study the sexual parts of the Louisiana iris as shown in the diagrams. The three style arms radiating from the center of the flower contain the stigmas or female parts on the underside and near the end of the style arm. To each side of the style arm's center line is a stigmatic lip, making six lips in all. In many varieties the two lips connect to form a single structure. The style arm itself is the connecting tissue between the stigmas and the ovary, where the female sex cells (egg cells or female gametes) are located. The ovary is barely visible on the new flower. Just under the style arms lie the anthers or male parts, which contain the pollen, which in turn contains the male sex cells or gametes. A normal Louisiana iris has three anthers, one under each of the three style arms. Each anther consists of two pollen sacs, one on each side of a slender

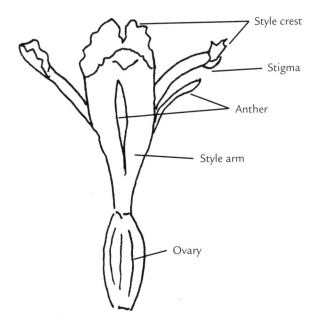

Dissected Flower

stalk or filament. All these parts, including the standards and falls, are tightly furled in the flower bud. The highly colored standards and falls, the most attractive parts of the flower, have no sexual significance. They serve only to attract bumblebees to pollinate the flowers. A short time after the flower opens the pollen sacs break open, or dehisce. The bumblebee enters the flower between the fall and the style arm in search of nectar. Pollen on the back of the bumblebee contacts the stigmatic lips and the bloom is pollinated. Pollen from many flowers may adhere to the back of the bumblebee, so the pollination is very random. During the peak of the iris season bumblebees are very plentiful and they are literally yellow with pollen.

The hybridizer provides the same function as the bumblebee but in a much less random and more scientific fashion. Based on desires, experience, objectives, and some knowledge of genetics, the hybridizer decides on the female and male parents, the pod parent and pollen parent, respectively. The female bears the seed and the male furnishes the pollen. (Hybrid formulas such as 'Wheelhorse' × 'W. B. MacMillan' name the pod parent first and pollen parent second.) Theoretically any fertile iris can function as either parent. Some irises set seed more readily as one parent than the other. Many hybridizers will make a cross both ways to optimize seed set. After choosing the parents, they follow this procedure:

Entire flower showing all parts intact.

Applying pollen to stigma.

Device for holding pollen. (A soft brush also works well.)

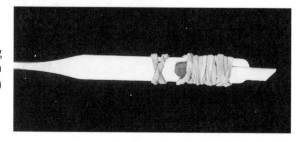

Emasculated flower with anther being removed for subsequent pollination.

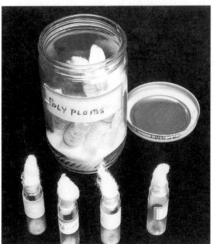

Pollen storage in low-moisture environment.

Resultant seed pods, which are usually mature in eight to ten weeks.

1. The female parent, the flower, is forced open when in the loose bud stage. Twist carefully in the direction counter to which the bud is furled. Early morning is the best time to open the flower. The falls will break off immediately, but you need not remove the standards. Remove the anthers with eyebrow tweezers and save the pollen in a "pollen bank" for use in future hybridizing. To save the pollen, place the anthers, pollen side up, on a small piece of paper indoors, and allow them to dehisce at least six hours. Be sure to mark the name or number of the bloom on the paper. Pollen left in open flowers is rapidly carried off by bumblebees and other insects. If pollen is not stored it may not be available when needed.

2. The bloom, prepared as described, should age about six hours before pollination to allow the stigmatic lips to loosen and the stigmas to become more receptive. The prepared blooms have little or no chance of being pollinated by bumblebees or other insects, for insects are unable to reach the stigma lips when the falls have been removed.

3. One method is to use a small firm brush to pollinate each stigmatic lip, forcing a very small quantity of the chosen pollen under the lip, between the lip and the style arm. If pollen is scarce, pollinate only one lip on each style arm. The pollen must rest within the gap between the lip and the style arm. You can construct a special tool that makes pollination easy. Attach an ordinary book match, broken end up, to a very thin wooden or metal handle about 6 inches (15.2 cm) long. Use a rubber band or plastic tape to secure the match, leaving about one-half the length of the match extending beyond the tip of the handle. Cut the tip of the match with a razor on about a 45-degree angle to form a sharp point on one side. Dip this point lightly into the pollen in the pollen bank, and a very small quantity will adhere. The point can easily be forced under the stigmatic lip. Use a damp cloth to clean the point between pollinations, and cut a new point after several repetitions. Replace the match periodically.

4. When pollination is complete, immediately and carefully tag the pollinated bloom with a weatherproof label that lists the pod parent × the pollen parent and the date the cross was made. Also keep a separate written record of each cross. Leave the label on the stalk until harvesting the seed pod, about three months later. Some hybridizers recommend that no more than two pollinations be made on each stalk, preferably on the uppermost and immediately lower positions. Others pollinate as many blossoms as possible. For those

irises that make two blooms at each position, pollinate only the first bloom to avoid confusion, or make the same identical cross on the second flower. With care, you may make a different cross on the second flowering position provided each is properly labeled. If you do not wish to pollinate the second flower, it may be best to remove it when it appears.

It is desirable to have pollen available when necessary, and a pollen bank serves this purpose. After the fresh anthers dehisce in about six hours, carefully remove the pollen to a small sheet of paper and then into a small dry bottle, about 1 ounce or less (5–10 cc) in size. Label and date the bottle and stopper it with a wad of cotton. Place several pollen bottles in a large screw-cap jar containing a 1-inch (2.5-cm) layer of solid dessicant on the bottom. Silica gel dessicant used for drying flowers is very satisfactory. Keep the pollen as dry a possible. Tightly cap the large jar and store it in the refrigerator. The pollen is available at any time and usually remains viable for a full hybridizing season.

Development and Growth of Seed

Within a very short time after pollination, amazing but invisible things begin to happen. The pollen grains "germinate" on the surface of the stigma and start to grow tubes called pollen tubes into the tissues of the style arms. These tubes grow into the ovary where they come into contact with the egg cells. The two male germ cells of each pollen grain are borne downward through the pollen tube and into the egg cell. One male germ cell fertilizes the egg cell to form the union between the chromosome set or sets of the male cell and the set or sets of the female cell. The combinations are $n + n = 2n$ for diploids and $2n + 2n = 4n$ for tetraploids (where n signifies a chromosome set). Random combinations of the many genes associated with the chromosomes determine the features of the new irises.

The second male germ cell, the one that does not fertilize the egg cell, unites with an endosperm-forming nucleus within the egg cell. This union yields the endosperm, which provides nourishment for development of the embryo and later the newly germinated seedling. The embryo and the endosperm are both contained in the hard pellet surrounded by the seed coat.

The ovary becomes the seed pod and development is fairly rapid. Within a few days the ovary begins to swell, and within a month or so the seed pod and seeds have reached near maximum size. But the seeds are not completely developed, and the pods will need staking. No specific rules give the time required for the seeds to develop fully and be ready for planting. This probably depends on both genetic and environmental factors. Some varieties develop seed faster than others. In southern Louisiana most pods are completely developed in eighty to ninety days after pollination. Never allow a pod to deteriorate, letting the seeds harden and fall on the ground. Hardened seed may be very difficult to germinate. When the pods are still green but have begun to yellow, remove the seeds and plant them. Some authorities have described mature seed as pale tan rather than white or cream-white in color. But germination seems equally good with cream, tan, or brown seeds as long as they are mature and they are planted shortly after harvest.

A typical diploid pod will average near thirty seeds, although some may produce less than ten or as many as fifty or sixty. A tetraploid pod will average ten to twelve seeds. Tetraploids very rarely produce over twenty seeds, but frequently less than ten and occasionally none. Some pod parents, both diploids and tetraploids, naturally produce more seeds than others. The number of seeds produced and planted is particularly important. With high quality parent stock and well-planned crosses it is much more important to have more seed from a given cross than a greater number of crosses. Due to the many genetic combinations and probabilities, forty to fifty seedlings will barely screen the potential of a given cross. Since 50 to 60 percent germination is a reasonable average, at least 100 seeds from every promising cross should be planted. Ideally several hundred seedlings should be grown and evaluated. Very promising combinations should then be re-evaluated more definitively by growing and evaluating at least 1000 seedlings. Unfortunately, this is not very feasible with diploids for most amateurs, and it is impossible with the present state of development of tetraploids.

When the pods have developed completely and have just begun to turn yellow or brown, remove the seeds and either plant them immediately or store them under dry conditions to plant the following spring. In mild climates such as Louisiana the seeds should be planted immediately. In cold climates, unless a temperature-controlled greenhouse is available, dry the seeds and store them in a cool, dry area. Some growers dust seeds with a solid fungicide prior to storage, but this is not necessary if the seeds are dry and air circulation is adequate.

Much work has been done and much has been written about various seed pretreatments such as refrigeration, soaking in various chemicals, leaching in flowing water, and many other techniques. All are designed to speed and increase germination. Some of these techniques are based on the theory that iris seed contains germination inhibitors which can be removed by these processes. All such procedures show variable effectiveness. Two specific steps may help germination. First, seed which has been subjected to dry storage should be rehydrated before planting. Place seeds in a stoppered bottle of water for two to three days prior to planting. Second, it may be useful to chip the seed coat at the hilum end, the point at which the seed was attached to the seed pod. Use your thumbnail to remove 10 to 15 percent of the seedcoat. The embryo-endosperm pellet should be visible and is normally light brown in color. A firm, sound pellet is necessary for germination, although soundness is not a guarantee of germination. Often, seed resulting from inter-series, inter-specific, or incompatible ploidy level crosses will be unsound and may be rubbery, watery, or lacking in embryo-endosperm pellets. Some growers theorize that chipping the seed coat allows better access for water to leach out germination inhibitors, but no evidence proves that such is the case. Either fresh or rehydrated seed can be chipped. Recent data from Sam Norris and Joe Mertzweiller indicate that complete removal of the seed coat and further nicking of the endosperm can markedly improve germination. Farron Campbell recommends soaking the seeds in water until the corky outer coat is ready to fall away, which can take as long as several months, leaving the seed pellet completely free of the outer coat.

Planting the seeds in plastic or hard rubber pots is preferable to planting in flats. A 6-inch (15.2-cm) diameter pot is ideal for planting all seeds from a single pod. Larger or smaller pots can also be used depending on the amount of seed. Planting in flats can lead to problems in maintaining the identity of many different crosses. And do not plant seeds directly in the ground. Container planting allows better control over environmental factors. The planting medium is not too important but should provide fertility, porosity, and reasonable moisture retention. A good mixture consists of equal parts well-decomposed manure and sand. Some growers prefer to use commercially available sterile planting mixtures sold under various trade names. Do not use strongly acid materials such as peat moss, for they are likely to cause the seeds to rot prematurely.

Set seeds from each cross one or two seed diameters apart in the pots, and press lightly into the planting medium. Cover the seed with at least ½ inch (1.3 cm) but not more than ¾ inch (1.9 cm) of planting mix, firming the soil to assure good soil-to-seed contact. Carefully label all plantings with weatherproof markers. Keep plantings moist but not soaking wet in a shaded or semi-shaded area where animals and pests cannot dig up the seeds. High temperatures, sunlight, and excessive moisture may cause rot. Heavy rains may dislodge the seed and cause them to rise to the surface if they still have the corky outer coat. It is most important that the container not dry out, for germination may be seriously inhibited.

In Louisiana, seed planted in mid-summer (late July) will germinate in mid-fall (about mid-October) or approximately three months later. Most germination will occur over a period of two or three weeks, but this may differ in other locations. The extent of germination cannot be predicted. Rotting of the seed is a principal cause of poor germination. Genetics is another controlling factor. Usually germination will vary from less than 10 percent for some crosses to almost 100 percent for others. Some may not germinate at all. About 50 to 60 percent is considered a good average first-year germination. Tetraploid seed is variable in germination.

In south Louisiana little germination occurs after December, but possibly 15 to 20 percent additional germination will occur about one year after the first period of germination. And slight germination is possible another year later. The grower must decide how long is appropriate to keep the seed plantings. During intervening summers, keep the plantings shaded and slightly moist.

Applications of a soluble fertilizer every two to four weeks will stimulate growth of small seedlings. Most importantly, protect pots and flats from excessive and prolonged cold, even in climates considered fairly mild. Temperatures below about 25°F (40°C) may kill the plants. Small seedlings in containers are much more vulnerable to cold than those in the ground.

When the seedlings are 6 to 8 inches (15.2–20.3 cm) tall they can be planted in the ground provided the severe cold is past. In Louisiana temperatures are safe about mid-February, but colder locations will be later. Remove the plants from the containers with the aid of a spatula or flat knife, taking all possible care not to damage the delicate root system. If you are to keep the seed plantings, take care not to disturb the seeds that have not germinated. If space is limited, start seedlings 6 to 8 inches (15.2–20.3 cm) apart in rows 10 inches (25.5 cm) apart. Under these conditions clumps may have grown into each other by bloom the second spring, but they can be traced by rhizome connections. With the best care, clumps will be up to 24 inches (61.0 cm) across in one or two years. Therefore if space permits, 24-inch (61.0-cm) spacing between seedlings is best.

The plants must develop a good root system before the hot summer arrives. About three months active growth in the ground is necessary for the seedlings to be "on their own." If time is short, it is probably best to keep the seedlings in the pots until late summer or early fall. Keep the seedlings shaded and well watered during the summer. Once the seedlings are established in the ground, their culture is identical to that for other Louisiana irises as described in Chapter 10. Some suggest that seedlings be kept at least three bloom seasons. Some will bloom after one full season in the ground, but many will require a second season. Those that have not bloomed after two or three full seasons are probably poor growers that should be discarded. But do not be too quick to discard seedlings.

Probably the most important and challenging part of the whole hybridizing operation is judging the seedlings. Experience is the best teacher. Rarely is a seedling so outstanding that registration and introduction are no question. Even in such rare cases the seedling should be grown for several seasons to be sure quality and performance are really what they seem. Send such seedlings as "guest irises" to other growers and locations for testing. An iris that performs well in one area may not in another.

A few irises will be good but borderline, borderline in the sense that they may or may not be significant improvements over varieties currently on the market. Retain such seedlings for additional testing, and after several more seasons, most will have been discarded. A very few can be registered and introduced and a few may be retained for hybridizing use. The hybridizer should always be sure that his new introductions are of top quality. Too many of today's new introductions do not represent enough improvement over existing cultivars. Chapter 9, "Objectives in Hybridizing," might be of help in evaluating your seedlings.

Most seedlings, possibly more than 99 percent, will not meet stringent quality requirements. They generally must be discarded to make space for new seedlings. Some growers destroy surplus seedlings to prevent inferior cultivars from getting into commerce. Others sell these in bulk quantities for landscape use. Many small growers give away discards to increase interest in Louisiana irises. It is a matter of ethics that the recipient not register or introduce such irises without permission of the hybridizer.

Embryo Culture

Embryo culture is one method capable of giving near 100 percent germination of iris seed. Completely remove the embryo from the seed and culture it under laboratory conditions on agar gel containing essential nutrients. Use a small bottle or test tube, and sterile conditions are absolutely necessary to avoid fungal contamination. This method is useful for germination of certain wide crosses and interspecific crosses which may be deficient in endosperm. Embryo culture is a very specialized technique not normally attempted by the average grower.

CHAPTER 6

History of Hybridizing to 1988

Early Years of Diploid Hybridizing

Among the earliest recorded hybrids in the *Hexagonae* were Dykes's 'Fulvala' and 'Fulvala Violacea'. They date from 1910 or earlier and were derived from *Iris fulva* × *I. foliosa* (*I. brevicaulis*). Magnificent color plates showing 'Fulvala' and the two parents are reproduced in *The Genus Iris*, in which Dykes states, "Evidence of the affinity of *I. fulva* and *I. foliosa* is found in the fact that the former proved to be readily fertile to pollen of the latter. Moreover the hybrid 'Fulvala' has proved to be not entirely sterile as is usually the case with hybrids between two widely separated species of iris. On the other hand we may take it that the two species are distinct, since the hybrid does not show 'dominance' in any character, but it is a distinct compromise between the features of the two parents." Dykes points to the three important features that were at play in the development of natural hybrids and the subsequent successes in controlled hybridizing: fertility among the species, resulting fertile F_1 hybrids, and incomplete dominance.

In 1918, E. B. Williamson crossed the same two species and gave us 'Dorothea K. Williamson'. This deep velvety purple hybrid is similar to 'Fulvala' and is reported to be pleasantly fragrant and to have the zigzag stalk characteristic of *Iris brevicaulis*. Although later hybridizing shows no documented use of 'Fulvala' or 'Fulvala Violacea', the hybridizing history of 'Dorothea K. Williamson' is most interesting. Hybridizing records show that this iris has appeared as a parent at least as often as any other Louisiana iris, and it has been in use over a longer period than any other—fifty years or more. Unfortunately, very few out-crosses were made to other Louisiana species or hybrids. Most hybridizing involved self-crosses or back-crosses to the parents. Preston

Hale carried out this approach, in some cases for three to five generations, and registered at least ten progeny. Most progeny were dark colored, but two were yellow. Philip Corliss registered five seedlings involving 'The Khan' and other parent complexes with 'Dorothea K Williamson'. No documented evidence shows that either the Hale or Corliss cultivars were further used in hybridizing. Sam Burchfield registered another offspring *Iris fulva* × *I. brevicaulis* in 1924. 'Huron Regent' was an unusual deep mahogany hybrid.

'Cacique' is another very old *Hexagonae* hybrid still in cultivation. According to Jim Rhodes of Glendora, California, 'Cacique' is a hybrid of *Iris fulva* × *I. hexagona* registered by S. S. Berry in 1924. It is a purple-violet self, not too different from Dykes's 'Fulvala', and is very vigorous and tolerant of a wide range of conditions. It has spread throughout southern California and is widely used in flower arranging. Although reported to be fertile, its further use in hybridizing is not evident.

Thomas A. Washington produced and registered many *Hexagonae* hybrids in the 1930s. At least a dozen are listed as *Iris fulva* × *I. hexagona* crosses, with colors varying from pink through rose and blue to red-purple. He used *I. vinicolor*—once considered a true species, but since determined to be a natural hybrid—and his crossing of 'Dorothea K. Williamson' × *I. brevicaulis* gave a velvety blue and creamy white progeny. It is uncertain which, if any, of the Washington hybrids entered the more advanced breeding lines. However, Washington is known to have been in contact with Frank Chowning, which makes plant exchanges highly probable.

As previously mentioned, J. C. Nicholls Jr. was strongly influenced by Small's work in the 1930s and registered many collected varieties and natural hybrids. He also crossed 'Dorothea K. Williamson' × self to register 'Calera' (1938) and 'Champagne' (1937). The latter was light yellow and slightly fragrant.

During 1933 to 1947 Eric Nies registered seven hybrids derived from white and purple *Iris hexagona*, *I. fulva*, and natural hybrids of the *Hexagonae*. Some unusual colors were represented in this group including white, yellow, and golden-bronze. As with Washington's early hybrids, Nies's irises have left no record of their disposition and future use.

Diploid Hybridizing, 1940 to 1988

Louisiana iris hybridizing set many great milestones between 1940 and 1988. Prior to 1940 only limited stock was available for hybridizing, and most work happened outside Louisiana. But the year 1940 set the stage for intensive hybridizing through Small's great work with irises, the discovery of *Iris nelsonii*, and the founding of the Society for Louisiana Irises.

Hybridizing felt the strongest impact from collecting in the 1940s and 1950s. To a slight extent hybridizing from collected parents still occurs, but most hybridizing after 1960 involves advanced generation hybrids as parents. Of the foundation stock collected before 1960, *Iris nelsonii* was utilized more than any other species or group. Natural hybrids, *Iris giganticaerulea*, and *I. fulva* were used to a considerable extent, but *I. brevicaulis* did not receive the hybridizing attention it deserves. *Iris hexagona* has received only limited attention in hybridizing. In fact, all references to *I. hexagona* as a parent are in serious doubt: many irises once considered to be *I. hexagona* have proven to be hybrids of *I. giganticaerulea* × *I. brevicaulis*. Only recently have taxonomic studies proven that *I. hexagona* is a true and distinct species. The only Louisiana iris hybrid that comes from a known *I. hexagona* cross is 'Lone Star' (1997) by J. Farron Campbell of Garland, Texas (discussed in Chapter 7).

Registration and documentation in the 1940s were still very limited. Most checklists refer to either species or a "collected natural hybrid" as parents. Only in those cases in which at least one parent is properly registered and named is it possible to consider the lineage in detail and draw specific conclusions about performance of parent stock.

In the following sections, contributions of the four species and the natural hybrids are given in terms of some of their best known progenies, particularly those that won the most prestigious award for Louisiana irises, the Mary Swords DeBaillon Award. The years between 1948 and 1985 saw only thirty-six DeBaillon Awards, meaning a great many of the best hybrid cultivars did not receive the award. (See Appendix C for a listing of the DeBaillon winners.) Although we discuss many of these unrewarded cultivars, it is not possible to do justice to them all. Virtually all present-day cultivars are complex mixtures of several species and natural hybrids. Often individual determinations reflect on the decisions made as to which species or groups are responsible for the major contributions. Scientific accuracy may be limited.

Contributions of *Iris nelsonii*

Many case histories are dependent on collected varieties or closely related cultivars of *Iris nelsonii*. Among the most interesting and complete stories is that of the beautiful white hybrid 'Clara Goula' (Arny, 1978), the 1982 winner of the DeBaillon Award and 1987 winner of the DeBaillon Medal. The hybridizing history leading to 'Clara Goula' is shown in the chart titled "The Royal Family of *Iris nelsonii*." 'Clara Goula' represents at least 50 percent *I. nelsonii* background, but its color does not exist in that species. Several hybridizers and collectors, including Caroline Dormon, Sidney Conger, W. B. MacMillan, Sam Redburn, Marvin Granger, G. W. Holleyman, and Charles Arny Jr., were responsible for the effort leading to 'Clara Goula'. The earliest identifiable ancestors were registered in 1943, but the hybridizing effort probably began at or near the peak of the collecting period, considerably before 1943, and continued to the introduction of 'Clara Goula' in 1978.

Four very important parents and DeBaillon Award winners themselves are intermediates in Chart 1: 'Violet Ray', 'Wheelhorse', 'W. B. MacMillan', and 'Charlie's Michele'. These are primarily descendants of the collected *Iris nel-*

Royal family of *Iris nelsonii*

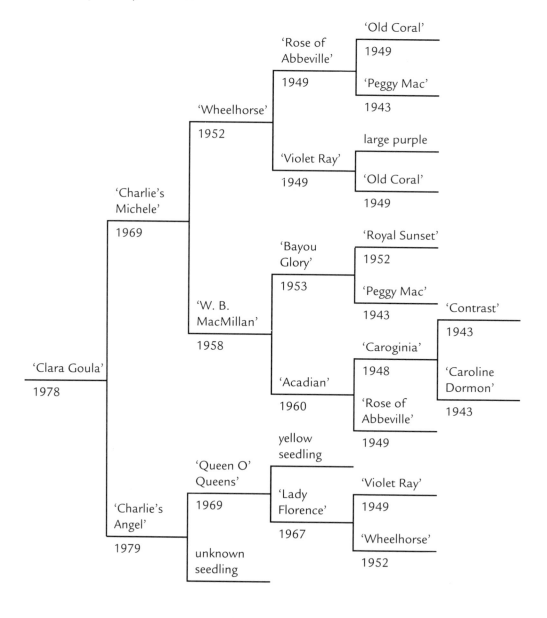

sonii, including 'Old Coral', 'Peggy Mac', and the natural hybrid 'Contrast', the first bicolor, which was collected by O. F. R. Bruce.

'Violet Ray', a pansy-purple with an extensive cream background (spray pattern) surrounding the signal, was introduced in 1949 by Caroline Dormon and remains popular to this day. It is most important as the pollen parent of 'Wheelhorse'; other important progeny from 'Violet Ray' include 'Breakthrough' ('Joyce's Choice' × 'Violet Ray'), 'Gulf Coast' ('Bramble Queen' × 'Violet Ray'), 'Gypsy Moon' ('Violet Ray' × 'Her Highness'), and 'Upstart' ('Rose of Abbeville' × 'Violet Ray'). 'Wheelhorse', a 1952 Caroline Dormon introduction, is a rose bitone considered by many to be the top parent of all the Louisiana irises. It and 'Louise Arny' are direct or remote parents more often than any others. Table 6 lists some notable offspring from 'Wheelhorse'.

'Wheelhorse' is most important as the pod parent of 'Charlie's Michele' but is even better known for the very broad gene pool it carries. G. W. Holleyman used 'Wheelhorse' extensively in his hybridizing. He is responsible for

Table 6. Notable offspring from 'Wheelhorse'

Cultivar	Parentage	Introduction	Hybridizer	Color Pattern
'Candle Glow'	'Wheelhorse' × *I. nelsonii*	1967	G. Holleyman	yellow-terra cotta
'Contraband Days'	('Bayou Sunset' × 'Gay Deceiver') × 'Wheelhorse'	1968	Granger	white-purple bicolor
'Charlie's Michele'	'Wheelhorse' × 'W. B. MacMillan'	1969	Arny	ruffled amaranth rose
'Frustration'	'Storm Signal' × 'Wheelhorse'	1960	G. Holleyman	violet on gold base
'Gee Whiz'	'Brandywine' × 'Wheelhorse'	1961	G. Holleyman	yellow with magenta veining
'King of Clubs'	smoky-colored seedling × 'Wheelhorse'	1973	Conger	low-growing red-purple
'Lady Florence'	'Violet Ray' × 'Wheelhorse'	1967	Redburn/ Granger	purple-veined yellow
'Louisiana Sambo'	'Wheelhorse' × 'Violet Ray'	1964	Neugebauer	yellow self
'Plain-Folks'	'Storm Signal' × 'Wheelhorse'	1961	G. Holleyman	veined rose bitone
'Royal Lady'	'Wheelhorse' × 'Her Highness'	1957	G. Holleyman	wisteria, darker blend

observing that yellow progeny often result from crossing 'Wheelhorse' with other irises having yellow coloring on the reverse side. This characterstic indicates a recessive gene for yellow, which has given several fine, large yellows and blended colors on yellow backgrounds. Among the blended colors are 'Candle Glow', 'Frustration', 'Gee Whiz', 'Lady Florence', and 'Louisiana Sambo'.

'W. B. MacMillan', a 1958 introduction, is another iris high on the list of choice parents. It is a red bitone hybridized by Sidney Conger from mostly *Iris nelsonii* parentage, including 'Rose of Abbeville', 'Peggy Mac', and the bicolor 'Contrast'. 'W. B. MacMillan' can be considered the end product of Conger's breeding to develop and intensify the flat, overlapping form of 'Peggy Mac'. Table 7 shows the most important descendants of 'W. B. MacMillan'.

'W. B. MacMillan' is the pollen parent of three DeBaillon winners, 'Marie Caillet', 'Charlie's Michele', and 'Ann Chowning', which also won a second time when the award was elevated to medal status in 1986. 'Charlie's Michele',

Table 7. Descendants of 'W. B. MacMillan'

Cultivar	Parentage	Intro-duction	Hybridizer	Color Pattern
Mary Swords DeBaillon Award winners				
'Charlie's Michele'	'Wheelhorse' × 'W. B. MacMillan'	1969	Arny	amaranth rose self
'Ann Chowning'	'Miss Arkansas' × 'W. B. MacMillan'	1977	Chowning	currant red self
'Marie Caillet'	'Acadian' × 'W. B. MacMillan'	1960	Conger	violet-blue bitone
Other important descendants				
'Miss Arkansas'	(*I. nelsonii* × *I. brevicaulis*) × 'W. B. MacMillan'	1978	Chowning	carnelian red self
'Dr. Dormon'	'La Reve' × 'W. B. MacMillan'	1973	Conger	orchid-mauve blend
'Charlie's Karen'	'Joyce' × 'W. B. MacMillan'	1972	Arny	beige-rose bitone
'Price Redmond'	*I. brevicaulis* × 'W. B. MacMillan'	1971	Arny	magenta rose
'Amber Goddess'	'Joyce's Choice' × 'W. B. MacMillan'	1963	Arny	amber bitone
'Melon Party'	(copper *I. brevicaulis* hybrid × 'W. B. MacMillan') × 'W. B. MacMillan'	1986	Chowning	orange

'Clara Goula', and 'Ann Chowning' may have been the three most popular Louisiana irises of the 1975 to 1985 decade. 'Ann Chowning' was the most popular of all.

'Miss Arkansas', a 1978 Chowning introduction, looms as another important hybridizing iris among the family of 'W. B. MacMillan'. It is already the parent of two DeBaillon winners, 'Ann Chowning' and Chowning's rose-pink 'This I Love'. It may not be entirely coincidental that the complex pod parent of 'Miss Arkansas' is *Iris nelsonii* × *I. brevicaulis*; Chowning was among the few hybridizers to make extensive use of *I. brevicaulis*.

The vigor, stamina, and current hybridizing performance of 'W. B. MacMillan' have raised a note of concern. Although this iris found extensive breeding use from 1963 to 1979, no progeny have been registered since 1979. It was almost exclusively a pollen parent. Some growers now report difficulties in growing and blooming 'W. B. MacMillan', suggesting it may be in a state of decline for unknown reason. It is important to determine if it truly is in decline and what factors may be involved. There are hybridizing alternatives that do not show decline. The same genetic "goodies" seem to be present in 'Miss Arkansas', and hybridizers should utilize 'Price Redmond' (*I. brevicaulis* × 'W. B. MacMillan'), which is similar in appearance but hardy to average growing conditions.

'Charlie's Michele', a 1969 Arny introduction, has contributed greatly to Louisiana iris hybridizing. Aside from being the pod parent of 'Clara Goula', it is also the pod parent of the 1984 DeBaillon Award winner, 'Monument', a ruffled white from Mary Dunn. Table 8 lists some of the more impressive progeny of 'Charlie's Michele'.

'Charlie's Michele' is a medium rose self with a large yellow crest and extensive ruffling, the first Louisiana iris to show ruffles. The ruffling feature seems to be semi-dominant and may be its greatest contribution to hybridizing. 'Clara Goula' is the most ruffled Louisiana from this period, followed by 'Buttermint Lace', 'Lavender Ruffles', and 'Monument', and it gave rise to current ruffled hybrids pioneered by Australian hybridizer John Taylor. Also noteworthy are the dark, velvety irises resulting from 'King Calcasieu' as the pollen parent. 'Charjoy's Mike' is unique in this group because of a fine silver edging on the petals with pink and cream-colored style arms. The progeny derived from 'Charlie's Michele' are expected to create excitement in hybridizing for a long time.

Charles Arny developed another landmark hybridizing iris from early breeding involving 'Peggy Mac', 'June Clouds', 'Lockett's Luck', and 'King's Gold'. Named 'Louise Arny' in 1956, this pastel lavender iris is somewhat small, about 5 inches (12.7 cm), flat to cupped, somewhat ruffled, and with great substance. An orange-yellow, dagger-like signal is outlined by a deep lavender zone. This unique iris became a mainstay in Arny's breeding program. While an exact parentage chart of 'Louise Arny' cannot be given, it is consid-

Table 8. Outstanding progeny of 'Charlie's Michele'

Cultivar	Parentage	Intro-duction	Hybridizer	Color Pattern
'Clara Goula'	'Charlie's Michele' × 'Charlie's Angel'	1978	Arny	ruffled cream-white
'Buttermint Lace'	'Charlie's Michele' × 'Charlie's Angel'	1979	Goula	ruffled pale cream
'Charjoy's Mike'	'Charlie's Michele' × 'King Calcasieu'	1977	Arny	purple with silver margin
'Charles Arny, III'	'Charlie's Michele' × 'King Calcasieu'	1977	Arny	violet-red
'Charlie's Tress'	'Charlie's Michele' × 'King Calcasieu'	1977	Arny	purple
'Lavender Ruffles'	'Charlie's Michele' × unknown	1979	Goula	ruffled light lavender
'Mary's Charlie'	'Charlie's Michele' × 'Mac's Blue Heaven'	1982	Dunn	ruffled red
'Monument'	'Charlie's Michele' × 'Ila Nunn'	1978	Dunn	ruffled white
'Elusive Butterfly'	'Charlie's Michele' × 'Pay Check'	1984	Ghio	lavender violet

ered to be at least 50 percent *Iris nelsonii* with the other species making up the remainder. 'Louise Arny' received the DeBaillon Award in 1961. By 1981, hybridizing with 'Louise Arny' had produced four DeBaillon Award winners and a host of other excellent irises almost too numerous to mention. The De-Baillon Award winners and only a few of the other outstanding progeny are listed in Table 9.

Much of Arny's hybridizing involved line breeding—crossing back to the original parents, siblings, or same plant—with collected cultivars such as 'Lockett's Luck' and 'King's Gold'. These and other pollen parents gave a wide spectrum of colors. Along with other outstanding progeny, 'Louise Arny' produced as interesting and spectacular a group of offspring as any Louisiana iris.

Other DeBaillon Award winners are closely related to collected clones of *Iris nelsonii*. 'Caddo' ('Lilyana' × 'Bayou Vermilion'), produced by Trichel and awarded in 1950, is red bronze with a conspicuous gold steeple-like signal. Its parent 'Bayou Vermilion' is a velvety crimson collected by MacMillan, which is most likely *I. nelsonii*. 'Cherry Bounce' ('Contrast' × 'Breeder's Red'), produced by Nelson in 1946 and awarded in 1951, is a wild, cherry-red self with a metallic luster. Its parent 'Breeder's Red', a red self with a metallic luster, is a col-

Table 9. Some cultivars from 'Louise Arny'

Mary Swords DeBaillon Award winners

Cultivar	Parentage	Introduction, Award	Color
'Bryce Leigh'	seedling × 'Louise Arny'	1977, 1981	pale lavender
'Eolian'	'Louise Arny' × 'New Offering'	1969, 1976	pale blue
'Mrs. Ira Nelson'	'Louise Arny' × 'G. W. Holleyman'	1969, 1973	mineral violet
'Ila Nunn'	'Louise Arny' × ('Snow Pearl' × 'Puttytat')	1969, 1972	cream-white self

Other outstanding progeny

Cultivar	Parentage	Introduction	Hybridizer	Color
'Brother Sam'	'Louise Arny' × 'Royal Lady'	1972	Arny	scarlet
'Faenelia Hicks'	'Louise Arny' × 'LSU Beauty'	1969	Arny	rose self
'Joyce's Choice'	'Louise Arny' × 'King's Gold'	1960	Arny	orange-yellow
'Mally Philips'	'Louise Arny' × 'Lockett's Luck'	1963	Arny	rose self
'Morning Treat'	'Louise Arny' × 'Lockett's Luck'	1960	Arny	salmon peach
'Mrs. Mac'	'Louise Arny' × 'Dora Dey'	1963	Arny	blue
'Myra Arny'	'Louise Arny' × 'Mistis'	1969	Arny	pink bitone
'Potato Chip'	'Louise Arny' × 'King's Gold'	1962	Arny	yellow-brown
'Snow Pearl'	'Louise Arny' × ('Holleyblu' × 'Buttercup')	1963	Arny	white self

lected *I. nelsonii* introduced by Nelson in 1949, but it was not registered with the American Iris Society. 'The Khan' ('Haile Selassie' × 'Cardinalis'), produced by Dormon in 1949 and given the DeBaillon Award in 1955, is a very dark, velvety black-violet with a huge, bright yellow signal. This sensational iris was the first with such deep contrast between color and signal. Its parent 'Haile Selassie' is a velvety, dark royal purple *I. nelsonii* collected by MacMillan in 1937 and introduced in 1943. It is second only to 'Peggy Mac' in hybridizing importance among the *I. nelsonii*. 'Cardinalis', cardinal red, veined crimson, is another *I. nelsonii* collected by MacMillan in 1943. And 'Delta King' ('Upstart' × 'Fire Alarm') × ('Upstart' × 'Fire Alarm'), produced by Hager in 1967 and given the DeBaillon Award in 1971, is a terra-cotta-red self. The parent irises are complexes of 'Upstart', from 'Rose of Abbeville' × 'Violet Ray', and 'Fire Alarm', from 'Cardinalis' × 'Haile Selassie', both Dormon irises. Accordingly, 'Delta King' is more than 50 percent *I. nelsonii*.

Contributions of *Iris giganticaerulea*

The tall, spectacular blue to white species, *Iris giganticaerulea*, is near equal in hybridizing importance to *I. nelsonii*. This is the most plentiful of all the species, and great numbers were collected and used in hybridizing. But only a handful were registered and introduced, thus the early hybridizing history leaves much to be desired. Most checklist references simply give *I. giganticaerulea* or *I. giganticaerulea alba* as the parents.

Hybridizers often sought "something special" about the particular *Iris giganticaerulea* they used. The white variant was fairly common and was used frequently. The semi-double 'Creole Can-Can' became the parent of all doubles, semi-doubles, and cartwheels, the form in which all six segments are essentially the same size, also known as the "all-falls" type. The triploid 'Ruth Holleyman' should have been used extensively but was not because of probable misunderstandings as to fertility—most triploids were believed to be sterile. The much more common blue *I. giganticaerulea* then took up the slack and gave many outstanding hybrid cultivars.

'Her Highness' is a white self with light green style arms. It was collected by William Levingston and introduced in 1957. It is probably the most important *Iris giganticaerulea* to ever be used in hybridizing. 'Her Highness' won the DeBaillon Award in 1959, and is one of only two collected Louisiana irises to do so. It is directly involved in two other award winners, 'Katherine L. Cornay' (1969) and 'Mary Dunn' (1977).

'Katherine L. Cornay' (Arny, 1962), 1969 DeBaillon Award winner, is a mineral-violet self with cream-white style arms. It is a spectacular and vigorous garden iris, having the parentage ('Louise Arny' × *I. giganticaerulea*) × 'Her Highness'. From 'Katherine L. Cornay' × self came another fine garden iris, the very large, pale pink 'Deneb' (Arny, 1969). 'Mary Dunn' (Hager, 1974), winner of the DeBaillon Award in 1977, is a very pale orchid-violet with the parentage 'Sidney Conger' × 'Her Highness'.

Among other contributions of *Iris giganticaerulea*, probably from the more common blue variety, are the DeBaillon Award winners 'Amethyst Star' and 'New Offering'. 'Amethyst Star' (DuBose, 1956), awarded in 1960, is a light rose-pink self from *I. giganticaerulea* × 'Contrast'. 'New Offering' (C. Davis, 1958) is very dark blue with darker violet veining and essentially no signal. Winner of the 1963 DeBaillon Award, it has the parentage 'Flat Top' × *I. giganticaerulea*. 'Flat Top' (C. Davis, 1953) is a pale wisteria-blue with very flat form. But it has unknown parentage. 'New Offering' is the pollen parent of 'Eolian' (Arny, 1969), a blue self awarded the DeBaillon in 1976. 'New Offering' is also the pod parent of 'Blue Shield' (Davis, Williamson, Ghio, 1966) a very dark, velvety blue. 'New Offering' and 'Blue Shield' are finding use in breeding dark, velvety blues and reds with little or no signal.

In the 1950s Claude Davis produced a remarkable series of about fifteen named cultivars by crossing *Iris giganticaerulea* and selections of *I. nelsonii*. The *I. nelsonii* parent was generally 'Haile Selassie' and sometimes 'Peggy Mac'. Due to classic hybrid vigor these were outstanding garden and landscape irises, among the most vigorous Louisiana hybrids ever produced. All were similar violet, purple, or red-purple, and a field planting was a memorable sight. Among these were 'Beau Geste', 'Kisatchie', 'Lafourche', 'Miss Louisiana', 'Plaquemine', 'Saint Bernard', 'Tiger', and many others.

'Clyde Redmond' (Arny, 1971) is a very dark blue self and winner of the DeBaillon Award for 1974. It is a top garden iris important in hybridizing and a very dependable bloomer. It is about 50 percent *Iris giganticaerulea* with the remainder including *I. fulva*, *I. brevicaulis*, and a limited contribution by *I. nelsonii*. The pod parent line of 'Clyde Redmond' consists of the blue and blue-violet hybrids 'Dora Dey' (Arny, 1955) and 'Puttytat' (Arny, 1958), developed from the old MacMillan seedling 'Bayou Sunset', a 1949 DeBaillon Award winner, and a blue *I. giganticaerulea* seedling. The pollen parent line started with 'Holleyblu' (Holleyman, 1952), a collected violet with a white border, probably *I. giganticaerulea*, and 'Buttercup', an obscure collected unregistered yellow, probably *I. fulva*. This seedling complex functioned as pollen parent with 'Louise Arny' to give 'Snow Pearl' (Arny, 1963), a low-growing white self. The genetic source of white is obscure but probably comes from the blue *I. giganticaerulea*.

'Clyde Redmond' has been widely used as a parent and has produced fine whites and blues. With 'Clara Goula' as pollen parent it gave the beautiful ruffled white self 'Acadian Miss' (Arny, 1980), thus indicating a recessive gene for white. Among the outstanding blues are 'Bit of Blue' (Arny, 1975), from a cross

Parentage of 'Clyde Redmond'

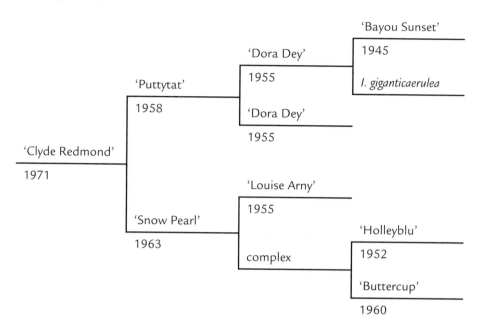

of 'Clyde Redmond' × 'Bayou Candelabra'; 'Charlie's Evangeline' (Arny, 1976), from a 'Gulf Surf' × 'Clyde Redmond' mating; 'Crayfish' (Betts, 1980), from a cross of 'Wood Violet' × 'Clyde Redmond'; 'La Perouse' (Raabe, 1976), by self-ing 'Clyde Redmond'; and 'Pledge' (Ghio, 1976), from the cross 'Clyde Redmond' × 'Sundown Shadows'.

Contributions of *Iris giganticaerulea* to hybridizing would not be complete without details of the collected cultivars 'Creole Can-Can' and 'Ruth Holleyman'. Both irises are unique. 'Creole Can-Can' was collected in 1956 by Marvin Granger and is a blue self, all-falls type, with no standards, some petaloids, and no two blooms identical. 'Ruth Holleyman' is one of only two known triploid Louisiana irises—the other is 'Triple Treat'. G. W. Holleyman collected 'Ruth Holleyman' in 1954 in the same general area of southwestern Louisiana as 'Creole Can-Can'. It is indeed fortunate these irises were collected, for beginning in 1957 a series of hurricanes devastated the Louisiana coast, destroying forever most collecting areas.

Through the untiring efforts and patience of Granger's hybridizing, 'Creole Can-Can' produced an outstanding line of unusual irises with many variations in form and color, including cartwheels, semi-doubles, and true doubles. 'Creole Can-Can' has no pollen but does set seed with pollen of normal irises to produce normal forms. Interbreeding and back-crosses are necessary to bring out the recessive gene for doubling. The blue-violet self 'Double Talk'

(Granger, 1973) provided proof that doubles could be bred from 'Creole Can-Can' by this approach. Another line involving out-crossing to 'The Khan' produced the dark blue, star-shaped, all-falls type 'Delta Star' (Granger, 1968). Introducing the genetic potential of 'Wheelhorse' and following with line breeding gave 'Creole Canary' (Granger, 1978), the first yellow double. Later out-crosses with 'Queen O' Queens' and 'Louisiana Sambo' and interbreeding ushered in a new era for doubles. An example is 'Rokki' (Granger, 1982), a chartreuse cream double which fades to white. 'Starlite Starbrite' (Granger, 1989), is a clear white semi-double with small yellow-green signals.

'Ruth Holleyman', a triploid variant of *Iris giganticaerulea*, is known to have only one direct descendant—the unregistered 'Baby Ruth' (Holleyman, 1966) from 'Ruth Holleyman' × 'Mistletoe Garnet'. Reasons for this lone descendant are not entirely clear but are probably related to fertility considerations. Most triploids are known to be sterile, which may have led to speculation that 'Ruth Holleyman' was sterile, which in turn probably explains the lack of interest by hybridizers. Unfortunately, this iris has disappeared from commerce. While many catalogs list 'Ruth Holleyman' today, none of them are triploid. Our only link to this iris comes to us through 'Angel Skin' (Neugebauer, 1968), which was used as a parent in the cultivars 'Medora Wilson', 'Rebecca Garber', and 'Royal Angel', all of which are still commercially available.

Contributions of *Iris fulva*

In 1812 *Iris fulva* was the second species in the *Hexagonae* to be discovered. It was collected extensively, but its direct contributions to hybridizing are limited, probably because outstanding collected and registered cultivars by Viosca, Nicholls, and Riggs found little or no hybridizing use and because the obvious superiority of *I. nelsonii*'s larger flowers with better form had far greater appeal to hybridizers.

The most noteworthy and direct contributions of this species are through the collected cultivar 'Maringouin Fulva' (Smith, 1943), a low-growing, intense yellow. This iris played a significant role in the development of yellow hybrids. Prior to the appearance of 'Maringouin Fulva', several lemon-yellow *Iris fulva* were collected in Arkansas in the 1920s and 1930s but were not registered. Other vague references to yellow *I. fulva* indicate this color variant in the species was not too rare. The yellow *I. fulva* is considered the source of yellow in the *Hexagonae*. The buff to brownish yellow colors of *I. nelsonii* are likely related to the original yellow of *I. fulva* in the evolution of *I. nelsonii*.

George Arceneaux initiated the main line of hybridizing with 'Maringouin Fulva' as shown in Chart 3, the parentage chart for 'G. W. Holleyman' and 'Dixie Deb'.

Parentage of 'G. W. Holleyman' and 'Dixie Deb'

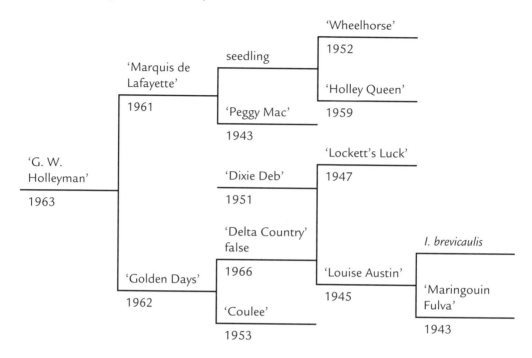

'Louise Austin', a low-growing, dark blue-purple (Arceneaux, 1945) re-sulted from *Iris brevicaulis* × 'Maringouin Fulva'. It is a reciprocal of the cross that produced 'Fulvala' for Dykes. 'Louise Austin' and 'Fulvala' are generally similar in size, form, and color. Frank Chowning then hybridized the collected natural hybrid 'Lockett's Luck' (Thibault, 1947) with 'Louise Austin' and pro-duced two yellows of note. Most important is the 1967 DeBaillon Award win-ner 'Dixie Deb' (Chowning, 1951). The other yellow is a sibling of 'Dixie Deb', distributed under the false name 'Delta Country'; it is not the iris originally registered under the name 'Delta Country' (Chowning, 1950), which resulted from 'Delta Country' false × 'Gold Dollar'. 'Dixie Deb' is a sulfur-yellow self, an excellent garden iris and most floriferous. Under conditions of good culture 'Dixie Deb' will often have six bloom positions and ten or more blooms per stalk, but the blooms are rather small at about 5 inches (12.7 cm).

It remained for *Iris nelsonii*-derived introductions to give further enhance-ment of the yellow line. The main source of this line is through 'Wheelhorse' and 'Peggy Mac' to produce 'Marquis de Lafayette' (Holleyman, 1961), which became the pod parent of 'G. W. Holleyman'. The pollen parent is 'Golden Days', a different type of yellow, from Chowning's 'Delta Country' false × 'Coulee' (Gorton, 1953). Levingston introduced 'Golden Days' in 1962 but never registered it with the American Iris Society. *Iris nelsonii* is not in the pollen parent line.

The introduction of 'G. W. Holleyman' (R. Holleyman, 1960), a chartreuse-yellow self, created a sensation. This was the first really large yellow in the *Hexagonae*, large yellows having been sought since the beginning of hybridizing. 'G. W. Holleyman' won the DeBaillon Award in 1966.

Table 10. Hybridizing legacy of 'G. W. Holleyman'

Cultivar	Parentage	Intro-duction	Hybridizer	Color Pattern
'Mrs. Ira Nelson'	'Louise Arny' × 'G. W. Holleyman'	1969	Arny	mineral violet
'Buffaroon'	'G. W. Holleyman' × seedling	1977	Raabe	buff-crimson bicolor
'Delta Sunshine'	'Dixie Deb' × 'G. W. Holleyman'	1971	Hager	yellow self
'E. H. Martyn'	'G. W. Holleyman' × seedling	1976	Raabe	yellow self
'President Hedley'	'G. W. Holleyman' × seedling	1980	Mertzweiller	yellow with brown overlay
'Uptight'	'Tressie Cook' × 'G. W. Holleyman'	1971	Arny	cream-yellow
'Papa Bear'	'Counterpoise' × 'G. W. Holleyman'	1983	Fritchie	yellow-brown

The hybridizing legacy of 'G. W. Holleyman' is very much in progress and has produced outstanding irises, many in various shades of yellow and brown. Arny's 1973 DeBaillon Award winner 'Mrs. Ira Nelson' has wide, overlapping flower parts and is slightly ruffled. Its flowers are borne on tall, sturdy stalks. Introducing more *Iris nelsonii* on the pollen parent side through the seedling complex rich in 'King's Gold' produced the impressive 'President Hedley'. This cinnamon-dusted yellow is among the most intensely color saturated of all Louisiana irises. A new form in a cream-yellow with upright standards, much as with bearded irises, is Arny's 'Uptight' ('Tressie Cook' × 'G. W. Holleyman'). 'Dixie Deb' × 'G. W. Holleyman' produced 'Delta Sunshine', a yellow self. The yellow-brown 'Papa Bear' ('Counterpoise' × 'G. W. Holleyman') and the bicolor 'Buffaroon' ('G. W. Holleyman' × seedling) are some of the more unusual colors. All the results from 1940 to 1988 further emphasize the importance of *I. nelsonii* for bringing larger flower parts and further color variety to hybrids in the *Hexagonae*.

Prior to the appearance of 'G. W. Holleyman', a different type of interme-diately sized yellow had been known for many years. These were typically soft, tall yellows with the flaring *Iris giganticaerulea* form. First was 'Kraemer Yellow' (Kraemer, 1943), a collected variety. Arceneaux hybridized two similar yellows, 'Aline Martin' and 'Helen Smith', both 1947 introductions. 'Coulee' (Gorton, 1953) was of the same type. Unfortunately, these irises have no parentage records. Later hybridizing by Fred Buchmann produced 'Lady Martha' (1996) and 'Lady Mary' (1968) from the parentage 'Barbara Elaine Taylor' × *I. fulva* (unregistered yellow). The pod parent is a collected white *I. giganticaerulea*. The progeny were all pale yellow, tall, and with the typical *I. giganticaerulea* form, a strong indication of the parentage of the early yellows.

Contributions of *I. brevicaulis*

Recorded and scientifically demonstrated contributions of *Iris brevicaulis* to hybridizing are limited by natural causes. *Iris brevicaulis* is the latest of the *Hexagonae* species to bloom, a full month after *I. giganticaerulea* and at least two weeks after *I. fulva* and *I. nelsonii*. This timing makes natural and controlled interspecific hybridization difficult unless the hybridizer resorts to stored pollen. Although Randolph did not find direct scientific evidence for *I. brevicaulis* in the constitution of *I. nelsonii,* neither did he rule this out.

Iris brevicaulis often grew with *I. fulva* and *I. giganticaerulea* in the *I. nelsonii* habitat. Out-of-season blooms are well known, giving good reason to believe that *I. brevicaulis* could have played a significant role in natural hybridization and in the evolution of *I. nelsonii*. In 1989 the *Bulletin American Iris Society* (No. 273, pp. 22–25) published the results of a six-year study of genetics and ecology confirming that *I. brevicaulis* did indeed contribute to the rise of *I. nelsonii*. For more details see Chapter 2.

Chowning's work leading to his DeBaillon Award winners, the spectacu-lar 'Ann Chowning' and 'This I Love', and their precursor 'Miss Arkansas' (1978), have been described. The same is true for 'Dixie Deb', 'Delta Country' false, 'Delta Country', and 'Gold Dollar'. These irises introduced the cold har-diness, later bloom season, and zigzag stalks of *Iris brevicaulis*, and 'Ann Chowning' has proven to be a popular and significant parent. Among Chown-ing's pure hybrids are 'Finders Keepers' (1966), a 12-inch (30.5-cm) tall, ivory-flecked blue; 'Trail of Tears' (1973), a 12-inch (30.5-cm) white self; and 'Petite and Sweet' (1986), also a 12-inch (30.5-cm) white self. All have the parentage *I. brevicaulis* × *I. brevicaulis*, although the source and color of the parents are not given.

Another group of Chowning's hybrids which were based on *Iris brevicaulis* also involved 'Cathedral Blue' (Caroline Dormon, 1944) and, to a slight extent,

I. nelsonii. This breeding line produced a taller group of irises, in the range of 30 inches (76.2 cm). Included are 'Tidewater' (Chowning, 1951), a lavender-blue with the parentage 'Cathedral Blue' × *I. brevicaulis*, and 'Spring Sorcery' (Chowning, 1951), a golden apricot with the same parentage. The Chowning cultivars 'Lake Maumelle', 'Little Rock Skies', 'Midnight Storm', and 'Pristine Beauty' involved 'Haile Selassie' or unregistered *I. nelsonii* cultivars in addition to 'Cathedral Blue' and *I. brevicaulis*. 'Pink Joy Roberts' (Roberts, 1954), a rose-pink self—which is an unusual color for *I. brevicaulis* and might go back to 1850 or earlier—was to play a significant role in modern hybridizing. Sidney Conger produced 'La Reve' in 1954, an oyster-white and lilac bitone from 'Pink Joy Roberts' × 'Bayou Sunset'. From 'La Reve' came 'Dr. Dormon' (Conger, 1973), a pastel blend of orchid and mauve ('La Reve' × 'W. B. MacMillan').

'Gulf Surf' (Arny, 1962), gentian blue with a yellow line signal on a white background, is from a cross of ('Louise Arny' × 'Dora Dey') × 'Pink Joy Roberts'. Some outstanding irises were bred from 'Gulf Surf', including the pale blue 'Ellene Rockwell', Arny 1973 ('Gulf Surf' × unknown); the Wedgewood-blue 'Charlie's Evangeline', Arny 1976 ('Gulf Surf' × 'Clyde Redmond'); and the white self 'Inez Conger', Arny 1973 ('Ila Nunn' × 'Gulf Surf').

This limited hybridizing history of *Iris brevicaulis* strongly suggests that this species has not been given the attention it merits. Three important characteristics of *I. brevicaulis* needing more exploitation include bud placement, floriferousness and stalk branching, and the late season of bloom. Many DeBaillon Award winners have poor bud placement—the buds do not exit the bud sockets properly and blooms are not exhibited well. The zigzag stalk of *I. brevicaulis* can do much to alleviate this problem. While many Louisiana irises are floriferous, many would be rendered even more beautiful by additional blooms and branching. These genetic features are present and seem fairly dominant in *I. brevicaulis*. The late bloom season may be most important of all—it produces improved hardiness, extends the bloom season, and produces blooms more likely to escape damage from spring freezes.

Contributions of Natural Hybrids

Thousands of natural hybrids were collected in the 1930s, 1940s, and into the 1950s. The hybridizing contributions made by collected irises cannot be measured, since only a very few were registered and introduced. It is possible that these contributions exceeded those of any of the species, except possibly *I. nelsonii*. Particularly during the years prior to 1960, about half the DeBaillon Award winners were not documented as to either parent, and many collected natural hybrids were likely involved as parents. The only collected natural hybrid to win the DeBaillon Award was 'Mary S. Debaillon' in 1948, the first year the award was given. 'Mary S. Debaillon' is an orchid-lavender-tinted rose-pink collected by Mary DeBaillon and later registered by Caroline Dormon. Three other collected natural hybrids 'Contrast', 'Cajan Joyeuse', and 'Lockett's Luck', also were to play important roles.

'Contrast', a bicolor with pale orchid standards and violet falls was collected by O. F. R. Bruce and was part of the original DeBaillon collection registered by Caroline Dormon in 1943. Hybridizing contributions to the DeBaillon Award winners 'Cherry Bounce' and 'Amethyst Star' are discussed in Chapter 1. 'Contrast' also served as pod parent of 'Adelaide Bradford' (Clark, 1949), an off-white with violet veining ('Contrast' × 'Mary S. DeBaillon'); 'Caroginia' (Conger, 1948), a pink-cream bicolor ('Contrast' × 'Caroline Dormon'); and 'Roses and Wine' (Conger, 1948), a pink-salmon bitone ('Contrast' × 'Caroline Dormon'). Although not DeBaillon Award winners, 'Caroginia' and 'Roses and Wine' made significant contributions to more advanced hybridizing. 'Caroline Dormon' (Ruth Dormon, 1943) is a rose-lavender of unknown origin.

'Cajan Joyeuse' (Thomas, 1942) is a rose-pink with darker rose veining and golden brown styles with gold edging. The most significant hybridizing contribution of this collected natural hybrid was as the pod parent of 'Saucy Minx' (Caroline Dormon, 1949), winner of the 1954 DeBaillon Award. 'Saucy Minx' is a pastel blend of rose red shading to soft yellow having the parentage 'Cajan Joyeuse' × 'New Orleans'. 'New Orleans' (Caroline Dormon, 1942) is a collected pink from the DeBaillon collection. 'Cajan Joyeuse' also functioned as pod parent for other pastel blends. 'Early Morn' (Conger, 1950) is a cream and old rose pastel from 'Cajan Joyeuse' × unknown. 'Easter Basket' (Caroline Dormon, 1946), a fuchsia-pink, is also from 'Cajan Joyeuse' × 'New Orleans'. 'Cajan Joyeuse' is in the more distant parentage of the Chowning hybrids 'Red Gamecock' (1977) and 'Tarnished Brass' (1966), which were used by Henry Rowlan and Richard Morgan to extend the Chowning line.

'Lockett's Luck' (Thibault, 1947), collected by Duval and Jestremski, is flesh-pink to mauve-pink and is another important natural hybrid. The most distinguishing feature of this iris is a conspicuous dark maroon outline surrounding a large diamond signal. This marking led to the original name 'Rattlesnake', a name soon considered inappropriate for so beautiful an iris. Hence the name change to 'Lockett's Luck'. Various modifications of this marking are frequently found in advanced generation progeny, indicating rather strong genetic dominance.

The hybridizing significance of 'Lockett's Luck' in producing 'Dixie Deb', 'Delta Country' false, and later 'G. W. Holleyman' is noted earlier in "Contributions of *Iris fulva*." Chowning produced 'Sheer Delight' (1954), a lavender pink with deep lavender surrounding a gold-line signal, from the parentage

'Lockett's Luck' × 'Accolade'. Arny obtained 'Morning Treat' (1960), a salmon-peach, and 'Mally Philips' (1963), an empire-rose self, from 'Louise Arny' × 'Lockett's Luck'. The beautiful wisteria-violet 'Midshipman' (Richard, 1949) resulted from 'Lockett's Luck' × unknown and has a yellow signal surrounded by a red-violet zone.

Other Mary Swords DeBaillon Award Winners

From 1949 to 1968, seven DeBaillon Award winners had little or no information about their background. Which species or natural hybrids were mainly responsible for producing these irises cannot be ascertained. Some may have been collected natural hybrids, but most probably grew from seed. Unfortunately, records were not kept or were lost. Such is to be expected in the early years of developing new hybrids. Table 11 lists these award-winning irises.

Table 11. Mary Swords DeBaillon Award winners with unknown parentage

Cultivar	Registrant	Introduction, Award	Color Pattern
'Bayou Sunset'	W. B. MacMillan	1945, 1949	soft rose with radiating signal
'Royal Gem'	Sally Smith	1947, 1952	dark velvety red-violet
'Wood Violet'	Ruth Dormon	1943, 1956	dark blue with small yellow signal
'Blue Chip'	Sally Smith	1950, 1957	medium blue self
'Dixie Dusk'	Lenora Mathews	1952, 1962	blue-black self
'Frances Elizabeth'	Sam Rix	1961, 1965	purplish bronze self
'Black Widow'	W. B. MacMillan	1953, 1968	black violet-purple, no signal

Most of the irises in Table 11 found little further use in hybridizing and gave few descendants. Some, like other early cultivars, are not available today. The only exception seems to be the unique 'Black Widow', considered by many to be the darkest Louisiana iris, and among the darkest of all irises.

The DeBaillon Award for 1978 saw a tie between the cultivars 'F. A. C. McCulla' (Arny, 1973), a beet-red self from a cross of 'Bayou Comus' × unknown, and 'Shrimp Creole' (Ghio, 1974), a shrimp-rose self from a cross of 'Delta King' × 'Tressie Cook'. The tie was not broken and no award was given.

CHAPTER 7

History of Hybridizing since 1988

The number of hybridizers of Louisiana irises increases each year as does the number of seedlings they introduce. These irises set seed easily, and the possibility of creating something new and different is greater than with the more highly developed bearded irises. It would not be possible to give credit to every person registering a Louisiana iris, but the following pages highlight some who have made great contributions in the past ten years. As exciting as the developments documented in Chapter 6 are the outstanding new innovations produced since 1988, an even more productive period. Many hybridizers have taken advantage of the advances made in the Arny line and have exploited them in amazing directions. For other than the Arkansas hybridizers, categorizing a hybrid as being predominantly derived from any single species is becoming increasingly impossible. Rather, most hybridizers are now dipping into derivatives of all species.

Contributions of Outstanding American Hybridizers

Mary Dunn stands out as the American hybridizer with the biggest impact on Louisiana iris hybridizing, with several DeBaillon Medals and Awards of Merit to her credit. Even more amazing is that Dunn had a very small piece of property, and she and her husband grew bearded irises and other perennials along with the Louisianas. She received her start with Louisiana irises as gift rhizomes from Melrose Gardens, and many of her own introductions stem from the Hager cultivars 'Full Eclipse' (1978), 'Dark Tide' (1981), and her namesake, 'Mary Dunn' (1974). Her dark-colored cultivars are among the most popular and important advancements, though most early efforts in this line involve simple intercrossing of the best available at the time, such as 'Blue

Shield' (1966), 'Black Widow', 'Full Eclipse', and 'Dark Tide'. From these came the very popular cultivars 'Bajazzo' (1981), winner of the 1992 DeBaillon Medal; 'Satchmo' (1987); 'Louie' (1988); and the incredibly dark ''Bout Midnight' (1989), which is among darkest irises produced in any color class. Later, Dunn crossed the ruffled Arny cultivars, such as 'Clara Goula', into the dark line, resulting in three outstanding sister seedlings: 'Extraordinaire' (1992), 'Far and Away' (1992), and 'Whistling Dixie' (1995), which resulted from crossing (('Blue Shield' × 'Black Widow') × 'Full Eclipse') × 'Clara Goula'. These three irises combine the extravagant ruffling of 'Clara Goula' with the darkness of Dunn's other cultivars. All grow well and have superb stalks and flower placement. They are already finding their way into the pedigrees of other outstanding dark irises.

Two other irises are prominent in Dunn's breeding efforts: 'Monument' ('Charlie's Michele' × 'Ila Nunn'), a white, was introduced in 1978 and won the DeBaillon Award in 1984; and 'Plantation Beau' (('Queen O' Queens' × 'Mrs. Ira Nelson') × 'Justa Reflection'), a mauve-purple, was introduced in 1985. Dunn combined these irises with all sorts of other colors to create a unique series of irises. Both have wide parts, light ruffling, good stalks, and excellent vigor and would be likely to produce good offspring, even from what may seem unlikely parents based on their color. 'Monument' gave rise directly to 'Coupe de Ville' ('Ann Chowning' × 'Monument'), a light rose-colored bitone introduced in 1991; 'Vive la Difference', a lavender-orchid bitone introduced in 1990; and a host of seedlings from a most fortuitous combination with Ghio's 'Handmaiden'. 'Plantation Beau' crossed with 'Wine Country' gave rise to such outstanding cultivars as the pink-toned 'Plantation Belle'. 'Even Handed' (1994), a light purple cartwheel, is the result of crossing 'Plantation Beau' × 'Easter Tide', and the clean blue 'High Flying' (1996) resulted from a cross of 'Plantation Beau' × 'Wine Country'. These are some of the most vigorous and healthy irises in the garden, due in part perhaps to the hybrid vigor obtained when crossing very dissimilar parent types. Several of Dunn's hybrids such as 'Delta Dawn', a 1983 introduction from ('Katherine L. Cornay' × 'Blue Shield') × 'Shrimp Creole', and 'Delta Twilight', a 1996 introduction from 'Fat Tuesday' × 'Cammeray', reflect their hybrid nature in the mixture of colors in their blossoms. Some of her irises display unusual blended colors found in no other Louisiana irises on the market. Examining some of Dunn's crosses indicates that any sort of cross between two quality Louisiana irises, regardless of color, might give some outstanding progeny.

The other major American hybridizer of the late twentieth century is Dorman Haymon. His lines were heavily influenced by his proximity to the dean of American hybridizers, Charles Arny. Haymon's use of Arny cultivars such as 'Fading Beauty' (1973), 'Ila Nunn' (1969), 'Acadian White' (1976), 'Valera'

(1980), and 'Easter Tide' (1979) is heavily in evidence by examining their pedigrees. Among Haymon's first introductions, the clean white 'Marie Dolores' (1988) and the red-purple 'Grace Duhon' (1988) are outstanding. 'Marie Dolores' ('Acadian White' × 'Ila Nunn') is a large white with extremely vigorous growth and remarkable production of bloom stalks. Aside from these characteristics, the bloom has an unusual dimple or twist in the falls and a bright orange signal, creating a unique look compared to other introduced white irises. 'Grace Duhon' ('Full Eclipse' × 'Ann Chowning') combines the velvet texture of 'Full Eclipse' with the more red hue from 'Ann Chowning'. Again this is a plant with excellent growth. The sibling to 'Grace Duhon', Haymon's 'Empress Josephine, is among the darker Louisiana irises available, but it is a slow grower by comparison to its sibling. It is marvelous when well grown. Haymon's 'Festival's Acadian' ('Fading Beauty' × 'Charjoy's Mike') introduced in 1990 was among the first dark irises with a distinct lighter halo and has much better growth than its parent 'Charjoy's Mike'. The chief value of this iris is as a parent, as it gives a high percentage of haloed offspring in all colors.

Haymon's later introductions include two seedlings from the cross of 'Valera' × 'President Hedley', 'Praline Festival' (1992) and 'Rokki Rockwell' (1992). 'Praline Festival' is really the color of pralines, created by a gold overlaid with fine brown lines. Even people who do not like brown irises are drawn to this flower. 'Rokki Rockwell' is a brilliant golden yellow with just a trace of brown upon opening. Both irises have five to six bud positions and multiple buds at each socket coupled with perfect placement of the blossoms. Combining a number of Arny and Haymon introductions in their pedigree, sister seedlings 'Camille Durand Foret' and 'Jean Bush' were introduced in 1994 from the cross ('Teresa Margaret' × ('Uptight' × 'Lucile Holley')) × 111-86- 1: ('Easter Tide' × 'Swamp Flame')—this last element denotes a seedling and gives the parentage. 'Camille Durand Foret' is a rich orange-gold self and 'Jean Bush' is a red with gold edges. Several of Haymon's new seedlings show extreme promise, and he is a regular winner for the best seedlings at the shows of the Society for Louisiana Irises in Lafayette, Louisiana. Some of these new irises combine the John Taylor irises, such as 'Dural White Butterfly', with Dorman's own lines.

Neil Bertinot also was influenced by his proximity to Charles Arny and the knowledge that 'Clara Goula' imparts ruffling to its progeny. 'Bellevue's Michelle' (1983), from 'This I Love' × 'Clara Goula', is a very good bitone rose-pink, and 'Bellevue Coquette' (1984), from 'Ila Nunn' × 'Clara Goula', is a fine rich lavender-blue. Both of these 'Clara Goula' derivatives are fine growers and have proven to be useful parents. Combining the brilliant purple 'Olivier Monette' (MacMillan, 1974) with the red 'Ann Chowning' gave Bertinot the brilliant red-purples 'Bellevue's Native Charmer' (1983) and 'Bellevue's Mike'

(1984). These are especially effective landscape plants, and their brilliant and unusual colors always attract garden visitors. A further cross of 'Bellevue's Mike' × 'Full Eclipse' gave one of the best darker irises of this vintage, 'Jeri' (1985). Winner of the DeBaillon Medal in 1994, 'Jeri' has outstanding vigor and exceptional stalks, with even low-positioned flowers opening perfectly. In addition, 'Jeri' is proving to be a fine parent for other dark-colored irises, with several introductions and more on the way.

Marvin Granger is a pioneer in hybridizing who has continued to produce quality irises. The double line from the collected iris 'Creole Can-Can' has continued with the production of two blue-purple true doubles, 'Instant Replay' (1982) and 'Flareout' (1992), and a cartwheel type in white, 'Starlite Starbrite' (1989). The production of a white from this line is an important break and comes from the use of the cream 'Queen O' Queens' crossed into the 'Creole Can-Can' family, and then intercrossing the derivatives to recover the white recessive color as well as the influence of the doubling. Granger is to be congratulated for working with such a difficult project and bringing it to fruition. His pinks are among his most popular irises. 'Kay Nelson' from 'Charlie's Michele' × 'Lafitte's Retreat', introduced in 1986 and winner of the DeBaillon Medal in 1995, is still a premier pink-toned iris. It combines a lovely ruffled flower with excellent plant habits and a superb stalk and is also proving to be a valuable parent. 'Danielle' (1991), a bitone pink with the falls edged lighter, is much shorter and late blooming. 'Deirdre Kay' (1991) is also shorter but of a very different shade of lavender-orchid, with a distinct sprayed signal area. Granger reports that a cross of 'Cajun Sunrise' × 'Margaret Lee' gave several excellent progeny in a variety of colors. Some of these may be future introductions.

The Arkansas hybridizers Richard Morgan and Henry Rowlan have relied heavily on the material of Frank Chowning in their hybrids, and hence have a greater proportion of hybrids derived from *Iris brevicaulis* and *I. fulva* than those lines of other hybridizers. Virtually all of the hybrids from these workers grow well even in the colder areas of the country and are useful in extending the popularity of Louisiana irises to less warm climates. In addition, many of the irises are shorter types which are useful for growing in front of the taller hybrids and in other garden situations requiring smaller plants. Many of Morgan's hybrids are descendants of a small white *I. brevicaulis* seedling from Frank Chowning known as 'Trail of Tears'. This has given some relatively shorter progeny with a bold signal patch. 'Midnight Spirit' (1992), a dark blue purple from 'Full Eclipse' × 'Trail of Tears', has a bold signal, and is an outstanding example of this kind of work. Another line is derived from the Chowning irises 'Missey Reveley' (1966), 'Little Miss Leighley' (1983), and 'Gold Reserve' (1977). All have reds and yellows blended together for interesting effects. Morgan has produced clear reds such as 'Parade Music', a 1986 introduction derived from 'Town Council' × 'Shines Brightly', and 'Cherry Cup', a 1989 introduction that resulted from a cross of 'F. A. C. McCulla' × 'Little Miss Sims'. He has also produced blended types such as 'Clown About' (1993) from 'Gypsy Moon' × 'Bayou Comus', 'Heavenly Glow' (1989) from ('Missey Reveley' × 'Ila Nunn') × 'Gold Reserve', and 'Kelley's Choice' (1993) from 'Town Council' × 'Shines Brightly'. All these blended types produce irises with intensified color on the petal edges. The intense green style arms of 'Heavenly Glow' (1995) combined with the yellow 'Sunny Episode' (Rowlan, 1984) produced the green-style-armed yellow 'Willow Mint' (1995). Two smaller blue irises of note are the light blue 'Lake Ouachita' (1992), the result of crossing ('E. Everett Caradine' × 'Clyde Redmond') × 'Bayou Waters', and the intense navy blue 'Lake Sylvia' (1993), the result of crossing ('E. Everett Caradine' × 'Clyde Redmond') × 'Trail of Tears'. These two irises show the ability of *I. brevicaulis* to produce blues of extreme clarity and intensity, unlike any other iris.

Henry Rowlan's hybridizing efforts have earned him two DeBaillon Medals. 'Frank Chowning', a bitone red from 'Ann Chowning' × 'Miss Arkansas', won the DeBaillon Medal in 1993. The plants of the Voodoo Series, derived from 'Black Gamecock' (Chowning, 1980), display the same outrageous vigor of their parent, but combine bolder signal colors and wider blossom parts. These are extremely effective garden irises. Rowlan's 1997 DeBaillon Medal winner, 'Voodoo Magic' ('Black Gamecock' × 'Dr. Dormon'), is a deep fuchsia-purple with large yellow signals. A cultivar in the Voodoo Series not descended from 'Black Gamecock' is 'Voodoo Queen', with the parentage 'Graceland' × 'Mentida'. It captures the rich coloring of 'Mentida' (Norris, 1981) but in a more ruffled modern-looking blossom. It is unfortunate that the parentage is unknown for both 'Black Gamecock' and 'Mentida', but it is generally agreed that *Iris brevicaulis* is in their lineage. Two outstanding pink irises, 'Pink Poetry' ('Bryce Leigh' × 'Winter's Veil') and 'Twirling Ballerina' ('Roll Call' × 'Clyde Redmond'), are more low growing than pinks from other lines. Both are lovely irises, but 'Twirling Ballerina' has truly unique coloring with its very deep red signal. Crossing these Arkansas-bred irises into the lines from other hybridizers may lead to fuller forms with more ruffling, and larger flowers on plants that are reliably hardy throughout the country.

Albert "Bobo" Faggard has long been a proponent of Louisiana irises in his corner of Southeast Texas. Three different irises are among his contributions to the group. The blue-violet 'Bayou Short Stuff' (1988) is among the finest of the smaller Louisiana irises and has better flower shape than most of this group. The Australian hybridizer Bernard Pryor is using 'Bayou Short Stuff' to develop a line of shorter irises. 'Ice Angel' (1991) is among the more unusual blue irises. It looks like a white iris with an overlay of the softest blue. 'Gulf

Moon Glow' is probably the best iris Faggard has produced. It offers an unusual combination of lavender-blue standards and greenish yellow falls. It is the greenest and cleanest of this color pattern.

J. Farron Campbell has quickly made himself known as a major hybridizer of the Louisiana iris. His breeding covers virtually the whole color range and involves lines not investigated by other hybridizers. Campbell's first introduction, 'Lone Star' (1997), is a cross of *Iris hexagona* × 'Clara Goula', and is the only marketed iris with this lineage. 'Lone Star' is a distinct cartwheel form of lavender-blue and has exceptional vigor and floriferousness, probably due to the wide nature of the cross. The as yet unregistered Richard Goula iris 'Lynn Hantel' ('Margaret Hunter' × 'Ann Chowning') has also proven very useful in Campbell's hybridizing, as it has the unusual intensified color at the petal edges also found in 'Margaret Hunter'. In a cross of 'Lynn Hantel' with 'Dural White Butterfly', Campbell selected two pink irises with darker edges, 'Babs Barnette' and 'Coushatta', that have the advantage of the fine form that comes from 'Dural White Butterfly'. A purple selection from this cross is also slated for introduction. A very nice near black iris is 'Atchafalaya' (1998), derived from 'Jeri' × 'John's Lucifer'. It has an open cartwheel form with light ruffling and an outstanding velvety texture. Other notable progeny from this same cross are being evaluated for introduction. 'Fiddle Dee-Dee' (1998) is a bright clear sunfast yellow with bright yellow-orange signals and branching stalks with a high bud count. The parentage of 'Fiddle Dee-Dee' is (('Ann Chowning' × 'Mrs. Ira Nelson') × 'C'est Si Bon') × 'Noble Planet'.

Campbell has also been working to produce new tetraploid lines by treating seedlings with colchicine. His efforts have produced several tetraploid plants with completely different parents from the Mertzweiller tetraploid lines. He hopes that by bringing *Iris brevicaulis* into the tetraploid lines cold hardiness will be greatly improved. Including crosses that bring greater color diversity into the tetraploid lines has also been a high priority. Work on the tetraploid lines is continuing, but it is a laborious undertaking.

Kevin Vaughn has developed an ambitious hybridizing program covering several color types. His first introduction, 'Red Velvet Elvis' (1997), combines the dark coloration of 'Jeri' with the red of 'Cajun Cookery' into a distinct red-black iris. 'Red Velvet Elvis' has proven to be a useful parent, already siring the beet-colored 'Bayou Borsch' from a cross with 'Extraordinaire'. 'Beale Street', from a cross of 'Bellevue Coquette' × 'Marie Dolores', captures the size of the pod parent, the vigor and shape of the pollen parent and a rich, fairly true, deep blue color. This iris has up to six bud positions with multiple buds at each position. 'Crawfish Pie' takes the red with gold edge theme of its parent 'Cajun Sunrise' and creates a redder and brighter petal interior. A most fortuitous cross of 'Heavenly Glow' × 'Kelley's Choice' gave an exciting group of seedlings that included two with distinct petal edges, 'Bananas Foster' and 'Razor Edge', and a clear chestnut-colored iris, 'Roasted Pecan'. A cross of 'Heavenly Glow' × 'Vermilion Queen' gave the clean lemon color with brilliant green styles of 'Lemon Zest'. All these 'Heavenly Glow' derivatives are on the shorter stalks characteristic of the Morgan line. Two of the most exciting of the new Vaughn registrations are the brilliant red spider type 'Arachnephobia' ('Black Widow' × 'Cajun Cookery') and the first registered iris with both a darker edge and a lighter halo, 'Creative Edge' ('Old South Ball' × 'Marie Dolores').

Most of Joseph Mertzweiller's work with tetraploids will be covered in Chapter 8, but Mertzweiller also produced a number of fine diploid irises. Foremost among these diploid hybrids is the red-brown with distinct gold edging, 'Cajun Sunrise' (1993). It resulted from a cross of a yellow MacMillan seedling and a red-purple Mertzweiller seedling. Although he lost this iris, it not only survived but burgeoned in Marie Caillet's pond in Little Elm, Texas. 'Cajun Sunrise' is already finding its way into the pedigrees of Louisiana irises and appears to be an average to better-than-average grower in most regions. Two very good Mertzweiller garden irises are the white 'Good Doctor' (1993), from a cross of 'Ashley Michele' × 'Clara Goula', and the blue and yellow bicolor 'Just Helene' (1991), named for his charming wife from a cross of 'Harland K. Riley' × unknown. Although not as ruffled as some introductions of this period, their growth and floriferousness are superior to other irises in these color classes. A cross of 'Acadian Miss' × 'Easter Tide' produced the clear blue with white halos named 'Bera' (1996). Like the other Mertzweiller irises, this is a very good grower, with none of the late-freeze problems often found in 'Easter Tide' derivatives.

Other new hybrids of this period include a rather diverse group of hybridizers. Archie Owen's 1987 introduction 'Exquisite Lady' ('Clara Goula' × 'Mrs. Ira Nelson') is an outstanding example of the halo pattern in rich lavender blue edged with silvery white. It appears to be a good doer in most areas of the country and is justly popular. Ben Hager's 'Cajun Cookery' (1990) is probably the outstanding bright red iris of the day. It has a simmering color of a near cerise red and small signals outlined in black. The parentage is (('Delta King' × 'Acadian') × ('Mistletoe Garnet' × 'Delta King')) × a 'Cajun Country' sibling. It is proving to be an outstanding parent as well. Ken Durio is more known for his work with tetraploids but several of his red-toned irises from the orange side, including 'Daniel' (1988), are outstanding in their brilliance of color.

Pat O'Connor's 'Feliciana Hills' (1992), named for an area just north of Baton Rouge, Louisiana, is among the better pink irises. Wide, large, and full, it is a considerable improvement on its parent, Arny's 'Deneb', and a much better grower. O'Connor's ice-blue-white 'Southdowns' (1993) and its medium blue seedling 'River Road' (1993) are both worthwhile additions to the blue class.

Kirk Strawn has recently introduced a number of cultivars derived from both the Arny and Chowning irises. In addition, extensive use was made of a Bertinot iris, a sister seedling to 'Bellevue's Native Charmer' and 'Bellevue's Mike', that was named 'Kirk Strawn'—with the parentage of 'Olivier Monette' × 'Ann Chowning'. Two of the favorites among this group include 'Charlene Strawn' (1996), an enormous mauve-pink derived from a cross of 'Mrs. Ira Nelson' × 'Kirk Strawn', and 'Julia Strawn' (1996), a purple with distinct white backs to the standards and falls and clear white style arms from a cross of 'C'est Magnifique' × 'Charjoy's Mike'. Many of Kirk's irises have remarkable plant habits and vigor.

The Australian Revolution

Perhaps the most significant change among Louisiana irises since 1988 did not occur in their homeland of North America but in a land far from where the species originated. The Australian coastal climate is much like that of coastal California, an area where Louisiana irises grow readily, especially when supplemented with extra moisture. In these essentially frost-free climates, growth and increase of the Louisiana irises are much greater than even in their native Louisiana. Australian interest in Louisiana irises had been growing even before the publication of the first edition of this volume, chiefly due to the importation of seed from several nurseries and hybridizers in North America. Later, cultivars were imported, and with the arrival of the improved Arny cultivars in the early 1970s, the stage was set for a revolution in the iris.

The principal player in this revolution was John Taylor, a co-owner of Rainbow Ridge Nursery with his brother-in-law Graeme Grosvenor, who is primarily a hybridizer of bearded irises. Taylor received 'Clara Goula' even before its introduction as a gift from Charles Arny with the suggestion that the iris should be useful as a parent. Heeding this advice, Taylor set upon a program of cross and line breeding that resulted in cultivars with extreme ruffling and flower forms never before seen among Louisiana irises. Along with the new forms emerged color breaks such as halos, striping of petals as found in the Ensminger and Kasperak bearded irises, laciniated petal edges, and new double forms unrelated to the 'Creole Can-Can' line. These new characteristics were probably due in part to the recovery of recessive characters that could only be detected through intensive inbreeding. For example, in the pedigree of 'Margaret Lee', the Arny iris 'Charlie's Michele' appears five times. Another factor possibly responsible for these breaks is the raising of larger numbers of progeny in a saturation program, which utilizes a single parent in many different combinations. Even those most prominent American breeders mentioned above do not raise large quantities of seedlings and have relatively small seedling patches. Small numbers of progeny only hint at the possibilities present within a given cross. Although the progress with Louisiana irises had been steady in the United States, it was clear that larger numbers of seedlings and a serious hybridizing program held the key to creating dramatic advances. Taylor's hybridizing efforts have been rewarded with Australasian Dykes Medals for 'Koorawatha', 'Helen Naish', 'Jazz Ballet', and 'Dural White Butterfly'. These and other Taylor irises have markedly increased interest in Louisiana irises around the world.

Tracing any of the Taylor lines reveals his ability to capitalize on his breakthroughs. In his line of blues, a cross of two Arny irises, 'Bit of Blue' × 'Clara Goula', gave the very clear blue 'Cammeray' (1986), combining the more ruffled form of 'Clara Goula' in a blue flower. A cross of 'Cammeray' with Arny's 'Secret Spell' gave the blue with heavily textured veining, 'Flight of Fantasy' (1988). 'Malibu Magic' (1990) is the next progression in this line, combining his fine white Dykes Medalist, 'Helen Naish', with 'Flight of Fancy'. The result is a pale blue flower with darker veins and precise ruffling, combining ruffling factors now on both sides of the pedigree. 'Malibu Magic' is being used by numerous hybridizers around the world in creating a perfect blue iris. Taylor's yellows show a similar series of progressions in quality. 'Dural Charm' (1982) resulted from a cross of 'Charjoy's Anne' × a yellow Arny seedling from Katherine L. Cornay and was a significant advancement in terms of bud count and branching in yellow Louisiana irises. A cross of 'Dural Charm' and 'Clara Goula' produced 'Koorawatha' (1986), an outstanding ruffled gold flower with extraordinary bud count and placement. Besides being a wonderful iris in itself, 'Koorawatha' is also a marvelous parent. Two direct descendants, 'Alluvial Gold', ('Koorawatha' × 'Watch Out') introduced in 1991, and 'Classical Note' ('Koorawatha' × 'Helen Naish'), introduced in 1990, represent improvements in size and vigor over their illustrious mother. 'Alluvial Gold' is also proving to be an exceptional parent. Other new Taylor yellows are coming from other breeding lines, too, as 'Koorawatha' was incorporated into other colors to secure the ruffling and branching. The heavily ruffled and shorter cream-colored 'Spanish Ballet' (1992) is a result of segregation of the yellow color in crosses between colored irises.

The line leading to the production of the elaborately ruffled 'Margaret Lee' in 1991 is actually a combination of efforts in the white and yellow irises, too. 'Helen Naish' (1982), a cold white with elaborate ruffling and large blossom size, was the result of crossing 'Clara Goula' × 'Charlie's Ginny'. 'Dazzling Star'

(1987), a pink-toned cartwheel form, came from a cross of 'Koorawatha' × 'Lucile Holley'. The cross 'Dazzling Star' × 'Helen Naish' resulted in an amazing group of heavily ruffled irises with wonderful substance, including the clear pink 'Dancing Vogue' (1993), the red with yellow edges 'Gate Crasher' (1992), the rosy-purple 'Surprise Offer' (1994), and the rose with lighter edges 'Margaret Lee' (1991). Aside from the ruffling, both 'Gate Crasher' and 'Surprise Offer' frequently produce double blossoms even though these irises are unrelated to the Granger doubles. They are further distinguished in that the doubling does not result in the loss of functional anthers as do the Granger doubles. Since the doubling of the blossoms is not consistent, it is considered a fault according to the official judging standards of the American Iris Society. This does not mean that these irises are not worthy of a place in the garden, however, or that they cannot be useful in hybridizing. 'Margaret Lee' has proven to be a tremendous breeder, a clear trend among the introductions from Taylor in the late 1990s. 'Going South' (1993), 'Knight's Treasure' (1995), 'Guessing Game' (1994), 'Better Watch Out' (1996), 'Watch for It' (1995), 'Fashion World' (1996), 'Dural Bluebird' (1993), and numerous others are the result of direct combinations of 'Margaret Lee' with other irises. Besides the combination with 'Dazzling Star' to produce the 'Margaret Lee' family, 'Helen Naish' has been utilized as a parent in many other successful matings as well. A cross of 'Uptown' × 'Helen Naish' produced the orchid-pink 'Art World' (1987) that captures the unusual color quality of 'Uptown' in a more modern-appearing blossom. 'Jazz Ballet' (1988), a cartwheel lavender bitone with distinctive green signals, resulted from a 'Secret Spell' × 'Helen Naish' mating. Perhaps the best garden iris in the white class is the ruffled clear white 'Dural White Butterfly' (1989), from a cross of the Arny pink 'Screen Gem' × 'Helen Naish'. Like its illustrious parent, 'Dural White Butterfly' is proving to be a marvelous parent for many colors despite being a rather difficult iris on which to set pods.

Heather Pryor was fortunate to have the best of John Taylor's line to begin her own. At the outset, her goal was to produce an orange Louisiana iris, and her first crosses involved the new Taylor irises 'Desert Jewel', 'Alluvial Gold', and 'Gladiator's Gift', all in warm tones that might create an orange iris. Success came quickly with the introduction in 1995 of the ruffled orange-gold 'Bushfire Moon' ('Alluvial Gold' × 'Gladiator's Gift'). In the path towards her goal, Pryor produced other colors besides the elusive orange: 'La Stupenda' (1995) is an improved version of 'Desert Jewel' from crossing 'Desert Jewel' × 'Noble Planet', 'Garnet Storm Dancer' (1996) is a small, very ruffled deep maroon derived from 'Gladiator's Gift' × 'Designer's Dream', and 'Charlotte's Tutu' (1995) is a ruffled rose-red cartwheel from 'Desert Jewel' × 'Noble Planet'. She also produced some lighter colors in those initial crops: 'Crushed Ice'

(1996) is a creamy version of its parent 'Dural White Butterfly', which was crossed with 'Alluvial Gold', and 'Frosted Moonbeam' (1996)—cream with an all-over glitter that makes it truly appear frosted—is the result of 'Dural White Butterfly' × 'Designer's Dream'. Several irises in pink tones also resulted from this line of breeding. 'Playful Minx', a pastel pink bitone with rose-pink veining, was introduced in 1996, but unfortunately only the pod parent, 'Lucile Holley', is known. 'Prix D'Elegance' ('Dazzling Star' × 'Jazz Ballet'), a ruffled dusky rose-pink with the distinct signal pattern of 'Jazz Ballet', was introduced in 1997. As you might expect from pedigrees involving 'Gladiator's Gift' and 'Desert Jewel', red-toned products also occurred in abundance. 'Jazz Hot' and 'Hot and Spicy', both introduced in 1997, also capture the ruffling and substantial characteristics of progeny of 'Gladiator's Gift'.

Pryor has since strayed into the blue lines with the 1998 introductions of 'Captain Gates' and 'Deep Sea Quest', resulting from a cross of 'Koorawatha' with the navy blue but finicky-growing 'Sea Lord' (John Taylor, 1990). She also recovered several small-flowered progeny, especially from the selfing of 'Gladiator's Gift'. 'Little Nutkin' (1995), a very ruffled clear brown, is a singular example. Heather's husband Bernard Pryor has taken on these smaller sorts as his own breeding project and has already produced two 1998 introductions, 'Love Me Do' and 'Mischief Maker', from 'Bayou Short Stuff' × 'Spanish Ballet'. Heather and Bernard raise approximately 3000 seedlings each year. That high quantity coupled with an ingenious breeding program foreshadows more wonderful things from the Pryor lines in the future.

The Pryors and John Taylor are not the only Australian success stories. Bob Raabe has been breeding Louisiana irises for many years. His clear blue 'Sinfonietta' (1986) from a cross of 'Bethany Douglas' × ('Clara Goula' × 'Gatewood Princess') and his yellow-haloed mauve-pink 'Gerry Marsteller' (1988) from a cross of 'Uralba Mist' × 'Trionfo' are among the most popular Louisiana irises in the United States in their color classes. The irises of John Betts have not found their way to the United States, but the little blue 'Crayfish' (1980) from a cross of 'Wood Violet' × 'Clyde Redmond' is a favorite with many (although many Americans would expect an iris named crayfish to be red). It is a good companion at the front of the border among the small red and autumnally toned hybrids from the Arkansas hybridizers. Craig Carroll's 'Our Parris' (1989) is a very delicate blend of sunset hues over a cream ground and is a good grower in most areas of the United States. It has a parentage of ('Marie Caillet' × 'Gypsy Moon') × 'Myra Arny' and appears to be a useful parent when breeding for blended color patterns. Janet Hutchinson's fine addition to the amoena class, 'Popsie' (1995), combines near white standards and rosy purple falls. A result of crossing her own introduction 'Soft Laughter' × 'Buxom', 'Popsie' has already been a top prize winner in Australia and is gaining popularity in the

States. Her 1991 introduction, 'Honey Star', is like a more pastel version of 'Praline Festival' and is a rambunctious grower.

At the turn of the twenty-first century, interest in Louisiana irises is at an all time high in Australia, and more breeders are taking up the cause of hybridizing these plants. Heather and Bernard Pryor's irises are being introduced directly in the United States, and importing of other Australian hybridizers' introductions quickly follows their release Down Under.

Interest in hybridizing Louisiana irises seems to be increasing each year. New interest often comes from hybridizers experienced with other iris types who are just beginning to appreciate Louisiana irises. The Louisianas' relative ease of culture and freedom from disease are attracting many more hybridizers to the cause.

CHAPTER 8

Tetraploid Hybridizing

All living things inherit characteristics from their ancestors. Several hundred years ago Carolus Clusius, while writing about bearded irises, stated, "A long experience has taught me that iris grown from seed vary in a wonderful way." It has often been said, "They still do." Although all Louisiana iris seeds are very similar in appearance, progeny from these seeds differ significantly in appearance and performance. This variation in offspring is the very basis of hybridization.

In hybridizing Louisiana irises, breeders attempt to create more spectacular flowers, different flower colors, unusual color patterns, increased plant vigor, and numerous other features. Achievements have been noteworthy in hybridizing over the past six or seven decades. With significant improvements in flowers, foliage, and growth habit, Louisianas promise to offer new appearance and higher performance in the future.

Cells, Chromosomes, and Genes

A general review of cells, chromosomes, and genes should benefit individuals who grow plants, particularly those who grow them from seed. The cell is the smallest complete unit of life or living matter. All living organisms are made of countless billions of these basic structural units. This applies to Louisiana irises as well as to our own bodies.

Although cells throughout an organism are widely differentiated, accomplishing unique roles and carrying specific chemically coded information, they all share the common trait of being able to reproduce themselves by the process called cell division. Living cells are distinguished from nonliving matter—such as very large chemical units (so-called macromolecules) of plastics, rubbers, fibers, and so on—by their ability to reproduce themselves.

A typical cell of a higher organism has numerous structures which may be observed with a microscope. The most significant part of the cell is a dense mass, located near the center of the cell, called the nucleus. The nucleus is the "control center" and regulates all cellular activities. In the resting state, the nucleus appears to be made of a substance resembling a fine net. This is called chromatin, and the net is sometimes referred to as the chromatin network. The cell nucleus and chromatin network undergo profound changes at the time of cell division.

Rapid and continuous cell division is possible in only two locations within a plant. All plant growth originates in irises and similar monocots either in the growing point or meristem and the root tips. Above-ground growth is centered in the meristem or meristems, while below-ground growth takes place in the root tips. Cells in other areas of the plant may enlarge considerably but do not divide. When cell division occurs, the chromatin network changes into a number of rod-shaped structures called chromosomes. Chromosomes may be quite variable in size and shape. With appropriate staining and magnification, chromosomes are readily distinguishable in number, size, and shape.

Cells in all tissue of a specific organism contain the same number of chromosomes. The number of chromosomes for different organisms may be similar or quite different. Even if chromosome numbers are the same, or similar, the coded messages contained in each chromosome are unique for the organism involved.

Depending upon species, Louisiana iris cells contain forty-two or forty-four chromosomes. In most organisms, the chromosomes may be grouped into sets of nearly identical members. Two such sets of twenty-one or twenty-two chromosomes have been observed in Louisiana irises. The number of such chromosome sets has special significance and is considered to be more important than the number of individual chromosomes in each set. For Louisiana irises, the forty-two or forty-four total chromosome number is called the diploid or 2n number, since it is the sum of two identical sets. Therefore, $2n = 42$ or $2n = 44$. Triploids have three chromosome sets, 3n, and tetraploids have four chromosome sets, 4n. Chromosomes may be counted and the number of sets determined when observed at the proper state of cell division. The segment of biology dealing with cells, cell structures, and chromosomes is called cytology.

Chromosomes contain genes. Genes are chemically coded units of heredity or inherited characteristics. Genes are lined up along the chromosomes, and many genes are on each chromosome. The study of heredity or genetic combinations that occur in fertilization and seed formation is the science of genetics.

Genetic information, or the genetic code, carried on chromosomes is contained in the chemical referred to as DNA (deoxyribonucleic acid). DNA is not a single chemical but a combination of many chemicals. Each organism has its own DNA, its own genetic code. The DNA structure is similar to an infinitesimally small spiral staircase containing many thousands or hundreds of thousands of steps. A small number of simple chemical units constitute the sides and steps of the staircase. The number and order of these simple chemical units are highly specific to the organism and gene. The combinations are virtually limitless. Even though chromosomes may be similar in appearance, they are unique in the coded genetic information they carry. Identical chromosomes in each set contain the same coded information. The code or gene for red color is a particular specific combination or order of chemicals in the DNA. A very small change in this order may change the shade of red or may give a gene for a different color. The study and possible modification of DNA is the science of genetic engineering. Although this science is controversial it holds much promise for the future.

Chromosome Cycles

Plants have two chromosome cycles. One cycle involves vegetative growth and development, and the other involves flowering and seed formation (sexual reproduction). Genetic information is stored, replicated, and transmitted from one generation to the next by these cycles.

The meristem and root tips of diploid Louisiana irises contain 2n or two sets of chromosomes. Cell division proceeds in several stages. In the first stage distinct chromosomes appear from out of the chromatin network. In the next stage chromosomes duplicate themselves and become double. This state in which each chromosome is joined to its duplicate is a very transient situation. The double chromosomes form a line at the cell center, then are pulled apart to each end of the cell by fiber-like structures. Half of each double chromosome moves to the opposite end of the cell, where they again form a chromatin network. The rest of the cell divides, and a cell wall forms between the two new chromatin networks. Two new cells now each have the same 2n chromosome sets of the original cell. The exact same genes are present in each new cell. In this way the identity of the organism is preserved as it grows. This process is called mitosis or mitotic cell division. Mitosis occurs in all plants, repeatedly and countless times, from their beginning until death. It is important to note that mitosis duplicates the 2n chromosomes, creating the very transient condition in which the parent cell has the 4n chromosome number prior to completing division and forming two 2n cells.

The other chromosome cycle involves reproduction by means of seed formation. This type of cell division is of most concern to plant hybridizers. When floral buds are initiated, much earlier than they can be seen with the eye, sex cells or germ cells (pollen cells and egg cells) form. Chromosomes do not reproduce themselves during this stage, rather homologous chromosomes from the two sets pair up. The 2n chromosome number is maintained to this point. The chromosome pairs migrate to the center of the cell, the individual chromosomes are drawn to opposite ends of the cell by fiber-like structures, and the cell divides, as in mitosis. Each chromosome ultimately goes to a separate cell, and each of these cells now have a reduced, or n, chromosome number (one set contains 21 or 22 chromosomes for diploid Louisiana irises). This n chromosome number is called the haploid chromosome number, and the process is called reductive cell division or meiosis. The cells produced in this way are the sex cells, also called the germ cells or male and female gametes (pollen cells and egg cells).

Each gamete carries one complete set of chromosomes (n) with one complete complement of genes. The 2n chromosome number is restored through fertilization, when chromosomes of the egg cell unite with those of the pollen cell. Although the number of chromosomes are usually the same for each parent, the genes are entirely different. Each set of chromosomes in the gametes has now completed its mission of transmitting its special heritage of genes to the new generation. This causes "irises grown from seed to vary in a wonderful way." Further development of the embryo and the germinated seed proceeds by mitosis, which continues as the seedlings develop into mature plants, when the chromosomes then repeat the cycle of meiosis, flowering and transmitting their gene complement to the next generation.

Ploidy Level of Louisiana Irises

The "standard" form of many plants, and particularly Louisiana irises, is the diploid or 2n level. Only limited study has been made of the chromosomes of Louisiana irises. We are forced to resort to analogy to other chromosome studies of irises, particularly the bearded irises. L. F. Randolph of Cornell University made limited studies on Louisiana iris chromosomes. Randolph counted and studied chromosomes of bearded irises and many other types in addition to the Louisianas. Chromosome counts made by Randolph for the Louisiana iris species are: *Iris fulva* (2n = 42), *I. brevicaulis* (2n = 42 or 44), *I. giganticaerulea* (2n = 44), *I. hexagona* (2n = 44), and *I. nelsonii* (2n = 42).

The series *Hexagonae* is a remarkably homogeneous series—all species are diploids with nearly identical chromosome numbers. Natural hybrids with forty-three chromosomes were found in southwest Louisiana in sympatric or neighboring locations of *Iris fulva* and *I. giganticaerulea*. Similarly Randolph substantiated Viosca's identification of most of Small's "species" as natural hybrids. Randolph was also able to show that the *I. nelsonii* were diploids of hybrid origin.

Although almost all Louisiana irises are diploids, two triploids (3n) are known to have existed. The triploid 'Ruth Holleyman' was a collected *Iris giganticaerulea*. This iris was a giant, usually 50 to 60 inches (127–152 cm) tall and pale blue in color. G. W. Holleyman collected this plant in the Louisiana marshes and it was registered in 1954. A triploid *Iris brevicaulis* was registered as 'Triple Treat' (Welshans and Hager, 1972). Although the history of this iris is obscure, Welshans reported the plant was growing on the grounds of his home in Indianapolis, Indiana, when he moved there in 1946. 'Triple Treat' could have been collected in Indiana, or a nearby state, prior to 1946. It is known that *I. brevicaulis* and *I. fulva* have been found in the past in the upper Mississippi Valley in the states of Arkansas, Missouri, Ohio, and Indiana. Randolph reported a chromosome count of 3n = 64.

Efforts to locate the true 'Ruth Holleyman' have not proven successful. The plants currently on the market under the name are diploid. A few descendants of 'Ruth Holleyman' are still in existence and were discussed in Chapter 6. 'Triple Treat' has also disappeared. As far as it is possible to tell, no hybridizing whatsoever was done with 'Triple Treat'.

Unfortunately, Louisiana irises with a higher ploidy level, specifically tetraploids, were not found in the wild. With the decline of wild populations, it is highly unlikely that tetraploids will be found. The importance of tetraploids can only be inferred by analogy to bearded irises. Tetraploidy offers many advantages in plant breeding. Each gene is represented four times rather than twice, which offers a much wider range of genetic features and translates into larger sizes, improved substance, deeper colors, new color combinations and patterns, new forms, and other desirable features. In addition, though triploids are usually infertile, tetraploids are generally fertile because of the ability of 4n chromosome sets to divide equally into 2n sets.

A study of bearded irises brings a greater appreciation of these facts. Hybridizing of bearded irises was completely revolutionized within about four decades. New introductions changed almost completely from diploids to tetraploids.

Advent of Tetraploid Louisiana Irises

Through the untiring and patient work of Joseph Mertzweiller, tetraploid Louisiana irises became a reality in 1973. The diploid (2n) irises used to create the tetraploids (4n) were very beautiful and colorful advanced-generation hybrids. Conversion was achieved through the use of colchicine to create chimera plants, plants made of tissues of differing genetic composition. These chimeras were then hybridized, and eventually stable tetraploid progeny were produced.

New growth shortly after colchicine injection, showing typical swelling and distortion.

Typical offset development several weeks after colchicine injection.

Chimera showing mostly tetraploid in upper part and mostly diploid in lower.

PRESSED FLORAL PARTS 'WHEELHORSE' CHIMERA (1970)

STANDARD NO. 1   STANDARD NO. 2   STANDARD NO. 3

FALL NO. 1   FALL NO. 2   FALL NO. 3

ANTHER (OUTLINES)

Pressed flower detail of previous photo.

Typical tetraploid style arms, resulting from colchicine injection.

Typical diploid style arms.

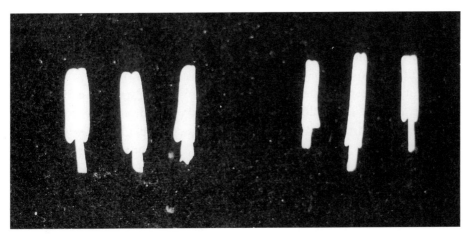

Tetraploid anther on left, resulting from colchicine injection; diploid anther on right.

Colchicine is able to convert diploids to tetraploids by its effects on a small cellular structure called the microtubule. A cellular function of microtubules is to move the chromosomes during mitosis. In a colchicine-treated iris, the cell progresses normally into mitosis, doubling the number of chromosomes (from forty-two to eighty-four or forty-four to eighty-eight) in anticipation of cell division. The cell progresses to the stage known as prometaphase in which the chromosomes are fully condensed in the center of the cell. At this point, both colchicine-treated and untreated cells are tetraploid, as the cell has twice the chromosomal content of the normal diploid cell. In a cell not treated with colchicine, the microtubules would then be involved in moving the chromosomes to the two poles, so that two new diploid cells can result. Because colchicine disrupts microtubules, the colchicine-treated cell is unable to separate the chromosomes back into two diploid cells, so the cell remains at the tetraploid level. When the colchicine solution is washed out of the cell, the cell retains its tetraploid level permanently. Many other compounds disrupt the mitotic progression just like colchicine, including the commonly used herbicides trifluralin and oryzalin, and can be used as safer alternatives to colchicine in inducing tetraploidy.

Further tetraploid hybridizing (4n × 4n) and selection should bring out the best tetraploid features and lead to still greater improvements. Unfortunately, progress has been slow. Some reduction in fertility and far fewer seeds per pod limits the ability to produce 4n seeds and seedlings. Producing a tetraploid seed currently requires about six times the effort compared to a diploid seed. Although this ratio is improving, it will remain a serious problem for some time to come.

Advantages and Disadvantages of Tetraploids

The conversion of diploid plants to tetraploids confers both advantages and disadvantages on the species. An obvious advantage is size. Tetraploid cells are about 1.4 times the size of diploid cells, resulting in about a 50 percent gain in the size of a tetraploid flower compared with a diploid blossom. Along with the increase in size is an increase in substance. Similarly, leaves increase in size and thickness, becoming more sturdy and weather resistant during the course of the season. Tetraploid Louisianas clearly stand out at midsummer by their greener, healthier foliage compared to the majority of diploids. Genetically, tetraploids have the advantage of four copies of each gene at every locus, compared with the two copies present in the diploids. Thus tetraploids potentially have more combinations of characters at a given locus than a diploid. Although such potential is often not realized or not useful, combinations of patterns, such as the enormous variation in plicata patterns in bearded iris, would be a genetic advantage in terms of improved Louisiana iris flowers. Characters that increase with copy number might also allow for more expression in a tetraploid compared to a diploid. For example, production of very dark irises may be due to over-expression of the genes involved in anthocyanin production and could allow for deeper shades towards true black. Some characters in bearded irises seem only to be expressed in tetraploids, such as the gene for lycopene production that results in the tangerine pinks in bearded irises. It might be possible that similar conversions of diploid Louisianas with these characters could result in baby-ribbon pinks comparable to those in the bearded irises.

With tetraploidy also come some disadvantages, especially in the first few generations from the diploid conversions. Although the increase in substance in tetraploids allows the blossoms to remain open for up to five days, this same increase in substance sometimes results in falls that fail to open properly. The falls may curl up at the tips or stray above the horizontal. Not all tetraploids have this opening problem; 'Professor Neil' and 'Sauterne' both open well, with the petals lying flat or even recurving slightly. In early generations after conversion, the tetraploids are often less fertile than the diploids from which they arose. Fertility loss has been a problem in the tetraploid Louisianas. The lower fertility may be due to aneuploidy or less-than-full sets of chromosomes that sometimes result from colchicine conversions, as well as the chromosomal complexities of tetraploid segregation that are not found in diploids. Indeed, tetraploid Louisianas generally produce fewer pods from a pollination and fewer seeds per pod. Improvements in pod-setting on cultivars such as 'Professor Jim' and 'Professor Fritchie' and the more potent pollen of 'Nuka' indicate that later generations may be more fertile than those derived directly from chimeras. In tetraploid daylilies, great improvements in seed setting were obtained when plants were grown in shade rather than in full sun. Kenneth Durio found that setting of tetraploid Louisiana pods was much improved when the blossoms were shaded with 60 percent shade cloth under excellent cultural conditions, with adequate moisture being most critical. Over 2,000 seeds of tetraploids were harvested from crosses between and selfing of 'Professor Ike' and 'Professor Claude'. Several important breaks resulted from this group, including the first red tetraploid, 'Bayou Rouge', the first yellow, 'Sauterne', and the first haloed cultivar, 'Ragin' Cajun'. Unfortunately a number of the sister seedlings were lost due to a hard freeze that destroyed some irises in pots, including some whites that are still rare in the tetraploids.

Recovery of recessive genes is also a problem. Whereas 3:1 ratios are obtained from selfing an individual carrying a recessive gene (Aa) at the diploid level, this same ratio becomes 35:1 for selfing an AAaa heterozygote at the tetraploid level. Coupled with the lower fertility and smaller seed set, the recovery of recessives is much less likely. Luckily, the first two tetraploids, 'Professor Claude' and 'Professor Ike', both carried the yellow recessives that allowed the production of 'Sauterne' and 'Welcome Change'. 'Snowy Change', the only white tetraploid Louisiana currently on the market, is the result of a similar recovery of a recessive from selfing the lavender 'Professor Paul'. 'Bozo' also regularly produces white offspring.

Tetraploid conversions in other genera are usually healthier and at least as vigorous and hardy as the diploids, if not more so. Tetraploid Louisiana irises are generally considered more tender than the diploids. They are especially susceptible to late freezes when all bloom stalks may be lost or severely stunted. However, two growers in Kentucky and one in Indiana have had good luck growing tetraploids in those climates, indicating that it is not just cold temperatures that cause this problem, rather, cold temperatures at a time of active growth. In an attempt to make tetraploids more hardy, seedlings of 'Black Gamecock' were converted but were not noticeably any more cold resistant than other tetraploids derived from *Iris nelsonii* or *I. giganticaerulea*.

With low seed set, poor germination, and lack of cold hardiness, tetraploid Louisiana irises still have hybridizing problems. Certainly the diploids offer the most profitable route for further hybridizing at this time. However, we have before us the transformation of the bearded irises and the smaller, still on-going movement in the Japanese and Siberian irises to convince us of the worth of tetraploid hybridizing.

Tetraploid Update

Compared to the dramatic progress in diploids since 1988, the progress in tetraploids has been much less dramatic, due in part to the small number of serious breeders participating in this work. Still, they have made progress in the variety of colors and forms that occur in the tetraploids, and they have extended the genetic material beyond just the two initial tetraploids, 'Professor Ike' and 'Professor Claude'.

Joe Mertzweiller was the most productive tetraploid hybridizer, with several more of the Professor series introduced. This tradition was initiated by naming the first two tetraploids for Professors Ike Nelson and Claude Davis, who were instrumental in Mertzweiller's interest in producing tetraploid Louisiana irises. 'Professor Marta Marie', named for Marie Caillet, is the pinkest available tetraploid, an old-rose-pink self with the broad form and substance expected from tetraploids. 'Professor Marta Marie' is the result of an induced chimera of 'Wheelhorse' × 'Professor Ike'. Mertzweiller's 'Professor Neil' represents a vast improvement in the quality of red Louisiana irises. It is a bright medium red with a bold thumb print signal. This iris, despite its tremendous substance, opens perfectly with none of the up-flipped falls so often noted in other tetraploids.

'Professor Barbara', named for Barbara Nelson, represents an important advancement in yellow tetraploids, with exceptional form and well-branched stalks. Growth is slower on this cultivar than either 'Professor Neil' or 'Professor Marta Marie', although still acceptable in performance. 'Professor Fritchie', named for Charles Fritchie, while not as shapely as 'Professor Barbara', is a superb yellow garden iris with abundant increase, strong growth, well branched stalks, and high floriferousness. 'Professor Fritchie' converts the superb Mertzweiller diploid 'President Hedley' into the tetraploid gene pool. 'President Hedley' has proven a marvelous parent at the diploid level, and it is hopeful that 'Professor Fritchie' will have these same attributes at the tetraploid level. 'Professor Fritchie' appears to be among the most fertile tetraploids yet produced.

Kenneth Durio has continued to produce new tetraploids descended from his seedlings that are all the result of intensive crossing of 'Professor Claude' and 'Professor Ike' in the late 1970s and early 1980s. 'Whooping Charlie' is a medium to light red-violet with a showy signal and very good opening habits. This is a very healthy plant and vigorous grower. 'Nuka' is probably the best-branched and -budded tetraploid now available, with blossoms in a clear shade of red-violet with a slightly lighter edging. Because branching and bud count are often low in the available tetraploids, 'Nuka' could be an important parent for imparting better branching to the tetraploids. Luckily, 'Nuka' seems to be more fertile than the majority of tetraploid Louisiana irises. 'Swamp Monster' is the most striking recent Durio registration because of its deep blue-violet color with lighter petal edges. It has a large, very fully formed blossom with excellent opening qualities.

Few tetraploid registrations by other breeders have occurred since 1988. 'Coorabell', from the Australian breeder Bob Raabe, is from 'Magistral' ('Professor Claude' × self) crossed back to 'Professor Claude'. It is probably the premier deep purple tetraploid Louisiana iris introduced to date and has very good growth habits. Two other tetraploids, 'Snowy Change' and 'Kentucky Cajun', offer qualities not available in other introduced tetraploids. Barry Clark's 'Snowy Change' is a near white, the palest tetraploid on the market, derived from selfing the light lavender 'Professor Paul'. Unfortunately, like its parent 'Professor Paul', 'Snowy Change' blooms very late, reducing its usefulness as a pollen parent. 'Snowy Change' is also a very poor grower for many, although it has performed well for others. 'Kentucky Cajun', besides offering new blood lines into the tetraploids through the cold-hardy and highly vigorous diploid 'Mentida', also introduces the first real ruffling in the tetraploid Louisiana irises and a lovely dark blue-purple coloration. And 'Kentucky Cajun', because it was hybridized by Samuel Norris in Kentucky, may prove more adaptable to colder climates than other currently available tetraploids.

Although relatively few hybridizers are working seriously on tetraploids, seedling patches have produced several exciting developments that have not yet been released. Blossoms with colors closer to pink than 'Professor Marta Marie' are appearing in seedlings from both the paler reds, such as 'Professor Jim' and 'Bayou Rouge', and the pale lavenders, such as 'Bowie' and 'Professor Paul'. Reverse bicolors appear in the subtle forms of the Durio tetraploids 'Sauterne' and 'Welcome Change'. The standards display an infusion of lavender to purple, while the falls have no or little anthocyanin. Seedlings from 'Professor Fritchie' × 'Sauterne' in several hybridizer's seedling patches have produced stronger reverse bicolors than 'Sauterne' itself, nearing reverse blue-violet amoenas. In addition, this cross has given yellows with better color and form than either parent. Besides the white 'Snowy Change', other whites have been obtained from the cross of 'Professor Fritchie' × 'Professor Paul' and, more surprisingly, from selfing the blue-purple 'Bozo'. White flowers are extremely useful in crossing for other colors or patterns, as the influence of 'Clara Goula' in the diploid crossing demonstrates.

Interploidy and Wide Crosses

Gametes of tetraploid plants carry a full set of chromosomes and are thus able to contribute a balanced set of chromosomes from the parent to the progeny. Hence, if a tetraploid is crossed to a tetraploid of a compatible species, the hybrid will contain a balanced set of chromosomes from both parents and produce a fertile tetraploid hybrid individual with a full set of chromosomes from each parent. The standard dwarf bearded irises are this kind of hybrid. Occasionally, a diploid × tetraploid cross will result in a fertile hybrid when the diploid plant produces an unreduced diploid gamete. Kenneth Durio took advantage of this phenomenon to produce the outstanding hybrid 'Little Caillet' by crossing a blue *Iris virginica* selection with the tetraploid Louisiana iris 'Bayou Rouge'. Although resembling the *I. virginica* parent in color and foliage, the shape, substance, and size of the flower reflect the influence of the Louisiana iris parent. The fertility of this iris is a full amphidiploid or allotetraploid, combining a full diploid set of chromosomes of the *I. virginica* parent with the diploid complement of chromosomes from 'Bayou Rouge'. (This conclusion is based upon the fertility of the hybrid; cytological analysis would be necessary to confirm it.) Seedlings from 'Little Caillet' vary some in plant habit and bloom size but little in color, as might be expected from the amphidiploid condition. Now crosses between other colors of *I. virginica* and the tetraploid Louisianas should allow a more complete color range of these very attractive and useful hybrids.

In 1985 Joseph Mertzweiller began a deliberate program of crossing diploids with tetraploids. The initial goal was to increase the genetic diversity in the tetraploids, as unreduced gametes (2n) in the diploid parent would combine with the normally produced diploid gametes of the tetraploid to produce tetraploids directly. In other crosses, aneuploids, triploids, and even diploids might result. This sort of crossing program is even more difficult than tetraploid × tetraploid crossing because of the high number of failed crosses and low number of seeds. However, Mertzweiller's results indicate that such an effort is worthwhile.

The first introduction from Mertzweiller's work, 'Creole Rhapsody', combines the fine Mertzweiller diploid 'Colorific' with a tetraploid seedling. 'Creole Rhapsody' retained the amoena coloration of 'Colorific' but has a wider form and heavier substance than the diploid plant, indicating the influence of the tetraploid parent. Although no chromosome count has been made on 'Creole Rhapsody', it appears to breed as a diploid or perhaps an aneuploid with close to a diploid complement. A Vaughn cross of 'Charge d' Affaire' × 'Creole Rhapsody' produced highly fertile amoena and bicolor progeny. 'Creole Rhapsody' is a very difficult pod parent, however, which is an indication that Mertzweiller's initial cross was not contaminated. Two other introductions with similar sorts of diploid × tetraploid pedigrees are Albert Faggard's 'Bulldog Blue' and Mary Dunn's 'Cuisine'. The appearance of these irises reflects the looks of the tetraploid pollen parent in increased size and substance. 'Cuisine' is a difficult pod parent, which may indicate an unbalanced chromosome complement. The production of these irises with heavy substance from diploid × tetraploid crossing indicates that further crossing of this type would result in outstanding irises, despite the difficulty of this approach.

The immediate future of tetraploid Louisianas depends on increased hybridizing interest and usage of the 4n cultivars now available and production of additional fertile 4n cultivars, preferably with little or no genetic relationships to current lines. Implementation of these methods must come from individual hybridizers and growers willing to put forth the required increase in time and effort. Several methods appear to produce new and fertile 4n cultivars, including the colchicine method and methods involving use of fertile 3n or 4n cultivars crossed with 2n cultivars. Admittedly, the colchicine method is long and tedious, but many improvements should be possible with the techniques described. Hybridizing routes depend on the functioning of unreduced gametes of one parent. While this depends on undetermined probabilities, the possibilities were thoroughly demonstrated many years ago with the bearded irises. Efforts and rewards should be great.

CHAPTER 9

Objectives in Hybridizing

This chapter considers the details of choosing parents and establishing breeding lines and the basics of flower color genetics in Louisiana irises. The mechanics of hybridizing—pollen transfer from one blossom to another and the subsequent formation of seed pods—are described in Chapter 5.

Practices and Methods of Hybridizing

Many people are under the misconception that hybridizing requires advanced knowledge of genetics and large amounts of space to grow seedlings. Although these both may be considered assets, Mary Dunn, Joseph Mertzweiller, and Charles Arny, some of our most successful hybridizers, had relatively small areas for seedling growth, yet all won the American Iris Society Hybridizer's Medal and produced numerous award-winning irises. Arny and Mertzweiller may have had a working knowledge of genetics, but many others like Mary Dunn used instinct or an artist's eye in selecting parents. Hybridizing ornamental plants is really a combination of science and art. Without the ability to judge beauty, all the scientific training is relatively useless. It is not surprising that individuals with a good appreciation for beauty and a healthy imagination are often just as successful as those with formal training.

Hybridizers of Louisiana irises, and of other plant groups as well, find success through the following practices and methods. Many examples sighted in this chapter are based on the work of Kevin Vaughn.

Pick an Objective in Your Breeding

Although it might seem exciting to breed all colors and patterns, you may make more progress choosing just a few objectives and concentrating on them.

A beginning hybridizer might pick areas of emphasis that other hybridizers have not chosen. For example, less work has been done with doubles, spiders, and short, smaller flowers of any color. Patterned blossoms received less attention than self-colored ones until about 1986. However, the relatively small number of active Louisiana iris hybridizers makes this a more open area of iris hybridization. Even areas being pursued by others could still yield valuable and unique results in your hybridizing program.

For example, Vaughn's red-black line started from an inspiration in similar work in the tall bearded irises—Gordon Plough had created exceptional red-black bearded irises, such as 'Edenite' and 'Study in Black', by crossing reds with blacks. Both good quality reds and near blacks existed in the Louisianas but none with the sultry red-black color of 'Edenite'. Creating this color became an early objective of Vaughn's. Heather Pryor chose to work toward the color orange, another color that was only dreamed of at the beginning of her work.

Among the plants in your garden, you may have admired a particular cultivar but wished it had more branches, grew better, or produced more flowers with better form and substance. These are ready-made hybridizing objectives. Also, breeding for hardiness for your particular area and climate could be a worthwhile objective.

Collect Parents for Breeding Stock

Now that you have an objective, obtain a number of parents that will lead toward it. Attending conventions and reading comments in plant society newsletters and bulletins will help you select cultivars that represent the best characteristics for the particular goal you have chosen. These will not only be useful as parents but also as benchmarks to compare with your own seedlings. Assemble this collection of potential breeding material together in the garden so that variations in growth and other characteristics may be compared side-by-side and to concentrate the hybridizing effort to a single area.

Generally, the newer a cultivar the more desirable it is in terms of a breeding program. Thus, obtaining breeding stock may take some capital investment, but this investment will bring a return as the newer varieties will have advances on which to capitalize. Older varieties with especially unusual characteristics or that have not been exploited as parents are definitely worth using. On several occasions Vaughn used thirty- to forty-year-old parents, and others have used collected species to good effort.

For the red-black project Vaughn bought all the near-black dark purples and all the available reds. A few older cultivars such as 'Devil's Dungeon' and 'Black Widow' were included for their unique aspects. Few reds offered desirable characteristics other than color, which left only 'Cajun Cookery', 'Parade Music', and a couple of 'Ann Chowning' seedlings for use as red parents.

Choosing Parents and Making the Crosses

Now that you have assembled the potential parents for your breeding objective, cross those that most closely meet your goal. Try not to combine parents with the same faults, as it is likely that all the offspring will have these faults as well. Irises with poor substance should be avoided, as invariably their progeny are of similar substance. However, if an iris of poor substance is the only plant with a particular characteristic, choose an especially heavily substanced mate. Ideally, choose parents with no obvious faults, but in general, balance the assets of both parents and hope for the best.

Some parents produce superior offspring in almost all matings. Plant breeders call this characteristic "high specific combining ability." These plants may not even be the best in their color class. For example, 'Classical Note' on most counts is a better yellow than 'Alluvial Gold', yet nearly all seedlings from 'Classical Note' have been ordinary whereas all from 'Alluvial Gold' have been exceptional. Plants with the ability to give superior progeny are listed below for each color class. Also invaluable for selecting parents are the American Iris Society Registrations and Introductions checklists which tell what other hybridizers have found successful by investigation.

At this point, consider how many named cultivars and seedlings you want to grow based on available garden space. With diploids, about 90 percent of the crosses take, and thirty seeds is generally an average cross. Germination is generally 30 to 50 percent unless improved germination methods are utilized. Also transplanted seedlings show some loss. Of course, if you obtain more seed or seedlings than you have room for, simply plant out only those crosses you consider most likely to produce superior offspring. Seed retains its viability for at least several years if stored dry, so other crosses not planted may be saved for a year when the seed crop is poor.

Growing the Seedlings

Grow seedlings in a manner that will exhibit their individual characteristics. A poorly grown seedling is impossible to evaluate, especially for characteristics unrelated to the blossom. For example, in the disastrous spring of 1996 in the central southern United States, few irises bloomed normally due to a severe late freeze. Vaughn retained his entire seedling crop for an additional year to evaluate them under more normal conditions.

Louisiana iris seedlings require abundant moisture and nutrients to perform optimally. Prepare seedling beds by incorporating organic matter and fertilizer, especially where seedlings will be crowded. And a watering schedule that guarantees 1 inch (2.5 cm) of water per week significantly improves the chances of seedling bloom.

Evaluation and Further Crossing

As the seedling crop blooms, you will note both superior and inferior individuals within the crop. Although no individuals may be worthy of naming (and of course, naming any seedling should not be done until after at least several bloom seasons), recognize any that might have improvements useful for further breeding. One practice is to number the seedling and record information on its characteristics (color, form, size, branching, and so on) in a notebook. Characteristics of seedlings not to be retained can be recorded more cryptically. Some hybridizers prefer to use a hand-held cassette recorder while doing evaluations, then they transcribe the recordings later. Regardless of the method you choose to document seedlings, be thorough and consistent, evaluating the entire flower and the plant. Take the time to make a key to any abbreviations or special notations used in describing the seedlings. With time memory can fade, or someone other than yourself may need to decipher your notes. Numbering systems vary depending on the hybridizer, but Vaughn chose a coded system for tracking his crosses. Numbering the seedlings consecutively is an effective tracking method. For example, Vaughn assigned the code C-12 to the cross 'Jeri' × 'Cajun Cookery', then he numbered the seedlings from that cross—the plant eventually named 'Red Velvet Elvis' was the fifth seedling, designated as C-12-5. Louisiana iris seeds often germinate erratically, yet the code C-12 would designate siblings from this cross that germinated and bloomed in another season. Many people use a year designation in their seedling crosses and number good seedlings as they bloom, for example 99-C-12-5 or 2000-C-12-1. Hybridizers develop their own unique coding systems for tracking seedlings, sometimes making them self-evident, sometimes deliberately cryptic.

Comparing state-of-the-art blossoms in a particular color class side-by-side with your seedlings is helpful in the evaluation process. Other knowledgeable local iris hybridizers may have useful or helpful opinions. Avoid "falling in love" with your seedlings and becoming blind to their faults. If possible, photograph every seedling that you number. With modern auto focus cameras and a macro lens, almost anyone can take decent photographs or slides. A visual record as well as a written record is extremely helpful in evaluating seedlings.

Now that a crop of seedlings has bloomed, what is the next step in the process? If a superior seedling that is towards the objective blooms, you have several options. You may cross back to either parent to intensify the traits from the initial cross, or you may cross to unrelated plants that might add other desirable traits. For example, in the cross of 'Jeri' × 'Cajun Cookery', the goal was red-black. Seedling C-12-5, 'Red Velvet Elvis', fulfilled this color goal, so little was to be gained from crossing back to either parent. Rather, 'Red Velvet Elvis' was crossed with varieties that might add more ruffling and size while retaining the red-black color. Crosses to 'Charles Arny, III', 'Extraordinaire', 'Far and Away', and other ruffled black-purples produced several successes with deeper ruffling, increased size, and the desired red-black color.

In another case, a cross of 'Bellevue Coquette' × 'Marie Dolores' aimed to combine the size and blue color of the pod parent with the vigor of the pollen parent. One seedling, 'Beale Street', captured the attributes of the pod parent; however, a back-cross of 'Beale Street' to 'Marie Dolores' was made to try for a blue iris possessing the impressive plant vigor of 'Marie Dolores', which is among the most vigorous Louisiana irises ever. Both clear blues and whites with larger size and the vigor of 'Marie Dolores' resulted. Crosses were also made to unrelated irises to gather new characteristics for the line, such as the tight ruffling of 'Obvious Heir'.

The above two scenarios for further crossing represent the two basic methods of plant breeding: out-crossing and line breeding. Out-crossing brings together different sets of genes, and when the breeder is lucky, the right combinations give superior offspring. Line breeding allows intensification of particular traits without diluting the traits of interest by crossing to unrelated individuals. A potential problem with line breeding is that deleterious recessives may also gather, leading to a loss of vigor. Because Louisiana irises are known for their ability to grow and rapidly develop into clumps, vigor should be a concern of anyone pursuing line breeding.

Specific Color and Type Recommendations

Each of the colors and patterns in Louisiana iris blooms have areas of strength and possible areas for improvement. Here is a list of those strengths and weaknesses as well as a list of parents that produce high-quality offspring consistently for each color group.

Whites. White is a most advanced color class, with outstanding examples of form, substance, and vigor. Areas of possible improvement include whites with contrasting styles, laciniation, or deeper veining (such as 'Cotton Blossom'). Parents with proven ability in these areas include 'Marie Dolores', 'Dural White Butterfly', and 'Helen Naish'.

Yellows. Many yellows have excellent form and substance, but color fast-ness is a problem, especially in the deeper shades towards bright gold and orange. Muddiness, with anthocyanin coloring overlaying the yellow, is also a problem in some of the deeper shades, although when the effect is even as in 'Praline Festival', it produces pleasing caramel to brown tones. Green style arms are available in a small number of yellow cultivars. Some cultivars exhibit snakey stalks, a legacy from 'G. W. Holleyman' breeding, although yellows with excellent stalks may be found. Joe Mertzweiller's 'President Hedley' was a major breakthrough in this color class. It has sired such fine varieties as 'Praline Festival' and 'Rokki Rockwell'. Currently useful parents include 'Alluvial Gold', 'Rokki Rockwell', 'Spanish Ballet', 'Noble Planet', 'Willow Mint', and 'Praline Festival'.

Blues. Blues in Louisiana irises come from two sources. Larger ones are derived from *Iris giganticaerulea* and are generally more towards lavender-blue. Smaller ones generally of a brighter hue are derived from *I. brevicaulis*. A wonderful goal would be the production of larger blues with the clarity and brilliance of the smaller varieties. A few cultivars show contrasting style arms of green or white, which developed into blues with different shades. Vigor is good in 'Clyde Redmond' and in varieties derived from it, such as 'Sea Knight' and 'River Road', and is a characteristic worth carrying into other varieties. Blue is dominant to white, and whites often carry co-pigments that make blue irises appear bluer. Thus, a way to obtain superior blue irises is to cross white irises of excellent form and substance onto blue irises of outstanding color. Worthwhile blue parents include 'River Road', 'Sea Knight', and 'Beale Street'.

Reds. Like the blues, reds in Louisiana irises come from two species. Large-sized blossoms are derived primarily from *Iris nelsonii*, and smaller flowers are derived from *I. fulva*. Generally the reds from *I. nelsonii* breeding are fuller and more round and ruffled flowers. Most work with *I. fulva* was from northern hybridizers, because of the hardiness of these clones and availability. McGarvey's 'Devil's Advocate' and 'Devil's Scion' were bred in New York State in a Zone 4 garden and Preston Hale's 'Red Dazzler' was bred in Iowa. All were exceptional in northern climates, and 'Red Dazzler' is still widely grown. Despite the fact that Louisiana irises are among the few iris groups with good red coloration, relatively less emphasis has been placed on this color class in recent years. Advances in the flower form noted in the yellow and white classes may well be incorporated into the red parents. 'Ann Chowning' has proven to be an exceptional parent in this color class and some of its numerous introduced progeny may prove similarly useful. 'Gladiator's Gift', although a blend itself, regularly produces good red progeny. Ben Hager's 'Cajun Cookery' gives brilliant colors and size to its offspring.

Purples. Mary Dunn developed the blue-purple class to its present state by adding form and size that were previously unobtainable. Most are from the combining of ruffled paler colors from the Arny lines with purples such as 'Dark Tide', 'Full Eclipse', and 'Blue Shield'. Further advancement of this line could include developing these larger ruffled blossoms into near-black flowers. Cultivars such as 'Delta Prince' combine relatively dark petal color with contrasting white style arms. It is a combination that would be valuable in darker and more ruffled blossoms. Some parents with proven ability include 'Extraordinaire', 'Jeri', and 'Far and Away'.

Pinks. No pinks similar to the lycopene-containing pinks of bearded irises are found in the Louisiana irises, but a pink effect is obtained by light lavender-blues, orchid-pinks, and rose-pinks from diluting dark lavenders, purples, and reds, respectively. Advancements toward purer pinks are coming, and cultivars may be had with good form and substance in each of the approaches to pink. Parents of use in this class include 'Kay Nelson', 'Margaret Lee', and 'Dancing Vogue'. The older variety 'Medora Wilson' is exceptionally pink and may be worth combining with newer varieties. 'Margaret Hunter' has some of the best plant habits of any Louisiana iris and is still a useful parent for both pinks and for irises with plicate-like patterns.

Doubles and cartwheels. Marvin Granger produced a series of doubles from the collected *Iris giganticaerulea* 'Creole Can-Can'. This line has petaloid stamens that make crossing these cultivars as male parents virtually impossible. In very rare cases a minute amount of pollen will be found on the petaloid stamens. J. Farron Campbell of Garland, Texas, has had some success in obtaining seed using pollen from the petaloid stamens of Granger's 'Flareout'. Doubling in the Granger lines is a recessive characteristic, so crosses to unrelated varieties give predominantly single or cartwheel varieties (the latter perhaps indicating a partial expression of the doubling trait). More recently, cartwheels and doubles have appeared in the Taylor line that have the advantage of male and female fertility, as the stamens are not petaloid. This wide-open field for hybridizing could be focused on improving consistency and blossom symmetry. Considering the progress made in Japanese irises and daylilies with double segments, this goal should be obtainable. Useful parents in this area include 'Creole Can-Can' derivatives such as 'Double Talk', 'Gate Crasher', 'Surprise Offer', 'Aunt Shirley', and 'Geisha Eyes'.

Halos and edges. One of the most popular additions to the Louisiana iris hybridizing effort has been the production of irises with lighter halos and deeper edges. Halos appear to be a combination of yellow or white parents and an anthocyanin-containing parent, although not all of such combinations result in offspring with halos. Considering the high quality of yellows and whites, transfer of the form and substance of these cultivars into haloed offspring should be easily obtainable. Less is known genetically about those with darker petal edges, although at least some of these appear to give edged progeny in crosses to other edged and non-edged progeny. Some of these varieties give effects not unlike plicata patterns in bearded irises. Parents known to produce haloed progeny include 'Exquisite Lady', 'Margaret Lee', 'Cajun Sunrise', 'Bera', 'Crawfish Pie', and 'Charge D'Affaire'. Useful parents for edges include 'Lynn Hantel', 'Kelley's Choice', 'Desert Jewel', and 'Margaret Hunter'.

Amoenas and variegatas. Although amoenas are relatively rare in the Louisianas, preliminary results indicate that at least some of this type are dominant to self-colored blossoms. Amoenas in purple, lavender, pink and yellow are currently available and several yellow-red variegatas have been produced from the Taylor and Arny breeding lines. Substance has been a problem in this color class, although recent examples in seedling patches show good improvement in these categories as well. Parents that have proven useful for improving substance include 'Bayou Mystique', 'Vermilion Queen', 'Glowlight', and 'Bellevue's Michelle'.

Patios. Shorter Louisiana iris cultivars are often designated as patios for their potential in edging low areas, such as patios, where taller cultivars would be inappropriate. Many of the Chowning, Rowlan, and Morgan cultivars that involve either *Iris brevicaulis* or *I. fulva*, or both, in the pedigree are shorter irises with smaller blossoms. Because of this pedigree, they are often among the hardier cultivars. Not all of the patios are derived from this line of breeding, however, as Faggard's 'Bayou Short Stuff', Arny's 'Geisha Eyes', and Pryor's 'Little Nutkin' are smaller, shorter segregants from *I. nelsonii* and *I. giganti-caerulea* breeding. Attention should be paid to keeping the smaller blossoms in proportion to the shorter stalks. 'Gladiator's Gift', 'Bayou Short Stuff', 'Heavenly Glow', and 'Kelley's Choice' have consistently produced smaller progeny and are useful parents in this line of breeding.

Flower Color Genetics of Louisiana Irises

Although a complete discussion of flower color genetics is beyond the scope of this book, an elementary presentation of basic color genetics should be helpful in planning crosses for a given flower color. Some results from specific color types are presented above in the various color classes. Refer to the chapters prepared by Ken Kidd in *The World of Irises* (Warburton and Hamblen, 1978) for a more detailed description of genetic principles.

Two major types of pigments are responsible for the colors in Louisiana iris blossoms: carotenoid pigments that give the yellow colorations and anthocyanin pigments that give the blue, purple, and red colors. Carotenoids are mainly insoluble compounds localized in structures called chromoplasts, and anthocyanins and their related pigments are water soluble and present in the vacuole of the cell. Blossom colors are the result of the presence or absence of each of these pigment types. For example, red coloration is due to the presence of both carotenoid yellows and red-purple anthocyanins to give the visual effect of red. As you increase the amount of bluer pigment overlaying the yellow, the effect turns more to brown than red. Thus, by adjusting the amount and presence of these pigments, a complete rainbow of colors may be produced.

In general, the presence of a particular kind of pigment is dominant to the absence of that pigment. For example, crossing a blue iris (contains anthocyanins) with a white iris (contains no anthocyanins) results in blue progeny. Crossing yellows (contain carotenoids) to whites (contain no carotenoids) results in yellow. Crossing an iris that has a particular pigment with one that does not generally results in progeny with a paler shade than that present in the parent having the particular pigment. White irises often contain accessory pigments that modify the color of the primary pigment by forming complex pigment mixtures in the vacuole. Thus, often a cross of white to blue will produce either bluer blues or more lavender-toned irises as a result of these co-pigments inherited from the white parent.

Two major kinds of anthocyanin pigments are present in the Louisiana iris. One, called delphanin, is a glycoside of the bluest anthocyanidin delphinidin (named for the discovery of its presence in delphinium blossoms) and is the major anthocyanin found in bluish irises. Ensatin, a glycoside of malvidin first discovered in Japanese irises, is the redder of the two anthocyanins and is present in greater quantity in red irises. Red-purples, such as 'Professor Ike', have approximately equal quantities of these two anthocyanins as well as some underlying carotenoid pigment. Because red-purples contain all the pigments and presence is dominant to absence, this color often results in crosses of Louisiana irises.

All white irises are not identical biochemically, as there are many steps in the biochemical pathway to produce anthocyanins. Blocking any of these steps will result in an anthocyaninless iris. White variants of several of the species (*Iris giganticaerulea, I. brevicaulis,* and *I. nelsonii*), when crossed, give rise not to whites but to blues and red-purples. For example, the cross of 'Ila Nunn' × 'Clara Goula' gave the blue 'Bellevue Coquette'. Each of the white parents lacks a specific step in the pathway to produce the anthocyanins, and each lacks a different step than the other parent, but the hybrid between the two obtains both steps required to produce anthocyanin. A real-life analogy would be the making of a stew. Without either meat or vegetables no stew could be produced, but combining the two ingredients allows for stew. In this case, the stew is the production of anthocyanin pigments. Crosses between white flowers that have the same type of deficiency would always produce more white flowers.

Plate 1. *Iris hexagona* watercolor by
Georgene Wood.

Plate 2. *Iris fulva* watercolor by Georgene Wood.

Plate 3. *Iris brevicaulis* watercolor by Georgene Wood.

Plate 4. *Iris giganticaerulea* watercolor by Georgene Wood.

Plate 5. *Iris nelsonii* watercolor by Georgene Wood.

Plate 6. A native stand of *Iris fulva* in the Atchafalaya Basin in south Louisiana. Photo by Joseph Mertzweiller.

Plate 7. Planting in a shallow pond at the Rabalais garden in Arnaudville, Louisiana. Photo by Joseph Mertzweiller.

Plate 8. A natural planting of Louisiana irises at Mercer Arboretum and Botanic Garden in Houston, Texas. Photo by Charles Mann.

Plate 9. Louisiana irises bordering a walkway at Mercer Arboretum and Botanic Garden in Houston, Texas. Photo by Earl Olsted.

Plate 10. Louisiana irises at Mercer Arboretum and Botanic Garden in Houston, Texas. Photo by Charles Mann.

Plate 11. Plantings in and along the banks of shallow ponds at the Copenhauer gardens in DeRidder, Louisiana. Photo by Marie Caillet.

Plate 12. 'Peggy Mac' collected near Abbeville, Louisiana, by W. B. MacMillan and registered in 1943. Photo by Hager-DuBose.

Plate 13. A white *Iris giganticaerulea* collected in the marshes below Lake Charles, Louisiana. Photo by Marie Caillet.

Plate 14. 'Bayou Vermilion', an *Iris nelsonii* hybrid collected by W. B. MacMillan near Abbeville, Louisiana, and registered in 1943. Photo by Hager-DuBose.

Plate 15. 'Mary S. DeBaillon', a hybrid collected by Mary Swords DeBaillon and registered by Caroline Dormon in 1943. Photo by Hager-DuBose.

Plate 16. 'Lockett's Luck', a natural hybrid collected and registered by Thibault in 1947. Photo by Farron Campbell.

Plate 17. 'Creole Can-Can', a semi-double *Iris giganti-caerulea* collected by Marvin Granger in the marshes below Lake Charles, Louisiana, in 1956. Photo by Marvin Granger.

Plate 18. 'Bayou Bandit' (Campbell and Weeks, 1998), a near brown *Iris fulva* collected near Baton Rouge, Louisiana, by Jeff Weeks. Photo by Farron Campbell.

Plate 19. 'Louise Austin' (G. Arceneaux, 1945), a first generation cross of *Iris brevicaulis* and *I. fulva*. Photo by Hager-DuBose.

Plate 20. 'Cherry Bounce' (Nelson, 1946), an early red. Photo by Farron Campbell.

Plate 21. 'Black Widow' (MacMillan, 1953) showing spider form. Photo by Farron Campbell.

Plate 22. 'Dixie Deb' (Chowning, 1951) growing in the Goula garden in Lafayette, Louisiana. Photo by Marie Caillet.

Plate 23. A planting of 'Marie Caillet' (Conger, 1963) in the Simpson garden near Baltimore, Maryland. Photo by Doris Simpson.

Plate 24. 'Finders Keepers' (Chowning, 1966), an early cross of *Iris brevicaulis* × *I. brevicaulis*. Photo by Kevin Vaughn.

Plate 25. 'Dr. Dormon' (Conger, 1973). Photo by Joseph Mertzweiller.

Plate 26. 'Colorific' (Mertzweiller, 1979) blooming with spider lilies (*Hymenocallis liriosme*) in the Caillet garden near Dallas, Texas. Photo by Marie Caillet.

Plate 27. 'Mentida' (Norris, 1981), a species cross. Photo by Farron Campbell.

Plate 28. 'Double Talk' (Granger, 1973) with semi-double form from 'Creole Can-Can', a collected *Iris giganticaerulea*. Photo by Marie Caillet.

Plate 29. 'Ann Chowning' (Chowning, 1977), among the most popular Louisiana irises. Photo by Farron Campbell.

Plate 30. 'President Hedley' (Mertzweiller, 1980). Photo by Joseph Mertzweiller.

Plate 31. 'Acadian Miss' (Arny, 1980). Photo by Farron Campbell.

Plate 32. 'Ruth Sloan' (Sloan, 1984) with pendent form. Photo by Marie Caillet.

Plate 33. 'Amber River' (Sloan, 1985) with ruffled and overlapping form. Photo by Marie Caillet.

Plate 34. 'Ashley Michelle' (Mertzweiller, 1987) growing on the banks of a pond in the Caillet garden near Dallas, Texas. Photo by Marie Caillet.

Plate 35. 'Exquisite Lady' (Owen, 1987). Photo by Joseph Mertzweiller.

Plate 36. 'Old South' (M. Dunn, 1986). Photo by Farron Campbell.

Plate 37. 'Koorawatha' (Taylor, 1987), showing ruffling and stalks with many buds. Photo by Marie Caillet.

Plate 38. 'Kay Nelson' (Granger, 1988). Photo by Marie Caillet.

Plate 39. 'Heavenly Glow' (Morgan, 1989). Photo by Farron Campbell.

Plate 40. 'Grace Duhon' (Haymon, 1988). Photo by Farron Campbell.

Plate 41. 'Cherry Cup' (Morgan, 1989). Photo by Farron Campbell.

Plate 42. 'Twirling Ballerina' (Rowlan, 1988). Photo by Farron Campbell.

Plate 43. 'Gertie Butler' (Arny, 1990) showing recurved form. Photo by Farron Campbell.

Plate 44. 'Festival's Acadian' (Haymon, 1990). Photo by Marie Caillet.

Plate 45. 'Starlite Starbrite' (Granger, 1989), a semi-double. Photo by Marie Caillet.

Plate 46. 'Just Helene' (Mertzweiller, 1991). Photo by Marie Caillet.

Plate 47. 'Sea Consul' (Taylor, 1990). Photo by Farron Campbell.

Plate 48. 'Deirdre Kay' (Granger, 1991) Photo by Joseph Mertzweiller.

Plate 49. 'Feliciana Hills' (O'Connor, 1992). Photo by Paul Gosset.

Plate 50. 'Praline Festival' (Haymon, 1992). Photo by Marie Caillet.

Plate 51. 'Rusty O' (Arny, 1992). Photo by Farron Campbell.

Plate 52. 'Our Parris' (Carroll, 1990), Photo by Farron Campbell.

Plate 53. 'Extraordinaire' (M. Dunn, 1992), Photo by Farron Campbell.

Plate 54. 'Rokki Rockwell' (Haymon, 1992), Photo by Farron Campbell.

Plate 55. 'Noble Planet' (Taylor, 1990), Photo by Farron Campbell.

Plate 56. 'Aunt Shirley' (Mertzweiller, 1992) showing very large flowers with signals on all parts. Photo by Marie Caillet.

Plate 57. 'Vermilion Queen' (Goula, 1993). Photo by Farron Campbell.

Plate 58. 'Kelley's Choice' (Morgan, 1993) showing plicata pattern. Photo by Farron Campbell.

Plate 59. 'Cajun Sunrise' (Mertzweiller, 1993) with yellow style arms and a yellow halo on contrasting red-brown flower parts. Photo by Marie Caillet.

Plate 60. 'Far and Away' (M. Dunn, 1992). Photo by Kevin Vaughn.

Plate 61. 'Julia Strawn' (Strawn, 1996). Photo by Kevin Vaughn.

Plate 62. 'Good Doctor' (Mertzweiller, 1993) with flaring and overlapping form. Photo by Farron Campbell.

Plate 63. 'Josephine Shanks' (Taylor, 1992), a near pink with overlapping segments. Photo by Graeme Grosvenor.

Plate 64. 'Obvious Heir' (Taylor, 1991) showing very ruffled and overlapping form. Photo by Graeme Grosvenor.

Plate 65. 'Charge D'Affaire' (M. Dunn, 1992) with an edging or halo. Photo by Kevin Vaughn.

Plate 66. 'Lucy Payens' (Taylor, 1992), a bitone. Photo by Graeme Grosvenor.

Plate 67. 'Gate Crasher' (Taylor, 1992). Photo by Graeme Grosvenor.

Plate 68. 'White Umbrella' (Taylor, 1990). Photo by Farron Campbell.

Plate 69. 'Going South' (Taylor, 1993). Photo by Farron Campbell.

Plate 70. 'Real Treasure' (Taylor, 1993). Photo by Graeme Grosvenor.

Plate 71. 'Camille Durand Foret' (Haymon, 1994). Photo by Farron Campbell.

Plate 72. 'Silencio' (Taylor, 1994), ruffled with a halo and signals on all parts. Photo by Graeme Grosvenor.

Plate 73. 'Gulf Moon Glow' (Faggard, 1994). Photo by Marie Caillet.

Plate 74. 'Bera' (Mertzweiller, 1996). Photo by Farron Campbell.

Plate 75. 'Knight's Treasure'(Taylor, 1995). Photo by Kevin Vaughn.

Plate 76. 'Willow Mint' (Morgan, 1995), intense yellow with green style arms. Photo by Perry Dyer.

Plate 77. 'Fashion World' (Taylor, 1996). Photo by Graeme Grosvenor.

Plate 78. 'Crushed Ice' (H. Pryor, 1996). Photo by Farron Campbell.

Plate 79.'Garnet Storm Dancer' (H. Pryor, 1996). Photo by Kevin Vaughn.

Plate 80. 'Playful Minx' (H. Pryor, 1996). Photo by Farron Campbell.

Plate 81. 'Prix D'Elegance' (H. Pryor, 1997). Photo by Kevin Vaughn.

Plate 82. 'Frosted Moonbeam' (H. Pryor, 1996). Photo by Farron Campbell.

Plate 83. 'Dural Breakaway' (Taylor, 1997). Photo by Graeme Grosvenor.

Plate 84. 'Sweet Cosette' (Taylor, 1997). Photo by Graeme Grosvenor.

Plate 85. 'Joie De Vivre' (H. Pryor, 1997) with signals on all parts. Photo by Farron Campbell.

Plate 86. 'Whispered Promise' (H. Pryor, 1996) showing a break in color. Photo by Farron Campbell.

Plate 87. 'Lone Star' (Campbell, 1997). Photo by Farron Campbell.

Plate 88. 'Red Velvet Elvis' (Vaughn, 1997). Photo by Kevin Vaughn.

Plate 89. 'For Zoe' (Taylor, 1997), ruffled, with signals on all parts. Photo by Graeme Grosvenor.

Plate 90. 'Braemer' (Taylor, 1997). Photo by Graeme Grosvenor.

Plate 91. 'Jazz Hot' (H. Pryor, 1997). Photo by Heather Pryor.

Plate 92. 'Hot and Spicy' (H. Pryor, 1997). Photo by Farron Campbell.

Plate 93. 'Better Believe It' (Taylor, 1998). Photo by Graeme Grosvenor.

Plate 94. 'Lemon Petticoat' (H. Pryor, 1997). Photo by Farron Campbell.

Plate 95. A stalk of 'Deep Sea Quest' (H. Pryor, 1998) showing flower placement. Photo by Heather Pryor.

Plate 96. 'Fiddle Dee-Dee' (Campbell, 1998). Photo by Farron Campbell.

Plate 97. 'Lemon Zest' (R. Vaughn, 1998). Photo by Kevin Vaughn.

Plate 98. 'Sorrento Moon' (H. Pryor, 1998). Photo by Heather Pryor.

Plate 99. 'Our Dorothy' (H. Pryor, 1999). Photo by Heather Pryor.

Plate 100. 'Atchafalaya' (Campbell, 1998). Photo by Farron Campbell.

Plate 101. 'Razor Edge' (R. Vaughn, 1998). Photo by Kevin Vaughn.

Plate 102. 'Roasted Pecan' (R. Vaughn, 1998). Photo by Kevin Vaughn.

Plate 103. 'Bananas Foster' (R. Vaughn, 1998). Photo by Kevin Vaughn.

Plate 104. 'Creative Edge' (Vaughn, R 1998). Photo by Kevin Vaughn.

Plate 105. 'New Vogue' (H. Pryor, 1998). Photo by Pryor.

Plate 107. 'Chuck Begnaud' (Haymon, 2000) with an edging or halo. Photo by Marie Caillet.

Plate 106. 'Great White Hope' (Haymon, 2000) showing upright standards or bearded iris form. Photo by Marie Caillet.

Plate 108. 'Professor Barbara' (Mertzweiller, 1992), an early yellow tetraploid. Photo by Marie Caillet.

Plate 109. 'Professor Neil' (Mertzweiller, 1992), a near red with very large yellow signals. Photo by Kevin Vaughn.

Plate 110. 'Professor Fritchie' (Mertzweiller, 1995), a very tall and hearty tetraploid. Photo by Marie Caillet.

Plate 111. 'Kentucky Cajun' (Norris, 1995), the first ruffled tetraploid. Photo by Marie Caillet.

Plate 112. 'Creole Rhapsody' (Mertzweiller, 1998), an interploid or cross between a diploid and a tetraploid. Photo by Marie Caillet.

Plate 114. Arrangement and photo by Carolyn Hawkins.

Plate 113. 'Little Caillet' (Durio, 1998), an interspecific cross of a tetraploid Louisiana iris and *Iris virginica*. Photo by Marie Caillet.

Plate 115. Arrangement and photo by Pat Norvell.

Plate 116. Arrangement and photo by Pat Norvell.

CHAPTER 10

Culture

Louisiana irises are perfectly suited for water and bog culture but readily adapt to most garden situations. Professionals studying the natural habitat of the species have given great insight into adapting these moisture-loving plants to the garden, but everyday gardeners have been the real key in taming and moving these native American wildlings into our landscapes. Adaptability is the factor that makes for a great garden plant, and Louisiana irises have proven themselves to be extremely adaptable. They are grown around the world under a very wide range of climates, soils, and cultural practices.

Location

It is important to pay attention to the movement of the sun when deciding where to position any plant. Irises bloom best when they receive a maximum amount of sunlight—at least six to eight hours per day during the active growing season. Irises tend to grow during the cooler times of the year in the fall and spring with a period of inactivity during the hotter and colder times of the year. A full-sun location is ideal unless you live in an area where summers tend to be long, hot, and dry. In this case, some afternoon shade may be beneficial. Areas of deciduous shade may be acceptable, but avoid areas of heavy shade—the irises will grow, but bloom will be reduced greatly. Naturally low spots where water tends to stand are excellent sites for locating beds if the light requirements are met.

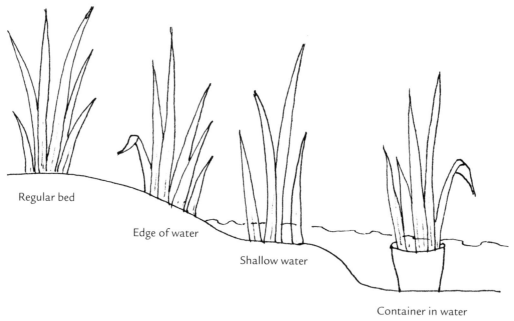

Regular bed

Edge of water

Shallow water

Container in water

Suitable Locations for Louisiana Irises

Soil

For many years growers assumed that Louisiana irises needed acidic soil. This assumption has proven to be inaccurate. In 1945 Ira S. Nelson wrote an article for the magazine *Home Gardening*, reporting on his study of the cultural requirements and the natural habitats of Louisiana irises. The popular belief that the wetlands of the southern United States, chiefly in south Louisiana, have soil that is both very acidic and rich in nutrients did not prove true, according to Nelson. In fact, the pH was found to be much closer to neutral and in many areas to be on the alkaline side, especially those areas that once supported the huge populations of *Iris giganticaerulea,* which are generally ancient oyster beds. He also noted that the swamp muck that produced the most amazing iris growth was far less fertile than the average garden soil in the region. He reached several conclusions that have proven accurate: (1) soil pH for garden culture is not too important so long as it is not extremely alkaline or extremely acidic; (2) the less fertile swamp soil was able to support rampant iris growth due to the suspension of nutrients in the standing water, making the nutrients readily available to the irises; and (3) the most critical time in maximizing growing conditions comes during the fall and spring growing seasons.

The average gardener does not have a bog or swamp in which to grow Louisiana irises, instead planting them among other plants in mixed beds. Learn as much as possible about the soil before planting or making amendments. Home test kits are readily available but may be less than accurate if you are not familiar with using them. Consider having a soil test done by a reputable laboratory. Consult your local county agent at the Cooperative Extension Service or local branch of the U.S. Department of Agriculture for locations and advice. The cost is usually not prohibitive, and in some areas basic testing costs nothing for property owners. Realize that you are likely to spend a great deal more money adding unneeded amendments than it would cost to have the soil test run. Soil conditions can vary greatly over very small areas. Your soil may be very different from that of your closest neighbor based on how the property was readied for building by the addition of fill dirt for leveling the site.

Adding organic matter to the soil is likely to be beneficial, especially for heavy feeders like Louisiana irises grown in the garden. For rhizomatous plants, course material is not desirable. The best sources of organic amendments are finished compost, brown Canadian peat moss, mushroom compost, alfalfa pellets, and shredded leaves. Grass clippings can be used, but green clippings will rapidly deplete nitrogen from the soil. Adding nitrogen along with green matter helps offset the problem. Avoid fresh manures, fresh sawdust or wood chips, and domestic black peat moss from the northern United States. While organic matter works wonders on the soil, it lowers the pH very little. A soil pH of 7.5 or greater may warrant amendments to increase the acidity. Soil pH can be lowered by adding sulfur-based compounds or acidifiers such as aluminum nitrate. Amendments will need to be added on a regular schedule to maintain a lower pH level. If the pH is lower than 6.0, you may need to make the soil a little more alkaline. The ideal pH is 6.5. The addition of garden lime is the most effective means of raising soil pH, and this product is readily available at nurseries and garden centers. Lime will also need to be added at regular intervals to maintain the higher pH.

Tight or heavy clay soils do not present a problem; in fact, they may have a distinct advantage in that they hold water very well. Adding copious amounts of organic material to sandy soils will increase water retention but will need to be an ongoing process. Products on the market designed to hold water in the soil are reported to work well. Cost may be prohibitive for treating a large area, however. A solution often used in areas of extremely sandy soils, or where water usage is limited, is to plant in sunken or lined beds. This method allows water to pool around the irises, maximizing the effect of watering. Lining the bed with a plastic or rubber liner will give the ultimate efficiency in watering. Construction can be a great deal of work since an ideal depth for such a bed is 14 inches (36.5 cm), but some people have had great luck with lined beds no deeper than 6 inches (15.2 cm). Children's plastic wading pools can be used to great advantage as liners. The work and expense of preparing such beds must be weighed against the long-term cost and availability of water. Before creating a sunken or lined bed, consider forming micro-zones that will allow you to grow plants with very different watering requirements in a relatively confined area.

Water

Ideally, never allow Louisiana iris beds to go dry, but they need not be kept soggy. The only exception to this rule is for roughly one month after planting, or until appreciable new growth has begun. During this period, keep the soil fairly wet to get plants established. Once the plants have settled in, keep the soil as evenly moist as possible. Mulching is the most efficient aid in achieving this goal and is discussed below. Prime growth time for irises is in the fall and spring. Hence, dry spells are more serious during these seasons. Louisiana irises also show more winter damage when they experience dry conditions during very cold weather. Summer is the natural dormant period for the species growing in native habitats, but growth is optimal only when the rhizomes are prevented from dormancy by adequate watering in hot weather. When watering is required, at least 1 inch (2.5 cm) of water at a time is recommended, roughly the same amount recommended for lawn grass during the summer. Less frequent but deep waterings are always better for the overall health and vigor of plants than frequent shallow watering. Deep waterings encourage plants to put down deeper roots, making them less susceptible to a brief dry spell or sudden change in temperature. To achieve a greater depth of soil moisture, pay careful attention to how quickly runoff begins when you water. When you notice that the water is not soaking in, stop watering and wait an hour or so, then start watering again. The time required to properly water your garden and the frequency of watering will depend on the composition of your soil. You can use a rain gauge to measure how much water has been applied.

Louisiana irises do love moisture, and there are many ways to apply water, but the two most common methods are overhead water from sprinklers and drip irrigation from soaker hoses. Mother Nature does it best, but can be fickle and not deliver when the plants need it the most. So, when in doubt, water. It is fortunate, and certainly no coincidence, that the prime growth periods of fall and spring also tend to be rainy seasons. Drip irrigation conserves water, but Louisiana irises love to have their foliage wetted during hot, dry weather. Plants that receive overhead watering have noticeably healthier-looking foliage throughout the summer than those that receive drip irrigation. Another factor to consider and check is the pH of the water. The frequency of application and strength of certain fertilizers and soil amendments may need to be adjusted to compensate for excesses in water pH.

Mulch

The easiest way to keep soil evenly-moist all the way up to the surface is to mulch. Mulching also regulates fluctuations in soil temperatures and greatly enhances water conservation. In hotter, dryer parts of the country where frequent irrigation would normally be required, mulching should be given a high priority. Mulching also protects the rhizomes, which tend to grow at ground level, from sunscald. And properly mulched beds present fewer weeds to pull, eventually breaking the weed-seed cycle.

Pine needles, sometimes called pine straw, is a top-notch mulch. It will not blow away or mat down, it lasts for several years, and it is attractive as well as aromatic in the landscape. In many areas of the country pine needles are easily obtained simply by raking. If this is not the case in your area check the local nurseries or home garden centers for baled pine needles—this is still a relatively new industry, but it grows with each passing year. Other mulch materials include hay, thrashed wheat and rice stalks, shredded leaves, shredded pine or cypress bark (not nuggets), and thoroughly-dried grass clippings.

A word of warning: hay is likely to contain huge amounts of weed seed and should be used with caution. Two methods will help prevent introduction of huge quantities of weed and grass seeds along with the hay. If time permits, several months before you need the hay place the bales out in the open and wet them down with a garden hose. Wet them gradually and every few days to maintain a sufficient moisture level to start the seeds in the hay germinating. In time, a mass of grass and weeds will be growing from the baled hay. At this point, stop the watering to kill the grass and weeds. This method is not totally effective but will greatly reduce the number of seeds left to germinate in the garden. Another method of controlling seed germination, which may be used in conjunction with the above method or on its own, is to use a commercial pre-emergent weed and grass control. Many such products are on the market and most will work to prevent germination of either broadleaf weeds or grasses; a few are designed to work on both. Pre-emergent controls are designed to prevent seed germination, not to kill existing weeds or other plant material. Be sure to carefully read and follow the application instructions.

Sunscald is considered a form of rot, and is a chief cause of poor bloom in Louisiana irises. In extreme cases the rhizome may be lost completely. Sunscald is the overheating of the rhizome due to direct exposure to the sun. This condition is easily prevented by a summer mulch. Planting the rhizome deeper is not a solution, but soil (about ½ inch, or 1.3 cm) may be used to cover the rhizome for protection from the sun if a suitable mulch is not readily available. The rhizomes of Louisiana irises like to be at ground level with the upper portion, from which leaves emerge, above the soil. Under natural growing conditions the rhizomes would be protected by grasses or other plants.

In very cold areas where winters tend to be long and extreme, a thick mulch applied prior to snow cover offers good winter protection. Winter mulching works a lot like summer mulch in that it helps prevent sudden and dramatic changes in soil temperatures. Leaves may be burned back from the cold, but this is to be expected in any area of freezing temperatures.

Planting and Transplanting

There was a time when the only way to obtain Louisiana irises commercially was through specialty iris nurseries and gardens. Thankfully, many commercial nurseries and garden centers are now offering them for sale as container-grown plants. The condition of the rhizomes affects planting times and methods.

Buying directly from specialty outlets is still the best way to obtain the very newest or hard-to-locate cultivars and species plants. Most specialty outlets ship plants bare-root in late summer or early fall and will not ship during the early spring when the plants are actively growing and blooming, or once winter has set in. Bare-rooted Louisiana irises need time to establish a healthy root system before cold temperatures set in. The same is true for the onset of summer temperatures that promote dormancy or greatly reduced growth. A good rule of thumb for determining the latest possible planting time is to plant at least three to four weeks prior to the average first freeze date for your area; however, the optimal interval would be to allow six to eight weeks for the plant to get established. Plant bare-rooted rhizomes in the spring only if absolutely necessary. This timing greatly increases the likelihood of losing the plant or disrupting the normal blooming cycle. Bare-rooted rhizomes are shipped in packages designed to ensure that they remain moist during shipment. Unpack them right away, and never allow them to dry out. Newly-received rhizomes should be soaked at least overnight and until planting. Make sure to keep the foliage above water so the rhizomes can breathe. Louisiana iris rhizomes can be held in water for lengthy periods without harm. If it is necessary to hold rhizomes in water for more than a few days, however, consider adding a general purpose water soluble fertilizer to promote new growth. Adding a root stimulator to the water is always a good idea regardless of how long the rhizomes are in water.

Container grown plants do have very distinct advantages over bare-rooted plants. Potted plants should have a healthy and extensive root system at the time of purchase, which allows planting at almost any time of year when the soil can be worked, even while the plant is blooming. Often, the root system has outgrown the pot and has begun to grow in circles around the pot. In this case, carefully pull the roots loose and spread them out to make better contact with the soil. Water them in with a root stimulator if possible. Remember that the roots will be concentrated in the immediate vicinity of the planting hole during the first few weeks after planting, so take care when watering to make sure water reaches this area.

All perennial garden plants need to be divided and replanted on a fairly regular schedule. The distance you allow between new plants can directly affect how often the rhizomes will need lifting, dividing, and replanting, but on average they need it every two or three years. Consider the method of cultivation when determining the spacing of plants. In the garden, allow space of at least 24 inches (61.0 cm) between different cultivars or adjoining plantings in the garden. Water and bog cultural practices are discussed below.

The preferred time to plant or transplant Louisiana irises is as the natural period of summer dormancy breaks at the end of summer or in early fall. Plants need enough time to re-establish a root system before winter sets in. Check for the average first-freeze date in your area and try to have all planting finished at least four weeks earlier. Planting or transplanting in early spring will diminish the quality of bloom and may lead to the loss of plants. Some growers advocate planting immediately after bloom and report excellent results. The key to their success is allowing time for a new root system to establish itself before the heat of summer causes the plant to slow or stop growing.

To lift and divide over-grown clumps of Louisiana irises, have on hand a pan or bucket of water, a sharp knife, scissors or garden shears, and a spading fork. Begin by pulling back the mulch and removing any old leaves that have died back. Trim the foliage with the scissors or garden shears by at least half at anytime before replanting, but doing so before digging them up will allow for a better view of the area. If you plan to hold any rhizomes for an extended period of time before replanting, wait and trim the foliage just before planting, or at least leave it slightly longer.

Spading forks tend to be the favored tool for lifting clumps, but in very loose soils a shovel would work just as well. Loosen the soil all around the clump before trying to break it apart. Rhizomes will tend to break away at the point where they emerge from the mother plant and would be removed with the knife, but do take care to avoid breaking them at some other point. Once the new-growth rizomes are removed from the old mother plant put them in a pan or bucket of water to prevent the roots from drying out. Rhizomes can

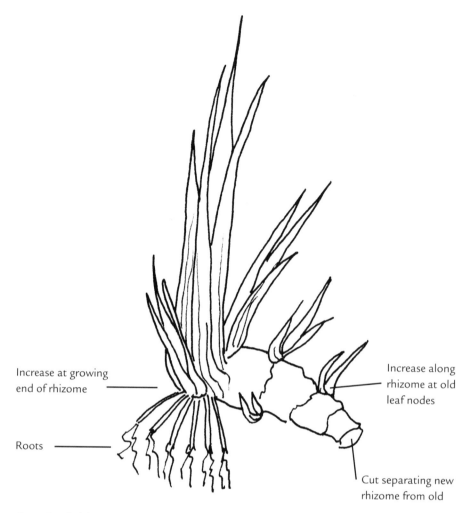

Increase at growing
end of rhizome

Roots

Increase along
rhizome at old
leaf nodes

Cut separating new
rhizome from old

Growth of Rhizome

be held in water for months without any ill affects, but you must leave adequate foliage to ensure the rhizomes can breath and you should add fertilizer to the water.

Not all rhizomes bloom, and not all rhizomes produce increase at the same rate or at the same season. Some cultivars increase in the spring while others may wait until the fall. Rhizomes that have bloomed are distinguishable by their blooming stalk. Once the new rhizomes are removed from a bloomed mother plant, it is normally discarded. In some cases you might wish to replant it to see if it will produce any additional new rhizomes. Very small new growth may be left attached to a portion of the old rhizome if it makes for easier handling. Rhizomes that did not bloom, though they were large enough to do so, should be replanted and given the opportunity to bloom the next season or produce more new plants. All good garden irises should produce a minimum of two new rhizomes.

Typical offset development in one season's growth.

Close-up of offset development.

Louisiana irises are typically generous increasers and will rapidly grow into a neighbor's space. Rhizomes should not be planted deeper than 1 inch (2.5 cm). Spacing between rhizomes of the same cultivar should be based on the length of a mature rhizome. Mature rhizome size varies greatly among cultivars, and can range from 3 or 4 inches (7.6–10.2 cm) to 12 inches (30.5 cm) or even longer. When buying new plants it may be difficult to know what constitutes a mature rhizome. In this case be generous and give them plenty of room to grow by allowing 8 to 12 inches (20.3–30.5 cm) between rhizomes. When dividing existing clumps, determine the size of the mature rhizomes of the plants that bloomed. To help keep the cultivars distinguishable, place a wooden divider in the soil between groups of different cultivars. If the rhizomes grow over the divider you can still determine the cultivar by the direction of growth. In mixed beds, other types of plants can act as dividers.

Re-establishing a root system as quickly as possible requires good soil-to-plant contact—make sure the soil is firmly pressed down around the plant, leaving no air pockets. One method of planting rhizomes is to make a small mound of soil in the bottom of the planting hole, then spread the roots over the mound before covering with soil. Watering the new planting is very important, and you might include a root-stimulating fertilizer. New plantings should never be allowed to dry out, and keep the soil fairly wet until appreciable new growth is evident.

Water and Bog Gardens

Gardening trends change from time to time, and a current craze is water gardening. For many years the Society for Louisiana Irises worked to dispel the idea that these irises had to be grown in water or bog culture. We did a very good job, and now find it necessary to point out that they are excellent subjects for the water or bog garden. People that grow Louisianas in garden beds and in bogs or water gardens report that, while they do well in the garden, growth, increase, stalk height, and the number of blooms per stalk is greatly increased in bog or water gardens. The bloom season also tends to be earlier in bog and water gardens. Variations in pH seem to be better tolerated in standing water. No appreciable problems have been reported by water gardeners in climates where bogs and ponds are frozen over for extended periods of time.

The first concern for planting Louisiana irises in a water setting is to ensure that enough foliage is above the water to permit the rhizomes to breathe. Container-grown plants should already have enough foliage to allow them to be planted right away. Bare-rooted plants will likely need to be planted in pots to allow sufficient foliage growth. At least as much foliage should be above the waterline as below, but two to three times more above the water is better. Each rhizome needs at least one mature leaf and one new leaf emerging, but more foliage is better. These requirements are especially important to observe when planting in pots and submerging them in water.

Water gardens with natural banks or planting shelves are easier to plant than pools completely lined with plastic or rubber. When planting around a natural lake, pond, or waterway, place rhizomes at the water's edge with the growing tip pointed into the water. The rhizomes will grow into the water and establish their own preferred growing depth. Increase seems to be optimal on plants that are in less than 1 inch (2.5 cm) of water; the rate dramatically drops as the water depth increases. As many matters pertaining to culture present opportunity for dispute, some growers claim increase is not adversely affected when plants are allowed to establish their preferred depth. Consider this factor when preparing planting ledges to maximize increase and quantity of bloom. Prepare a ledge that is like a naturally occuring bank, one that starts shallow and gradually deepens—the amount of slope will depend on the size of the pond.

Pinning the rhizome to the ground is something to consider, for it will keep the rhizome upright until roots take hold. The easiest and most readily available source of pins is a wire clothes hanger which can be cut and bent into the proper shape. Pins must be long enough to reach solid soil and curved to match the diameter of the rhizome without pinching it. Pinning rhizomes down is more critical when the water has a current but will also be helpful for keeping bare-rooted plants in place and upright around small ponds. Cultivars will need more room between them in a water garden, as growth is even more rampant than in regular garden beds.

Planting in containers for self-contained water gardens also requires that you pay careful attention to the amount of foliage above the water. The size of the container is extremely important as it will determine how many rhizomes you can plant and how often you will need to replant. Containers that are wider than they are deep will probably work better in most situations. The depth at which the container is placed can vary so long as foliage is sufficiently above the waterline. Fewer rhizomes are recommended when planting in containers since growing in water will likely produce rampant growth. If your water garden has koi or similar fish, make sure that you cover the container with mesh or other material such as rocks to keep the plants from being uprooted.

A bog situation is little different from regular garden beds when it comes to planting Louisiana irises. Growth will be more rampant, so allow more room between cultivars. Preparing the area for planting is likely to be much more difficult, however, especially if you want to add organic matter. And unless you know the bog will always stay damp, plan for a means of watering in the event the area goes dry.

Maintenance

A number of mistaken ideas about growing irises need to be dispelled. Regardless of the type of iris you grow, do not cut the foliage back or down after bloom. Without healthy foliage the rhizome cannot breathe or assimilate nutrients from the soil. No leaf should be removed until is has completely died back to the rhizome and pulls away easily. If you want to neaten unsightly foliage, take no more off than is absolutely necessary to get back to healthy foliage. Remove old bloom stalks immediately after they finish blooming. Louisiana irises are extremely fertile and will produce a great many seed pods that result from natural pollination by insects. The growing seed pods take energy away from the rhizome that could otherwise be used to nourish the new rhizomes that will come from the old mother rhizome. Once a rhizome blooms it begins to deteriorate and will not bloom again, but it will produce offsets that will bloom in following years. Remove the bloom stalk with a sharp knife or garden shears close to the point where the stalk emerges from the ground. With some irises you can simply snap off the bloom stalk near the ground, but this rarely works with Louisiana irises and is more likely to result in ripping the rhizome loose from the soil. If the stalks are allowed to remain until the seed pods reach maturity and drop seed into the bed you will end up with a garden full of seedling irises that you have never seen before and may not want.

Fertilizing

Maintain a regular fertilizing schedule in both spring and fall. Louisiana irises are very heavy feeders and benefit from heavier and more frequent applications of fertilizers than other types of irises. Applying concentrated water-soluble products with a hose-end sprayer is a quick and easy way to accomplish the task. The benefits are two-fold in that both the foliage and the roots absorb the fertilizer, which makes for a rapid green-up in the spring. Digging in solid fertilizer around plants is a laborious job that can damage roots and rhizomes, and it often needs to be done far earlier than other methods due to the increased time required by certain chemicals to work in the soil. Spring applications should commence four to six weeks prior to anticipated emergence of flowering stalks. Louisiana irises normally start blooming about two weeks after tall bearded irises. Use balanced fertilizers in spring, with sufficient nitrogen in the mix. Once bloom stalks emerge, cease fertilizing. Acidic fertilizers are available and are generally marked as "Azalea & Camellia" fertilizer. Slow-release fertilizers such as Osmocote are available in a number of formulas and do not require a lot of repeated applications. They also do not need to be dug into the soil. Fall fertilizer should include lower nitrogen and higher phosphate. As with planting, stop fertilizing three to four weeks prior to the first freeze date for your area. New plantings can be lightly fertilized once before winter sets in (with preferably a low-nitrogen, high-phosphate, high-potash material), but only after appreciable new growth has begun.

Fertilizer requirements may be even greater in water than in conventional culture, and fertilizers should be applied during the prime growth times of spring and fall due to the plants' more rapid growth in water culture. In water gardens that do not include koi or other types of fish, fertilizing is fairly simple. If fish are present then you must be more careful, placing heavy emphasis on organic and spike-type fertilizers that are inserted into the soil rather than broadcast. Some commercial fertilizers are formulated to be safe for fish, but they are generally available only at specialty outlets for water garden supplies. In natural water or bog gardens, composted materials and manures in the growing medium and as a mulch on shallow planting shelves can provide the required fertilizer.

Diseases and Pests

Louisiana irises are generally not bothered by any serious diseases or insect pests. The very fact that they evolved to grow and thrive in the bogs and swamps of the Deep South may be the key. Warm, wet climates tend to be very hospitable to insects, bacteria, viruses, and fungi. Louisiana irises are certainly not immune to all diseases or insect damage, but they are inclined to be far more trouble-free than their bearded relatives.

Diseases and pests that affect Louisiana irises vary based on climate and geographic location. If a problem arises that you are not familiar with, seek help. It is always wise to properly identify a problem before resorting to the application of chemicals. Help can be found from a number of sources. The Agricultural Extension Service or your county agent are available through most state universities or colleges of agriculture. Local nurseries or plants-people may also be good sources of advice. Members of garden clubs, especially iris societies, can be great resources for help and information.

If chemical treatments are required, read and explicitly follow the directions that come with the product. Never guess when it comes to chemicals. Mixing and combining various chemicals can be disastrous. It is better to make multiple applications of different chemicals than risk combining them. Adding a drop or two of liquid detergent, however, is safe. It acts as a surfactant which helps chemicals adhere to the surface of leaves. Many chemicals already include a surfactant. Be sure to add the detergent after the sprayer is filled or you may end up with more suds than liquid. The proper application and storage of chemicals should always be a top priority.

Nature seems to provide a "critter" for every occasion—some are more serious than others. They may range from the microscopic to something as apparent as the cat from next door. Some of the more common problems reported by growers of Louisiana irises are discussed below.

Iris Borers

Iris borers are not a problem in the warm climates of the Deep South, but can be a very serious problem in colder climates. Reports of iris borers attacking Louisiana irises have been limited to the colder regions of the United States.

According to *The World of Irises* (Warburton and Hamblen, 1978), "The iris borer probably occurs wherever irises are grown; however, it is rarely found as a far south as Nashville, Tennessee, or below the hardiness zone 7 (minimum temperature of 10°F, −23°C. They are generally considered to occur in eastern Canada from Maine to the District of Columbia, and west to Iowa."

The iris borer passes through four stages in its life cycle: egg, larva, pupa, and adult moth. They mainly do damage to the rhizomes but also to the leaves. In some cases they do no leaf damage and detection is difficult. Leaf damage usually consists of small pinholes or "bleeding" of young leaves. In dense clumps of irises the borer may travel underground from rhizome to rhizome without causing leaf damage. In this case, the first evidence of damage may be yellowing of central leaves which have rotted and can be pulled out easily. Examination of the rhizome will usually show it to be a hollow shell, the inside portion having been eaten by the borer. Such plants will not survive.

Chemical treatments are almost always required to eliminate iris borers in Louisiana irises. Systemic insecticides seem to offer the most complete method of control. Rather than make a specific recommendation for a chemical that can be used to fight borers, we suggest that you consult the sources mentioned above or read the labels on systemic chemicals that you find available for purchase.

Rhizome Rot

Rhizome rot can be caused by several bacterial and fungal agents. Fortunately, this is not a frequent problem with Louisiana irises, but it does occasionally occur and can spread rapidly. Rhizomes become mushy and may rot completely. Affected rhizomes generally give off a disagreeable odor. A few rhizomes or an entire bed may be affected. Rhizome rot can be caused by introduction of infected soil, humus, or manure into existing garden soil. Therefore, add only sterilized or fully composted materials to your soil.

If you detect rhizome rot, quick action is necessary to limit the infection. Dig up the plants immediately, cut away soft portions of the rhizomes and wash them with a fungicide and dilute formaldehyde solution, then plant them in another location. The infected area should be treated with a soil fungicide or a mixture of a fungicide with an agricultural bactericide according to directions.

Nematodes

Nematodes are microscopic worms. Not all nematodes are harmful to plants; indeed, some are considered beneficial. Harmful varieties infect roots, injecting digestive enzymes into them which cause the roots to become distorted. Roots infected with nematodes will develop knots or galls that cut off the flow of water and nutrients to the leaves. Plants infected with nematodes look stunted and new growth appears wilted or yellow. Fortunately, Louisiana irises are not a favorite of nematodes.

If you suspect that you do have nematodes, test the soil. Formerly, soil fumigants were the recommended control, but these products are no longer available to consumers. Nematicides are commercially available. Varying degrees of success have been reported with their use.

Leaf Miners

Leaf miners attack the leaves of Louisiana irises and are detected by the visible serpentine-like paths or trails left behind as chlorophyll is consumed, eventually turning the affected area white. Leaf miners are most active during late summer and the active growing seasons of fall and spring. Infestation typically occurs on the outer growth near the base of the leaves, but may occur higher up as well. All plants need healthy foliage to insure vigorous growth and top performance. Leaf miners are most often reported when plantings do not receive enough sunlight. Take time to note how many hours of full sun the irises receive. Moving the planting or trimming back limbs or foliage on other plants that block sunlight may be the answer to the leaf miner problem.

If the infestation is severe, diminished bloom and poorer overall performance of the irises may result, but the loss of plants is unlikely. The use of systemic insecticides works most effectively. Some growers advocate the removal of all infected leaves, but the cure in this case would seem to be as severe as the ailment since the result is the loss of foliage.

Rust

Rust is a fungal disease which appears as powdery red-brown speckles on the leaves. While very unsightly, rust generally is not a serious problem, but does affect the health of the foliage, which has a direct affect on the overall performance of the plant. Rust first appears as tiny yellow spots on the foliage before it finally breaks through to the surface. The infection will grow and spread as the temperatures turn warmer and humidity levels increase. Areas that tend to have fairly low relative humidity during summertime are not likely to have problems with rust. Louisiana irises that have blue-green foliage also seem to be less susceptible to rust than those cultivars with bright green foliage, suggesting that genetics may be a prime factor in the development of rust. Some growers also contend that excessive applications of high nitrogen fertilizers may spread or promote rust.

Controlling rust can be a problem. It is transmitted by spores which can be borne on the wind as a very fine dust and may remain active in the soil for extended periods of time. It is therefore very important to pay careful attention to garden cleanliness. Remove all infected foliage from the garden. Do not compost the infected leaves. Applications of fungicides are fairly effective in controlling rust. Fungicides are available in both topical and systemic formulations. A combination of both usually succeeds in eliminating rust from gardens. Wettable sulfur applied with a sprayer has also been reported to give good control. The key to controlling rust seems to be early detection and prompt action.

Rust on Louisiana iris foliage.

Close-up of rust spores.

Leaf Spot

Leaf spot has both fungal and bacterial forms. Fortunately, Louisiana irises are not reportedly bothered by bacterial leaf spot. Fungal leaf spot has been reported but is not considered a widespread or prevalent problem. Fungal leaf spot appears as small circular to somewhat oval-shaped spots that are watery or greasy in appearance. Over a period of several days the spots will enlarge to about ¼ inch (0.6 cm) and turn yellow or brown. Very often a distinct border of brown to red-brown appears. Fungal leaf spot is likely to occur only during very wet times of the year and will diminish as rainfall and relative humidity levels decrease. If the infestation is very severe during the spring, bloom quantity and color may be affected.

Fungal leaf spot is not considered lethal to the plant and will clear on its own as the weather changes. Keeping beds free of old leaves helps prevent recurrence. Some growers advocate the removal of any infected foliage. Spraying with fungicides may also slow or halt the advance of fungal leaf spot. Remove infected foliage from the garden and do not add it to the compost.

Cutworms

Cutworms can be a fairly serious problem. Damage is more likely to occur in the early part of the growing season as the new, tender growth begins to develop. These chewing worms literally cut down a plant at the base or chew holes into it. In some cases the cutworms will eat the tender new growth into the meristem area and kill the plant.

If the greenish brown caterpillars can be located they should be destroyed, but it is unlikely that most will be found. They can do much damage in a short period. Many general purpose insecticides can be applied as sprays or solid pellets and are effective against cutworms. Apply treatment as soon as evidence of the cutworms appears. The organic *Bacillus thuringiensis*, commonly known as Bt, may also prove to be effective.

Grasshoppers

Grasshoppers are voracious eaters and tend to appear at the height of summer in hot, dry regions of the United States. The damage done to the foliage of the irises depends on the population of the grasshoppers. Some years the damage is quite severe. Since the grasshoppers are constantly moving it does not do much good to attempt controlling them. Should you choose to fight the problem, liquid sevin or diazinon are both fairly effective sprays. The use of natural predators such as praying mantises has also been reported to be fairly effective.

Animal Pests

The lush foliage and plump rhizomes of Louisiana irises may prove to be too tempting for various pests to ignore. This is certainly not a problem unique to Louisiana irises, nor are they any more prone to attack than any other plant in the garden. Special problems may occur from armadillos, deer, rodents, rabbits, moles, voles, skunks, and even household pets. All the special cultural pitfalls that each grower might encounter are unforseeable. In situations that leave you at a loss for a solution, consult a fellow gardener in your vicinity. Chances are that they have faced the same problem. The Agriculture Extension Service is always a good place to start, regardless of the problem. And follow all instructions and local laws that might apply to the use of traps or poisons.

The highlight of any gardening experience is the final payoff when the plant produces flowers. Some garden pests do nothing but attack the blooms. The remedy depends on the nature of the attack.

Slugs and Snails

Slugs and snails are very active during the spring when the irises bloom, and attack under the cover of darkness. The damage varies in degree from a simple "sliming" to total destruction of the blossom. Slugs and snails are widespread problems.

None of the many remedies seem to be totally effective. Many baits are commercially available, but more and more concern is being raised about the toxicity of the products. Products such as diazinon or Dursban powder or crystals may also be lightly dusted around the base of the plants as a control, but here again there is a concern about the widespread use of such poisons. One organic method often reported to work well is diatomaceous earth. Several types are available but only the agricultural type should be used. Sinking small containers such as cups or tin cans into the soil and filling them about one-quarter full of beer also works very well for trapping and drowning slugs and snails. The biggest drawback to this method is how many traps must be set and the frequency with which they must be emptied and refilled.

Orthochaetae Larvae

This grub-like larva of the orthochaetae chews its way into the unopened flower bud and destroys the style arms and other sexual parts of the flower. Buds of the early-season cultivars seem to be the most often affected. When the blossom opens, it has a very distorted, malformed center, with brown or eaten center parts. The orthochaetae larvae is approximately ½ inch (1.3 cm) long and is white with two black dots. In the northeast United States it has been reported as a problem in Siberian irises.

The most effective control is to manually search for the grubs and destroy them, thereby eliminating the population from your garden. When the blossoms open the larvae may be found hiding down in the spathe. Growers of Siberian irises have also reported success through administering insecticides as the earliest buds emerge. The use of Bt may also prove to be an effective non-toxic control.

Verbena Bud Moth

The verbena bud moth deposits her eggs on the ripening seed pod. Once the larva emerges it eats its way into the pod until it finds the seeds. A sawdust-like material may be noted around the hole in the pod and a brown, empty pupa skin may protrude from the hole. The degree of infestation varies and larvae may destroy only a few seeds or the entire pod. Most growers of Louisiana irises will remove bloom stalks once bloom is over so the loss of seeds is not relevant. To a hybridizer, however, the loss of the seeds is a major concern.

The life cycle of the verbena bud moth is complex and control is difficult. Chemical control methods are not very effective. Many methods have been tried, and so far the most effective is to cover the seed pods with small paper bags. The bags are secured below the pod to the stem and the bag does not touch the seed pod. This method was nearly 100 percent effective.

CHAPTER 11

Landscaping with Louisiana Irises

Louisiana irises can serve a number of useful roles in the landscape. The upright foliage and stalks give the garden a strong vertical impulse. In large clumps, they provide valuable landscape anchors. The wide spectrum of colors and forms offers a tempting and versatile palette. In full bloom, a well-tended grouping gives the garden an image of bright butterflies fluttering in the breeze. Louisiana irises offer many fine qualities for discriminating gardeners.

Those with insufficient knowledge about these charming plants, however, may make conceptual and practical mistakes which bring out the worst features of the irises while hiding their best qualities. This chapter offers advice about how best to incorporate Louisiana irises into the landscape, whether the gardener is planting a display garden, a water feature, or simply trying to knit Louisiana irises into a mixed planting in a bed or border.

This chapter avoids the pitfall of offering too-specific advice. For example, companion plantings suitable in the southern United States may not be at all appropriate for gardeners in more frigid climates. Instead, the guidelines in this chapter focus on general principles. Specific plants are suggested only when they have demonstrated an ability to grow successfully in many climatic zones under a range of cultural practices.

Likewise, specific Louisiana irises are mentioned only infrequently. Iris selections for the garden depend primarily on characteristics such as height, color, bloom season, and vigor. Once you designate specific requirements for this or that iris planting, you are likely to find a large number of cultivars to fulfill your intent. Hence, this chapter only mentions cultivars as examples and for those rare cases in which only a handful of cultivars will fulfill a gardener's requirements. The color photographs in this book will help you select specific irises for plantings, and descriptions in commercial catalogs are also a helpful resource.

Before finalizing plans to incorporate Louisiana irises into the landscape, wise gardeners will acquire a thorough knowledge of their forms, growth patterns, and cultural requirements. This effort will help prevent mistakes, saving the time and frustration of making corrections further down the line as the garden begins to mature. The concepts of form, growth pattern, and culture are mentioned in this chapter only as they relate to specific landscaping decisions; other sections of this book provide more detailed discussions of these related topics.

Take into account the following few overall principles that apply regardless of the type of garden. Keep these principles firmly in mind before moving on to consider more specific goals for the various gardening applications—displays, water gardening, and mixed plantings.

First, Louisiana irises grow vigorously and require plenty of room. Remember that these irises come from species that, in natural settings, tend to form huge clumps. Before wetland drainage proceeded apace in southern Louisiana, vast areas of marshland were literally filled with *Iris giganticaerulea* spreading as far as the eye could see. Gardeners will enjoy the greatest success by allowing these irises to fulfill their evolutionary tendency to grow to large clumps. Where space is at a premium, choose from the limited range of smaller cultivars known for their tidy habits ('Lone Star' and 'Wood Violet' are archetypal examples), or be prepared to reset the Louisiana iris clumps each fall to prevent them from getting out of bounds.

Second, Louisiana irises are heavy feeders. They perform best only with supplemental fertilization, especially during the fall and spring growing seasons. This need affects iris siting. They must be accessible for fertilization, and they must not have to suffer appreciable competition for nutrients. Where competition is unavoidable—for instance, if irises are sited at the driplines of deciduous trees—you must be even more committed to providing adequate fertilizer to ensure optimum growth and bloom.

And third, Louisiana irises are often unsightly during high summer unless they are given the most thorough pampering. Even with the gardener's best efforts, Louisianas may fade and yellow during especially hot and dry summers. Again, this characteristic stems from genetic factors inherited from the species. Where species Louisianas grew in or along shallow waterways and marshes, they developed the ability to go dormant during southern summers, when oppressive heat tended to dry up or limit the available water. This tendency to have an "off" period during midsummer is not mentioned as an indictment of Louisiana iris plantings, for a number of gardening strategies can offset this problem. It is simply a warning that gardeners must take this characteristic into account in their planning.

Gardeners armed with these three seminal precepts are prepared to begin laying more specific plans for using Louisiana irises. These plans will vary depending on the type of planting you have in mind. Three types of gardens typically find uses for Louisiana irises: display or hybridizer's gardens, where the irises are more or less "rowed out" and planted by themselves without abundant companion material; bog or water gardens, where the natural environment of irises is most perfectly duplicated; and ordinary bed-and-border mixed plantings, where the selection of companion plantings is crucial to overall success.

Display and Hybridizers' Gardens

Here the irises are the focus of the garden. Many large botanical gardens offer a separate planting of Louisiana irises for display purposes, and more than a handful of iris enthusiasts also give Louisiana irises a separate place of their own in their private gardens. These plantings are heavily visited during bloom season but are more or less bypassed during other times of the year.

Most hybridizers, too, tend to grow their irises in utilitarian beds devoid of companion plantings or attempts at artistic presentation. Whether the goal is to provide a beautiful display of irises of many different varieties, or to gather the irises together in a serviceable planting that provides access for hybridization, many of the guidelines for designing the planting are the same.

The primary goal is access. Whether the iris beds are functional rectangles or more aesthetically pleasing curved shapes, the planning of walkways becomes almost as important as the beds themselves. The width of the aisles depends on how many visitors the garden is expected to accommodate at any given time, but a 24-inch (61.0-cm) width between beds is an absolute minimum. A 36-inch (91.4-cm) spacing is better, and 48 inches (121.9 cm) or more is ideal. Even though hybridizers require fairly little space to make crosses, working themselves among their irises, they should remember that hybridizers' gardens inevitably become display gardens, drawing a wealth of visitors during bloom time.

Remember, too, that it is easy to underestimate the number of guests who will visit, and thus the amount of space that will be required for these walkways. It is better to plan for wider rather than narrower aisles. Giving up potential bed space for walkways is sometimes a difficult decision for an enthusiastic gardener to make, but it is far better than having to widen walkways later, which inevitably means reworking the entire garden, plantings and all.

As for the iris clumps themselves, they are best developed in single rather than double rows within the bed. This, again, is because of the irises' tendency to form large clumps. A double row of iris clumps would have to be 6 feet (1.8

m) wide at a very minimum, and even then the clumps are likely to grow into each another. A bed 6 feet (1.8 m) or wider presents its own problems of access since you would inevitably have to walk in the middle of the beds, compacting the soil and potentially damaging roots, to perform routine tasks such as fertilizing, dividing rhizomes, and of course, hybridizing.

Although hybridizers may pass up opportunities to incorporate companion plantings into their iris garden, plantings intended solely for display purposes present a more satisfying composition when other plants are grown in and around the irises. Simply remember that the irises should stand front-and-center in the planting. The best plan here is also the simplest: merely choose good low-growing annuals and perennials to plant between the iris clumps or as edgings to divide the walkways from the beds. In form, these companion plantings should emphasize a horizontal rather than a vertical line, to contrast with the strongly vertical shape of the irises. And surrounding the garden with tall shrubs gives dimension and form to the overall garden.

Blocking off the garden with shrubs also has the advantage of "hiding" the garden from the remainder of the grounds during midsummer, when the irises are likely to sag and yellow somewhat. Remember, display gardens usually are visited only during bloom time, so they suffer no disadvantage when they are bypassed or ignored during other seasons. To further meet this goal, the display garden could be sited away from the main traffic areas of the larger garden or grounds, to a place where the display planting is not a prominent feature during periods of non-bloom.

Irrigation is a final factor to consider. It may consist of an elaborate drip system, an overhead sprinkler system, or simply a nearby waterhose you can put to good use when necessary. Just remember that all Louisiana irises not grown in wetland settings will require artificial irrigation, so plan the irrigation system from the outset, considering this feature just as important as the beds and pathways of the garden.

Water and Bog Gardens

Bog and water gardens most closely duplicate the conditions of the Louisiana irises' natural home, and it is here where the irises achieve their full glory. True, the irises grow well in regular garden situations; however, in wetland settings, they grow with greater vigor and display truly remarkable bloom.

As a result, the simplest treatment is also the most satisfying. Water and bog gardeners will obtain the best results by striving for a natural effect, giving the irises sufficient room to grow into truly monumental clumps along water's edge. This the irises will do with alacrity, especially when given adequate supplemental fertilization. In smaller gardens where space is more limited, the rhizomes will need digging and dividing fairly frequently. Furthermore, if you intend to keep cultivars growing separately, the clumps will need even more room between them than in ordinary garden situations.

As in display gardens, the primary challenge is access. The irises will grow readily along the shoreline and out into the water to distances depending on the water's depth. *Iris brevicaulis,* or hybrids with much *I. brevicaulis* in their backgrounds, will not thrive in deeper water and are good selections for growing just along the shoreline. Other varieties may grow well out into water up to 10 to 12 inches (25.4–30.5 cm) deep, and sometimes even deeper. In most settings like this, the irises are actually best viewed from the water, not from the shore.

A few approaches can optimize viewers' access to the irises. A berm rising from the iris planting elevates viewers, giving them a better vantage from which to look down into the overall clump. A more enthusiastic plan will include walkways or perhaps a footbridge built out over the water, giving the best views of the irises. The most practical idea may be to plant the irises along a narrow part of the water feature, so that the clumps can be well-viewed from the opposite shoreline.

The naturalistic look in companion plantings is also best for water and bog gardens. Choose native and introduced plant materials that grow best in your area. A full discussion of such plants would fill many pages and exceed the scope of this book, but given the great interest in water gardening in the present day, a wealth of resources are available to guide plant selection. As a general principle, avoid introducing too many vertical elements into the plan. The irises themselves tend to dominate the picture, and other plants similar to the irises in form—particularly those with strongly upright or arcing blade-like foliage—can bring a monotony to the landscape. Remember, too, that contrasts in foliage textures and shapes can bring a wealth of variety to the garden even when the plants carry undistinguished blooms, and water plants in particular offer a great many options for interesting, unusual foliage that is highly compatible alongside irises.

At other times, gardeners and landscapers will plan a formal water garden as an architectural feature in the more dressed portion of the grounds. In this setting, the naturalistic treatment suggested above may not be appropriate. Consider pot culture when the goal is a more limited clump of irises meant to be maintained in an exact position over the years. Pots should be broad and fairly shallow, and set so that the rim of the pot is no more than a few inches beneath the water's surface. Still, the iris rhizomes over time will tend to grow over the pot's rim and float outward on the water's surface. If this is a problem, simply remove the pot each fall, dividing and resetting the rhizomes—a fairly easy task with pot culture. In all but the harshest climates the iris pots can remain in the water over the winter, unless they will become encased in ice for prolonged periods.

Mixed Plantings

The vast majority of gardeners who use Louisiana irises incorporate them into mixed plantings in beds and borders. Louisiana irises are ideal for this purpose as long as they need not conform with settings contradictory to their nature. For example, a xeriscape garden is no place for Louisiana irises. Two decisions are paramount: siting the irises within the beds and choosing suitable companion plants, including those that will bloom with the irises and those that will bloom at other times. Other decisions, involving matters such as color selections and background plantings, are more easily left to individual taste.

In all rhizomatous plants, the rhizome is actually an underground stem that tends to creep underground or just at the surface, pushing outward toward the tips of the leaves. This characteristic is particularly pronounced in Louisiana irises, especially those with larger rhizomes. Hence, rhizomes planted near the edge of a bed should be pointed inward, or they will quickly grow beyond the bed and into the path. Over time, a clump of Louisianas may shift its position within the bed. In general, be careful to "aim" the rhizomes in the direction you wish them to grow. For a strong clump, position the rhizomes in a circle, with each rhizome radiating out from a central point.

Louisiana irises are not best for the front of a bed or border in a mixed planting. Exceptions include cultivars from the so-called patio class of Louisiana irises, which typically grow from 12 to 16 inches (30.5–40.6 cm) high and are not known for rampant spreading. The vast majority of Louisiana cultivars, however, are known for their statuesque height, from 36 to 42 inches (91.4–106.7 cm) tall and even taller. For the most part, their height alone argues for placing them further back in the border.

Another reason for siting them at the back is that iris foliage tends to flag in midsummer, taking on a yellow cast. Iris leaves are also a favorite target of grasshoppers, which tend to be at their worst during the warmest part of the year, leaving behind tattered and bedraggled foliage. Iris clumps at the front of the bed or border cannot hide, but those planted further back can be partially or even completely hidden in midsummer by some well-chosen companions that acheive their full height and bloom in summer, after the irises have already bloomed and faded from the scene. While the irises are blooming, these companions are just beginning their burst of growth and hence do not interfere with the enjoyment of the iris blooms. Rudbeckias, purple coneflowers (*Echinacea* spp.), and upright, fall-blooming sedums such as *Sedum* 'Autumn Joy' are excellent choices, but there are countless others, with the best selections dependent on the garden's particular climatic zone.

Likewise, a wealth of plant material is available to gardeners searching for companion plants to bloom at the same time as the Louisianas. Too-specific suggestions would be folly, since success depends so much on the individual gardener's goals and taste. But certain families of plants are inescapably successful when interplanted with irises. Upright selections include penstemons, poppies (*Papaver* spp.), annual larkspur (*Delphinium* spp.), and columbines (*Aquilegia* spp.). Lower growing selections include dianthus, alyssum, pansies (*Viola* spp.), and certain of the mat-forming spring-blooming phloxes.

Ornamental grasses, very popular in contemporary gardening, also make excellent companions for the irises. The best selections are those with thin, arcing foliage, such as the miscanthuses and pennisetums, for example. Some of these plants spring into growth quickly and make an impact at iris bloom times. Others are slower, arriving at their full glory in summer and fall. These later types may be valuable for their "hiding" function. In mild areas, a grouping of irises and ornamental grass remains persuasive, with the green iris foliage an effective contrast to the brown ornamental grass topped by its dried bloom scapes.

Background plantings that can be expected to bloom during iris season include many antique rose cultivars and the pure-white blooming mock orange (*Philadelphus* spp.), whose arcing branches and bright green foliage are a perfect foil for the irises.

Irises can be expected to grow well in mixed plantings, but be forewarned that they must be irrigated during dry spells. The irises are particularly sensitive to a lack of moisture during the fall and spring growing seasons. In mild areas, they also make significant growth over the winter, when other plants are dormant. In these areas, supplemental water may be required even during wintertime.

Regardless of the garden's purposes, Louisiana irises are useful and beautiful additions to the landscape. Gardeners armed with knowledge of these plants' habits and cultural requirements can greatly enhance their plantings by incorporating Louisiana irises.

CHAPTER 12

Flower Arranging with Louisiana Irises

Diversity in Louisiana irises makes them an arranger's delight. Louisianas can furnish all the design elements needed for outstanding results. It matters not whether the arrangement is for the home or a flower show. These irises even lend themselves to many of the traditional designs, particularly those in the oriental manner. They are perfect wherever large flowers or long stems are required to make a bold statement, since they tend to produce large flowers and have some of the tallest stalks in irisdom.

Mechanics of Arrangements

Size of bloom in Louisiana irises varies from small to very large. The available sizes are unlimited among the sizes of the buds, partially opened flowers, and fully opened flowers. Although blooms may vary from 3 to 7 inches (7.6–17.8 cm), the smaller blooms are preferred for arranging. Foliage, too, is to be found in many sizes. Bloom stalks may be from 24 to 48 inches (61.0–121.0 cm) in length and from a small to an extremely heavy circumference. Textural variations are found in both flowers and foliage. The foliage may be a shiny light green. In other cultivars it will be a blue-green with a lovely bloom. But the greatest textural differences are found in the flowers. Flower texture may be smooth, velvety, crepe-like, shiny, dull, or satiny. An exciting texture for almost any use can be found in blooms of Louisiana irises.

Hybridizers have introduced forms of Louisiana irises which greatly extend their use. Although the horticulture show winners tend to be large, round, and full, designers can find very different forms to be used full face or in profile. Louisiana iris blooms may be full and flat, flaring, drooping to slightly drooping, with nearly upright standards, or even spidery. Some flowers are tailored, others ruffled, or even fluted. Thus a selection can be made to create almost any desired pattern.

Pattern is also varied within the flowers. Signal patches may be a line, steeple-shaped, large and triangular, or a sunburst with lines of many lengths radiating into the falls. Some flowers have no obvious signal patch and many now have signals on both the standards and falls. Style arms may be of a contrasting color or may have large, fringed tips tinged a different color. Bicolors and bitones give still different patterns. A recent development in flower pattern is the edged or picotee bloom in which the edging is usually white or silvery but is sometimes yellow.

Just the foliage of Louisiana irises can supply almost any desired line. Some foliage is stiff and erect, some is gently curving. Because of its substance, most foliage can be manipulated to a zigzag or twisted line. The bloom stalks may be straight or slightly zigzag. A stalk of Louisiana irises with unopened flowers can be used for a dramatic line. With care, it is possible to cut a stalk into any length to use a bud or a fully opened flower. Hence, the length of the line of the bloom stalk is your choice.

Probably the greatest bonus from Louisiana irises is their color. Whites and pastels to very intense colors are found in the Louisiana irises. Unlike some of the other iris groups, Louisiana irises are found in near reds and orange, in tans and browns, in yellows and golds, and in the very darkest blue-purples and red-purples. Pale blues and lavenders are now being joined by the elusive pinks. They have no strong green but greenish whites and greenish yellows are to be found, and tints, shades, and tones of all the other hues. Perusing the catalog of a Louisiana iris grower will give an overview of the tremendous range of color available.

When planning an arrangement, think first of the location and background. Will it be against a wall and be viewed from one side only? Will it be near a high traffic area? Will it be on a coffee or dining table where it will be viewed from all sides? Do you want it to stand out or harmonize with its surroundings? How tall, wide, and deep will it need to be to fit well into its location? When you know the answers to these questions you will be ready to begin. These initial questions must be answered whether you are making an arrangement for home, church, hospital, flower show, and so on. In a flower show where a background niche is provided, it will determine the maximum height, width, and depth of your arrangement. You can, however, drape the background with whatever fabric and color will most complement your creation.

The shape of the container you choose will determine how you hold the materials in place. A vase that is low or rounded or that has a wide opening will need a needlepoint holder or something similar. For a transparent vase, you can wrap a needlepoint holder in aluminum foil to help hide it. A cylinder or deep vase can have chicken wire or florists foam wedged into it.

Creating a flower arrangement takes three steps. Establish the height and general shape with the first few branches or stems. This can be a triangle, curve, column, or mound composed of flowers or branches of nonflowering material. Next comes the focal area. It can consist of one or more irises, depending on the size of the arrangement and the color and size of the flowers. An odd number is usually preferred. Finally add any necessary filler material, which could consist of more iris branches, another variety of smaller flowers, ferns, or anything that will complement the composition.

The first branches or stems should be of varied lengths. Avoid a shape that looks something like rabbit ears on top. A good rule of thumb is for the longest branch or stem to be visible above the container to about one and one-half times the height plus the width of your vase. So, if you have a vase that is 12 inches (30.5 cm) tall and 5 inches (12.7 cm) wide, the visible part of your longest branch would be about 25 inches (63.5 cm) long. Cut the stem long enough so that it will reach the bottom or side of the vase where it is to rest. Keep the focal area of prize irises fairly low so the design will not look top heavy. Do not crowd them. Try to make sure that the arrangement does not look flat. Angle some stems to the front and others to the rear to create depth. Do not cut the stems too short. It is much easier, after inserting a stem, to find it is too long, remove it, and cut a little off, but once it is cut too short it is too late.

Filler material should complement the irises, not compete with them. If using secondary flowers, use a variety that is smaller. Baby's breath (*Gypsophila paniculata*) is good and readily available. Many spring-flowering plants combine well with Louisiana irises. Penstemons, phlox, annual larkspur (*Delphinium* spp.), daisies (*Bellis* spp.), some late *Narcissus*, and dogwoods (*Cornus* spp.), *Philadelphus*, and many other flowering shrubs are beautiful in combination with Louisiana irises. Some common wildflowers can be used successfully. Leaves make good filler, provided they are not too large. Louisiana iris leaves work well because they are slender and graceful. Use them in groups by cutting several in different lengths. Hold the bases of two or three together and insert them into the arrangement as a unit. Remember, the irises are your subject. Three to five different kinds of materials in your design is plenty.

A nice finishing touch for an arrangement in a low, open container is small river stones or marbles to help conceal the needlepoint holder. The flattened oval marbles are best because they will stay where placed. Just because you may have five beautiful irises, do not feel that you must use all of them. The spaces created with the materials are as important to the design as the flowers themselves. Some flowers do not respond well to crowding. The iris is one of these because it is very three-dimensional and rather fragile. One can look into it as well as at it. Other more flat-faced flowers such as daisies (*Bellis* spp.), chrysanthemums, and zinnias may easily be massed when a large area of color is desired, but not the iris.

With some repair and replacement, an arrangement of Louisiana irises can last for ten days. Each bloom, if the stalk is freshly cut, lasts for three days. Each bud position usually has additional buds, each of which will eventually open. Here are some suggestions for helping an arrangement to last longer:

1. For irises and other plant materials from your garden, cut them the evening before or early in the morning and place in water immediately.
2. When making the arrangement, keep a bowl of water at hand and cut the stems under water to help them take up water more readily and last longer.
3. Use florist's flower preservative or include a small splash of mouthwash in the container to help prevent the growth of bacteria in the water.
4. Strip all leaves off the underwater parts of stems to help keep the water fresh.
5. If the arrangement is kept for several days, change the water in the container every day or at least when the water becomes stagnant.
6. Rearrange plant material as old flowers fade and new buds open. Secondary material may fade faster and have to be removed or replaced. Louisiana iris buds that open in the arrangement will be slightly smaller and slightly less intense in color than those that open outdoors on the plant.

The cut flower industry is still new to Louisiana iris growers, but it is certain to expand in the future. Some countries already support a big market for the cut stalks. A grower in South Africa grows them by the thousands to sell as cut flowers, and a grower in south Louisiana has been selling them to local flower shops. Since stalks cut in bud are easy to handle and the first set of buds will all open perfectly, their potential as a cut flower is obvious.

Recommended Cultivars

No cultivar can be ruled out as a prospect for an arrangement, but if your Louisiana irises are for cutting, here are some recommendations. Those with smaller flowers may be easier to handle and use, such as:

'Dixie Deb' (yellow)

'Willow Mint' (yellow)

'Acadian Miss' (white)

'Gulf Shores' (deep
   blue-purple)

'No Data' (dark purple)

'River Road' (medium blue)

'Puttytat' (deep blue)

'Mentida' (cobalt blue)

'LSU Beauty' (salmon pink)

'Cherry Cup' (red)

I. fulva (various shades of red and
   yellow)

'Heavenly Glow' (orange)

'Little Nutkin' (tan-orange)

'Honey Star' (tan)

Cultivars that produce many stalks per rhizome will produce more for the space in the garden, such as 'Lone Star' (lavender-blue), 'Praline Festival' (yellow-tan), 'Bera' (blue purple), and 'Ice Magic' (creamy white). Louisiana irises with many buds and flowers will bloom longer. Examples of irises known to carry large numbers of buds per stalk are 'Delta Prince' (red-violet), 'Marie Dolores' (white), and 'Koorawatha' (yellow).

Society for Louisiana Irises

The Society for Louisiana Irises was organized in the spring of 1941 by a small group of collectors and growers of the North American native irises found primarily in the Gulf States. This meeting was held on the University of Louisiana, Lafayette, campus, which was in the center of the natural fields of the native irises. Present at that meeting were some of the future officers, writers, and workers in the organization, such as W. B. MacMillan, Joe C. Richard, Randolph Bazet, Lillian Hall Trichel, Caroline Dormon, Katherine Cornay, George Arceneaux, Percy Viosca, and Ira S. Nelson, who had just come to the university that spring semester as a horticulture professor.

Other charter members who contributed during the early period were Minnie Colquitt, Jackie Richard, Ruth Dormon, Eddie Arceneaux, Hamilton Robertson, William Fitzhugh, and Marie Caillet. Membership first came from Louisiana, but within a few years people from Texas, Mississippi, and Arkansas joined. More than half the current membership is from outside Louisiana and from a number of foreign countries.

The name given the organization was the Mary Swords DeBaillon Louisiana Iris Society to honor a leader among collectors and growers from 1920 to 1940. DeBaillon collected hundreds of selected species and natural hybrids throughout south Louisiana.

Most objectives set up by the organization in 1941 are still valid today. Those objectives were:

1. To stimulate interest in the planting and cultivation of the Louisiana native irises and to protect and preserve the native irises in their native state.
2. To exchange information among amateur iris collectors on collecting, cultivating, and hybridizing of native irises.

3. To collect and distribute the best available information on the subject of native irises.
4. To encourage investigational work that will have as its object the best nomenclature and development of new cultivars.
5. To assist in securing legislation and appropriations for conducting investigational and experimental work.
6. To cooperate with existing organizations interested in native irises.

These objectives were carried out during the early years, but some have had to be abandoned. With the development of the oil and cattle industries in south Louisiana, vast stands of the native irises were destroyed. The encroachment of cities and highways has further reduced the native habitats. The objectives of the Society for Louisiana Irises did result in some worthwhile projects during the early years, some of which have continued:

1. Planting collected species and hybrids for study and research. This developed into a test garden but was abandoned when collecting stopped in the 1950s.
2. An annual meeting in Lafayette, Louisiana, with a planned program and, by the second year, an iris show. The meetings and shows have continued.
3. Organized trips to the swamps to collect irises. But for a very few exceptions, trips are made now only for photographing.
4. Publications of interest to members and that contribute to the knowledge of these native wildflowers. The number of publications produced by the society has greatly increased in recent years.
5. Conducting investigational work and research. This work has led to the modern hybrids and tetraploids.

Some projects have changed, but some like the annual meeting and the publications have continued through the fifty-eight years of the society. Areas of the country outside Louisiana have seen an increase in the number of gardeners growing and hybridizing Louisiana irises. These areas will host the annual meeting in some years. Little Rock, Arkansas, was the first to offer their city as the site of the national convention. Conventions include garden tours, a flower show, seminars, a judges' training school, and fellowship. On average about 100 to 150 members attend these meetings with many coming thousands of miles.

The quarterly newsletter was started as a way to inform members of society business, meeting information, and news of the membership. Over the years it has developed into a bulletin on Louisiana irises, with articles on culture and cultivar performance, black and white pictures, advertising by dealers, and listings of new introductions. A membership in the Society for Louisiana Irises covers the cost of this newsletter. Membership also includes the society's special publications, bulletins with color photographs sent every three to five years. These publications are financed by funds raised through auctions and plant sales and by sales of this book. These funds also finance the printing of four-page color brochures that are distributed at iris shows, programs, and conventions.

The society has also published bibliographies on Louisiana iris topics and cultivar checklists. A revised checklist is due to be published by 2001 listing all the registered and introduced Louisiana iris cultivars to date. Such lists give date of introduction, parentage, awards, and a detailed description of each iris.

The society sponsors a number of other projects. Sets of slides are available on loan, each set sent with a script to read as slides are shown. The color slide archive holds pictures of the species, historical irises, and recent cultivars, along with slides of old and current iris gardens and people who have worked with the society since the beginning. The University of Louisiana, Lafayette, maintains an archive of papers, letters, and publications for the society. A display garden committee promotes private and public plantings for viewing of Louisiana irises during bloom. Members donate plants to these gardens and many donate their time to planting irises at botanical gardens. Information about these projects can be obtained by writing to the address below.

In 1948, the original name of the society was changed to the Society for Louisiana Irises. To preserve the name of Mary Swords DeBaillon, an annual award was established through the American Iris Society (AIS) for the Louisiana iris voted by official judges as the best in the nation. A bronze medal, provided by the Society for Louisiana Irises, is given with the award. For a complete list of the irises that have won this coveted award, see Appendix C.

The society became a Cooperating Society of the AIS in 1993. A meeting and program devoted to Louisiana irises is held during the AIS convention each year. The Society for Louisiana Irises helps finance the expenses for one officer to attend that convention for the purposes of conducting the meeting and presenting a program.

Membership in the Society for Louisiana Irises numbers about 500 people, including those from almost all the states in the United States plus other countries such as England, France, Germany, Japan, New Zealand, and Australia. A few members come from Canada, the Philippines, the Ukraine, and South Africa.

For information about the society, its membership, publications, and sources for obtaining plants via mail order, write to the Society for Louisiana Irises, P.O. Box 40175 USL Station, Lafayette, Louisiana 70504.

American Iris Society

The American Iris Society, founded in 1920, is a national organization for the advancement of all irises, including the Louisiana group. Membership extends beyond the United States and is currently past the 8000 mark. Although not specifically devoted to the Louisiana iris, the AIS promotes this group of irises and supports their specialty groups. Official registration of Louisiana irises by name and description is done through the registrar of the AIS. They train and supervise national judges for both exhibition and garden awards.

The AIS publishes four bulletins a year and many of these contain valuable information about Louisiana irises. They hold an annual convention each spring at peak bloom time for the location. Gardens on tour during the convention contain plantings of Louisiana irises as guest plants on display.

For information write to Membership Secretary Marilyn Harlow, P.O. Box 55, Freedom, California 95019-0055.

Species Iris Group of North America

The Species Iris Group of North America (SIGNA) is a section of the AIS devoted to the study of iris species throughout the world. This organization publishes excellent bulletins, maintains a seed exchange for members to grow new species, and sponsors research on the species. They are especially interested in the native irises of America and in the classification of those in the Louisiana iris group. They hold an annual meeting and program at the time and location of the American Iris Society Convention.

Information about this organization can be obtained by writing to President Carla Lankow, 11118 169th Avenue S.E., Renton, Washington 98059 or to Colin Rigby, 18341 Paulson Street S.W., Rochester, Washington 98579.

Popular Cultivars of Louisiana Irises

Popularity of iris cultivars depends to a great degree on distribution and the number and location of dealers that handle certain irises. Older cultivars have had wide distribution and thus are generally more popular throughout the world. Some very old irises that were once popular are no longer on dealer lists. Thus, some new introductions appear on popularity polls each year. The following cultivars made the top twenty-five favorites in the popularity polls conducted by the Society for Louisiana Irises each year from 1991 through 1998. You will note that some are old but continue to be in favor. They are grouped into color classes though some are difficult to place in any exact group.

White

'Acadian Miss' (Arny, 1980) medium tall; small ruffled pure white.
'Clara Goula' (Arny, 1978) large ruffled creamy white.
'Crisp Lime' (Dunn, 1983) large white with green throat.
'Dural White Butterfly' (Taylor, 1989) tall; ruffled pure white
'Ice Angel' (Faggard, 1991) tall; very large ruffled blue-white.
'Marie Dolores' (Haymon, 1988) medium height zigzag stalk; orange signal.
'Obvious Heir' (Taylor, 1991) zigzag stalk; very ruffled flowers.

Yellow

'Dixie Deb' (Chowning, 1951) tall stalks; small open-form flowers; hardy to minimum care.

'Koorawatha' (Taylor, 1986) multibudded tall stalks; very ruffled flowers.
'President Hedley' (Mertzweiller, 1980) large yellow-gold; pendent form.
'Professor Barbara' (Mertzweiller, 1992) tall; light yellow tetraploid.
'Professor Fritchie' (Mertzweiller, 1995) very tall; tetraploid.
'Rokki Rockwell' (Haymon, 1992) tall; large bright yellow blooms.
'Sun Fury' (Arny, 1980) medium height; slightly ruffled with green throat.

Tan, Brown, Apricot

'Heavenly Glow' (Morgan, 1989) red-orange with green signals.
'Honey Star' (Hutchinson, 1991) small-flowered cream and apricot; fast
    growing.
'Kelley's Choice' (Morgan, 1993) yellow with rose edging and veining.
'Little Miss Leighley' (Chowning, 1983) light gold with maroon-outlined
    signal.
'Praline Festival' (Haymon, 1992) yellow-tan with heavy veining.
'Valera' (Arny, 1980) apricot-buff with light green style arms.

Blue, Blue-Violet

'Clyde Redmond' (Arny, 1971) small clear blue; vigorous.
'Exquisite Lady' (Owen, 1987) mid lavender-blue with silver-white halo.
'Gulf Shores' (Dunn, 1982) medium height; ruffled deep blue.
'La Perouse' (Raabe, 1976) tall stalks; clear medium blue.
'Mac's Blue Heaven' (MacMillan, 1973) Blue violet with white style arms.
'Malibu Magic' (Taylor, 1990) Small ruffled blue-lavender flowers.
'Sea Lord' (Taylor, 1990) royal blue flowers; late blooming.
'Sinfonietta' (Raabe, 1986) tall; deep blue with slight ruffling; vigorous.

Purple, Red-Purple

'Bajazzo' (Dunn, 1981) red-violet; cartwheel form.
'Black Gamecock' (Chowning, 1980) short stalks; very dark late blooms;
    vigorous.
'Black Widow' (MacMillan, 1953) black-purple; open form.
'Empress Josephine' (Haymon, 1990) small very dark purple.
'Full Eclipse' (Hager, 1978) very dark purple.
'Grace Duhon' (Haymon, 1988) dark red-violet with yellow signal.

'Hurricane Party' (Haymon, 1988) tall; red-violet with darker markings.
'Jeri' (Bertinot, 1985) tall stalks; large dark blue-purple flower.
'Marie Caillet' (Conger, 1963) very tall stalks; blue-purple late flowers.
'Pegaletta' (Holleyman, 1963) medium purple; vigorous.
'Professor Ike' (Mertzweiller, 1975) red violet; vigorous; tetraploid.

Red, Near Red

'Ann Chowning' (Chowning, 1977) bright red with large yellow signal;
    hardy for minimum care.
'Cajun Cookery' (Hager, 1990) tall; dark red with narrow yellow signal.
'Cherry Cup' (Morgan, 1989) short stalks; small cherry-red late flowers.
'Freddie Boy' (Mertzweiller, 1974) large red and purple bitone.
'Parade Music' (Morgan, 1986) medium height; dark red.
'Professor Jim' (Mertzweiller, 1987) tall stalks; tetraploid.
'Professor Neil' (Mertzweiller, 1992) large red with large signal; tetraploid.

Pink, Lavender

'Aunt Shirley' (Mertzweiller, 1992) very large rosy lavender with yellow
    signal.
'Bubble Gum Ballerina' (Haymon, 1990) tall; ruffled lavender and rose
    bitone.
'Dancing Vogue' (Taylor, 1993) ruffled pink with yellow signal.
'Deirdre Kay' (Granger, 1991) pinkish lavender with cream sunburst mark.
'Feliciana Hills' (O'Connor, 1992) near pink with large yellow signal.
'Gerry Marsteller' (Raabe, 1988) pink and cream bicolor.
'Jazz Ballet' (Taylor, 1988) very ruffled violet.
'Kay Nelson' (Granger, 1988) ruffled light pinkish lavender.
'Lavender Ruffles' (Goula, 1979) ruffled light lavender.
'Margaret Lee' (Taylor, 1991) very ruffled pink and magenta bitone.
'Professor Paul' (Mertzweiller, 1982) pale lavender late bloom; tetraploid.

Variegated, Near Bicolor

'Cajun Sunrise' (Mertzweiller, 1993) dark red-brown with yellow halo and
    styles.
'C'est Si Bon' (Taylor, 1983) violet with large white spray pattern.

'Colorific' (Mertzweiller, 1979) white and lavender bicolor with green
    throat.
'Easter Tide' (Arny, 1979) variegated lavender-blue and yellow.
'Elusive Butterfly' (Ghio, 1984) lavender with large white spray pattern.
'Festival's Acadian' (Haymon, 1990) red-purple with yellow halo and styles.
'Gertie Butler' (Arny, 1990) lavender with yellow radial signals.
'Glowlight' (Taylor, 1988) white and purple bitone.
'Just Helene' (Mertzweiller, 1991) pale blue and yellow variegated.
'Lucy Payens' (Taylor, 1992) tall; apricot-yellow and red-purple.
'Marble Cake' (Taylor, 1993) marbled cream and violet.

Mary Swords DeBaillon Medal

The Mary Swords DeBaillon Medal is the highest award exclusively for Louisiana irises. The medal is given by the Society for Louisiana Irises, but is awarded and presented by the American Iris Society through its official judging system. About 1000 accredited judges vote for the awards each year for irises in all groups. Only registered and introduced Louisiana irises that have won an Award of Merit are eligible to win the DeBaillon Medal. Winners of the DeBaillon Medal are then eligible to receive the Dykes Medal. The Dykes Medal is not restricted to any type of iris and is considered to be the top award an iris can win in the United States.

The Mary Swords DeBaillon Award, as it was originally called, was established in 1948 by the Society for Louisiana Irises in cooperation with the American Iris Society. The name of the award honors an early collector of Louisiana irises in south Louisiana. She did much to preserve and promote the native flowers from 1920 to 1940. It was her name that in 1941 graced the original organization that has since become the Society for Louisiana Irises. Caroline Dormon, another early collector and hybridizer of the south Louisiana region and heir to the DeBaillon collection, designed the bronze medal that is given to the hybridizer of each year's award-winning iris.

Mary Swords DeBaillon Award Winners

1948 'Mary S. Debaillon' Caroline Dormon (collected)
1949 'Bayou Sunset' W. B. MacMillan
1950 'Caddo' Lillian Hall Trichel
1951 'Cherry Bounce' Ira S. Nelson
1952 'Royal Gem' Sally Smith

1953 'Violet Ray' Caroline Dormon

1954 'Saucy Minx' Caroline Dormon

1955 'The Khan' Caroline Dormon

1956 'Wood Violet' Caroline Dormon

1957 'Blue Chip' Sally Smith

1958 'Wheelhorse' Caroline Dormon

1959 'Her Highness' William E. Levingston (collected)

1960 'Amethyst Star' Sidney DuBose

1961 'Louise Arny' Charles W. Arny Jr.

1962 'Dixie Dusk' Lenora Mathews

1963 'New Offering' Claude Davis

1964 'W. B. MacMillan' Sidney Conger

1965 'Frances Elizabeth' Sam Rix

1966 'G. W. Holleyman' Ruth Holleyman

1967 'Dixie Deb' Frank E. Chowning

1968 'Black Widow' W. B. MacMillan

1969 'Katherine L. Cornay' Charles W. Arny Jr.

1970 'Marie Caillet' Sidney Conger

1971 'Delta King' Ben Hager

1972 'Ila Nunn' Charles W. Arny Jr.

1973 'Mrs. Ira Nelson' Charles W. Arny Jr.

1974 'Clyde Redmond' Charles W. Arny Jr.

1975 'Charlie's Michele' Charles W. Arny Jr.

1976 'Eolian' Charles W. Amy Jr.

1977 'Mary Dunn' Ben Hager

1978 No award. Tie not broken between 'F. A. C. McCulla' Charles W. Arny Jr. and 'Shrimp Creole' Joseph Ghio

1979 'This I Love' Frank E. Chowning

1980 'Ann Chowning' Frank E. Chowning

1981 'Bryce Leigh' Frank E. Chowning

1982 'Clara Goula' Charles W. Arny Jr.

1983 'Easter Tide' Charles W. Arny Jr.

1984 'Monument' Mary Dunn

No voting occurred in 1985 in order to change the award to medal status. The Louisiana irises eligible for the DeBaillon Medal in 1986 were the last eight DeBaillon Award winners. This number was reduced to the last six winners plus the Award of Merit winners in 1987, and to the last three winners plus Award of Merit winners in 1988. After 1988 the DeBaillon Medal winner was selected from the Award of Merit winners only.

Mary Swords Debaillon Medal Winners

1986 'Ann Chowning' Frank E. Chowning
1987 'Clara Goula' Charles W. Arny Jr.
1988 'Easter Tide' Charles W. Arny Jr.
1989 'Black Gamecock' Frank F. Chowning
1990 'Acadian Miss' Charles W. Arny Jr.
1991 'Rhett' Mary Dunn
1992 'Bajazzo' Mary Dunn
1993 'Frank Chowning' Henry C. Rowlan
1994 'Jeri' Neil Bertinot
1995 'Kay Nelson' Marvin Granger
1996 'Professor Jim' Joseph K. Mertzweiller
1997 'Voodoo Magic' Henry C. Rowlan
1998 'Bayou Mystique' Mary Dunn
1999 'Professor Neil' Joseph K. Mertzweiller

Glossary

Allele One of the two or more alternative states of a gene that occupy the same position (locus) on homologous chromosomes. Alleles are separated from each other at meisosis

Allopatric Growing in different areas or habitats

Alloploid A polyploid in which one or more sets of chromosomes come from different species

Allotetraploid A tetraploid derived from two species, having two diploid genomes from each species (alloploid)

Amphidiploid Synonym for allotetraploid. A hybrid between two species that has at least one complete diploid set of chromosomes derived from each ancestral species

Amoena Any iris having white standards and colored falls

Aneuploidy Having less or more than two complete sets of chromosomes

Anther The part of the stamen that contains the pollen

Anthocyanin Blue or purple pigments

Apogon A beardless, rhizomatous iris

Asexual (reproduction) Reproduction from rhizomes or stalks without the union of sex or germ cells

Back-cross Crossing of a seedling to either parent

Bee pod A seed pod resulting from bee pollination

Bicolor An iris with standards and falls of different colors

Bitone An iris with standards and falls of different shades of the same color

Blade The flat portion of a leaf or flower segment

Blaze Radiating lines or markings on the iris falls, often in combination with the signal

Blend Having different or mixed pigments in different parts of the flower segment

190

Brackish (water) Somewhat salty water

Bract A leaf at the base of the flower or flower cluster that often embraces or enfolds it

Branch (lateral branch) A secondary flowering scape or stalk

Carotenoid Yellow pigment

Cartwheel Flat flower form with standards and falls similar in size and markings

Cauline leaf Leaf growing from lower part of the stalk or stem

Cell The smallest unit of living matter

Chimera A plant having two types of tissue, e.g. diploid and tetraploid

Chlorophyll The green pigment in plants that is required for photosynthesis and growth

Chlorosis Yellowish leaf color caused by the lack or incomplete formation of chlorophyll

Chromatin Diffuse, net-like structure of chromosomes in the resting cell

Chromosomes Rod-like structures of the cell nucleus which carry the genes

Chromosome number Number of chromosomes in the nucleus of a specific plant cell; usually constant in each plant species

Clone A plant produced by vegetative reproduction from a single plant

Colchicine A naturally occurring chemical extracted from *Colchicum autumnale* and used in hybridizing to double chromosome numbers

Controlled hybrid A hybrid resulting from planned, usually manual, pollination

Copigment An additional pigment contributing to overall color

Cultivar A variety developed in cultivation, as distinguished from a naturally occuring botanical variety or subdivision of a species

Cytology The branch of biology devoted to the study of cells and cell structures, particularly the chromosomes

Dehisce An anther or seed pod's act of opening to permit escape of pollen or seeds

Delphanin Anthocyanin pigment producing a blue color

Diploid A plant with two complete sets of chromosomes (2n)

Deoxyribonucleic acid (DNA) Complex chemical structures which carry genetic information and compose chromosomes

Dominance A genetic condition which suppresses expression of other genes

Egg (cell) The female sex cell or gamete located in the embryo sac of the ovary

Embryo The new plant within the seed formed by sexual union of the pollen and egg cell

Ensatin Anthocyanin pigment responsible for a red-purple color

Enzyme A protein which catalyzes a chemical reaction, generally within a cell

Falls (also sepals) Outer perianth parts of the iris flower

Factor A gene which determines specific inherited characteristics

F₁ (seedling) The first filial generation from a cross

Fertilization Union of male and female sex cells to form the zygote from which the embryo develops

Filament The stalk of the stamen

Flare Spreading outward, near horizontal

Form The shape of a flower. Also, a botanical variant

Gamete The male or female germ cell or sex cell in seed formation

Gene Unit of heredity or part of the DNA of the chromosome

Gene pool The sum total of the genes, dominant and recessive, of a species

Genome In diploids, one haploid set of chromosomes with the genes they contain

Genus Taxonomic rank representing all the species in a group of related plants

Germ cell A gamete or sex cell

Germination Initiation of growth of a seed or pollen grain

Glaucous A surface appearing to be covered with white powder

Haft Constricted portion of the standards or falls

Halo A rim or band of color on the edges of falls and standards

Haploid Having only one set of chromosomes. The reduced or gametic chromosome number as present in sex cells of diploids

Heredity All qualities genetically derived from ancestors

Heterozygote Form having two different alleles for a given gene

Hilum Point of attachment of the seed to the seed pod

Homologous Chromosomes from different parents which associate in pairs in meiotic cell division

Hybrid Progeny of genetically unlike parents, e.g. from two species

Hybridization Formation of seed and offspring from unlike parents

Hypothesis A proposed working explanation for accumulated facts suggesting a general principle and subject to experimental testing

Inbreeding The result of repeated self pollination, sibling crossing, or intercrossing closely related individuals

Incomplete dominance A blend of inherited features intermediate between the features of the two parents

Inhibitor In genetics, a gene which inhibits the action of another gene

Interploid A cross between a diploid and a tetraploid

Interspecies A cross between two different species of the same genus

Karyotype Generally a drawing depicting the total number, size, and form of the chromosomes

Keel A ridge or midrib of a leaf or flower segment

Locus The position on a chromosome occupied by a particular gene

Lycopene Pink pigment in bearded irises

Meiosis Cell division leading to formation of sex cells or gametes; also known as reductive cell division because of reduction of the chromosome number

Meristem Undifferentiated plant tissue from which new cells arise by mitosis

Microtubule The cellular structure responsible for moving chromosomes in mitosis

Mitosis Cell division in somatic tissue cells in which the chromosome number remains constant

Monocot Shortened form of monocotyledon

Morphology Study of the form and development of form of a flower or organism

Mutation A change in genetic or chromosomal constitution often resulting from radiation

Natural hybrid A hybrid resulting from pollination by natural forces, e.g. by insects

Nucleus The body within the cell which contains the chromosomes

Ovary The egg-cell- or ovule-bearing structure at the base of the iris flower which develops into the seed pod after fertilization

Papillae Cells protruding from the surface of a flower segment resulting in velvety texture

Pedicel The stem of a single flower

Perianth The standards and falls of the iris flower

Perianth tube The tubular connection between the ovary and the perianth segments

Petals The standards or inner perianth parts of the iris

pH A scientific measurement of acidity, 7.0 indicating neutrality, below 7 acidity, and above 7 alkalinity

Pistil The complete female reproductive parts of a flower, the ovary, style, style branch, and stigma

Plicata A bearded iris pattern of white or light-colored edging on the flower segments

Pollen Male sex cells or gametes from the anthers of the flower

Polyploid Having more than two complete sets of chromosomes

Prometaphase A stage of mitosis in which the chromosomes have replicated but not yet divided

Pubescence Downy covering of fine hairs

Recessive A genetic or inherited characteristic that is suppressed completely or nearly completely

Rhizome A horizontal underground stem

Scape The flower stalk arising from the basal leaves

Segregation The separation of the chromosomes (and genes) from different parents at meiosis

Self An iris with standards and falls of the same color. Also, pollination of a flower with its own pollen

Sepals The falls or outer perianth parts of the iris

Sexual Propagation by seed involving the union of sex cells or gametes

Sheath Base of a leaf which wraps around the scape

Sib Sibling; offspring of the same parents

Signal A marking in yellow or orange located on the falls where the beard is located in bearded irises; signals vary from very large to almost absent

Somatic cell A body cell or tissue cell in contrast to a sex cell or gamete

Spathe A bract or small leaf subtending a flower or group of flowers. Inner and outer spathes may be present

Species A kind of organism. Species are designated by binomial names consisting of the genus and specific epithet in Latin, followed in formal botanical usage by the name of the author of the published description. Species names are written in italics

Stalk A lengthened part if the plant that carries leaves or flowers, often referred to as a stem or scape

Stamen The pollen-bearing structure, the filament and anther

Standards The more erect inner perianth segments, same as petals

Stigma In iris the under surface of the style, having the form of a ridge or lip which receives the pollen

Stoma An opening or pore in the epidermis of the leaves

Style The extension of the ovary which bears the stigma

Style crest The terminal edge or projection of the style

Subspecies (also subgenus, etc.) Subdivision of a species or other classification not sufficiently distinct to be classed separately

Sympatric Growing close together in the same natural habitat

Taxon In taxonomy, a category of classification of living organisms, such as family, genus, species, cultivar, and so on

Taxonomy The naming and classification of living organisms

Testcross A cross made to verify certain genetic features such as dominance, segregation, and so on

Tetraploid A cell having four sets of chromosomes (4n)

Theory A hypothesis demonstrated to be valid

Tissue culture Inducing growth of complete organisms from fragments of living tissue in a nutrient medium

Triploid Having three sets of chromosomes (3n)

Unreduced gamete A sex cell in which chromosome sets have failed to reduce, resulting in the same number of chromosomes as tissue cells (somatic instead of gametic chromosome number)

Variation All genetic differences that occur between seedlings and parents, or between clones of a species

Variegata The name of a diploid species of bearded iris, *Iris variegata*—with yellow standards and falls and variable red or red-brown veining—which has become a term used to decribe irises having any combination of yellow and red or red-brown coloring

Variety A cultivar with a common (English) name, or a taxonomic group within a species differing sufficiently to be given a (Latin) varietal name

Venation Pattern of veins in the leaf or flower segments

Virus Submicroscopic particles able to reproduce only in host cells. Viruses cause many plant and human diseases

Wide cross Cross between species with very different characteristics and different chromosome counts

Zygote The fertilized cell resulting from the union of male and female gametes

References

These references are from magazines and books that are available in most libraries. This is not intended to be a complete list of references for Louisiana irises. It would be impossible to list all the valuable publications produced by the Society for Louisiana Irises over the past sixty years. To date, the society has printed 172 newsletters, fifteen special publications, and other material with information on the irises. Such material that is available only at limited libraries and through members of the society is not included here. Newspaper articles also are omitted. Anyone doing serious research on Louisiana irises or the Society for Louisiana Irises should contact the society for access to further sources.

Alexander, E. J. 1934. Louisiana red irises. *Flower Grower* 21: 16.

Arbuckle, M. L. 1941. Notes of iris native to North America. *Bull. Amer. Iris Soc.* 80: 49–56.

Arceneaux, G. 1941. Breeding and propagation of Louisiana iris. *Bull. Amer. Iris Soc.* 82: 61–71.

——. 1947. Breeding Louisiana irises. *Home Gardening* 7: 92–93.

Arisumi, T. 1966. Colchicine-induced tetraploid and cytochimeral daylilies. *Jour. Heredity* 5: 254–261. Reprinted in *Hemerocallis Jour.* 20: 59–67.

Arnold, M. L. 1993. *Iris nelsonii*: origin and genetic composition of a homoploid hybrid species. *Amer. J. Bot.* 80: 577–583.

Arnold, M. L., B. D. Bennett, and E. A. Zimmer. 1990. Natural hybridization between *I. fulva* and *I. hexagona*: pattern of ribosomal DNA variation. *Evolution* 44: 1512–1521.

Arnold, M. L., C. M. Buckner, and J. J. Robinson. 1991. Pollen mediated introgression and hybrid speciation in Louisiana irises. *Proc. Natl. Acad. Sci. U.S.A.* 88: 1398–1402.

Arnold, M. L., J. I. Hamrick, and B. D. Bennett. 1990. Allozyme variation in Louisiana irises: a test for introgression and hybrid speciation. *Heredity* 65: 297–306.

Arnold, M. L., J. J. Robinson, C. M. Buckner, and B. D. Bennett. 1992. Pollen dispersal and interspecific-gene flow in Louisiana irises. *Heredity* 68: 399–404.

Arny, C. W. Jr. 1959. Louisiana iris impressions. *Bull. Amer. Iris. Soc.* 152: 12–14.

———. 1960. Variations in characteristics of Louisiana iris. *Bull. Amer. Iris Soc.* 158: 37–40.

———. 1963. Irises for the Southland. *Bull. Amer. Iris Soc.* 171: 31–35.

———. 1967. Louisiana iris silver anniversary heritage. *Bull. Amer. Iris Soc.* 186: 22–28.

———. 1970. The amazing Louisiana iris. *Bull. Amer. Iris Soc.* 198: 54.

———. 1974. Progress with Louisiana irises. *Bull. Amer. Iris Soc.* 214: 7–11.

———. 1979. Fashions in Louisianas. *Bull. Amer. Iris Soc.* 235: 57–61.

Baxter, J. 1975. Beauty from the swamps. *Your Garden* (March): 10–11.

Bender, S. 1993. No better iris than Louisiana's own. *Southern Living* (April): 68–72.

Bennett, B. D., and M. L. Arnold. 1989. A preliminary report on the genetics of the Louisiana iris. *Bull. Amer. Iris Soc.* 273: 22–25.

Brown, C. A., 1943. Louisiana Irises. *Flower Grower* 30: 215.

———. 1946. What is *Iris fulva*? *Bull. Amer. Iris Soc.* 102: 17–18.

———. 1972. *Wildflowers of Louisiana and Adjoining States.* Baton Rouge: Louisiana State Univ. Press. 30–32.

Burke, J. M., T. J. Voss, and M. L. Arnold. 1998. Genetic interactions and natural selection in Louisiana iris hybrids. *Evolution* 52: 1304–1310.

Caillet, M. 1951. Places of interest in south Louisiana. *Bull. Amer. Iris Soc.* 120: 9–11.

———. 1992. Flower forms and variations in Louisiana irises. *Bull. Amer. Iris Soc.* 286: 56–63.

———. 1996. Jazzy Louisiana irises. *Fine Gardening* (July): 22–29.

———. 1996. Louisiana beauties. *Neil Sperry's Gardens* (April): 24–29.

———. 1988. Spotlight Louisiana irises. *Flower and Garden* (April-May): 48–50.

———. 1988. What's happening to Louisiana irises. *Bull. Amer. Iris Soc.* 269: 19–24.

———. 1990. The Louisiana iris—great for problem areas. *Texas Gardener* (September-October): 30–33.

———. 1993. The Louisiana iris—a native water plant. *Pondscapes* (January-February): 6–8.

———. 1995. The Society for Louisiana Irises. *Bull. Amer. Iris Soc. Anniversary Issue* (May): 117–118.

Caldwell, S. Y. 1948. Louisiana haywride. *Bull. Amer. Iris Soc.* 110: 62–67.

——. 1949. Louisiana society promotes native iris interests. *Flower Grower* 36: 669.

——. 1949. The swamplands gift to the garden. *Holland's Magazine* 68: 29–30.

Campbell, J. F. 1991. Garden culture of Louisiana irises. *Amer. Iris Soc. Reg. 17 Newsletter* (March): 18–21.

——. 1993. A basic guide to recommended cultural practice. *Bull. Amer. Iris Soc.* 289: 20–23.

——. 1993. Observations of a beginning hybridizer. *Bull. Amer. Iris Soc.* 288: 34–35.

Campbell, J. F., and C. Fritchie. 1990. *Louisiana Iris Cultivars.* rev. ed. Lafayette, Louisiana: Soc. for La. Irises.

Chowning, F. E. 1952. The role of foliosa and other species in the creation of a hardier strain of Louisiana iris. *Bull. Amer. Iris Soc.* 127: 21–24.

Colquitt, M. 1943. Some rare native iris. *Bull Amer. Iris Soc.* 91: 11–12.

——. 1946. Iris in Shreveport. *Bull. Amer. Iris Soc.* 102: 23–27.

Conger, I. 1964. Louisiana irises, a challenge. *Bull. Amer. Iris Soc.* 173: 51–53.

——. 1973. The heritage left us by Caroline Dormon lives on. *Bull. Amer. Iris Soc.* 211: 75.

Conger, S. L. 1950. Again—progress with Louisianas. *Bull. Amer. Iris Soc.* 117: 53–54.

Cook, T. 1953. *Louisiana Irises, a Bibliography.* Soc. for La. Irises Special Publication.

——. 1967. Swamp flags come of age. *Bull. Amer. Iris Soc.* 186: 19–22.

——. 1972. *Revision of Louisiana Irises, a Bibliography.* Soc. for La. Irises Special Publication.

Cooper, J. 1988. Louisiana irises in Minnesota. *Bull. Amer. Iris Soc.* 269: 48–50.

Cornay, K. 1946. The Mary Swords DeBaillon Louisiana Iris Society. *Bull. Amer. Iris Soc.* 102: 6–11.

——. 1948. Bayou babble. *Bull. Amer. Iris Soc.* 110: 73–75.

Cottman, E. V. 1932. Some wildflowers of Louisiana. *Louisiana Conservation Review* (March): 16–17.

Cruzan, M. B., and M. L. Arnold. 1993. Ecological and genetic associations in an iris hybrid zone. *Evolution* 47: 1432–1445.

——. 1994. Assortive mating and natural selection in an iris hybrid zone. *Evolution* 48: 1946–1958.

Cruzan, M. B., M. L. Arnold, S. E. Carney, and K. R. Wollenberg. 1993. cpDNA inheritance in interspecific crosses and evolutionary inference in Louisiana irises. *Amer. J. Bot.* 80: 344–350.

Davis, C. W. 1951. Louisiana iris, culture and propagation. *Home Gardening* 11: 85.

———. 1952. Cultural requirements of Louisiana native iris. *Bull. Amer. Iris Soc.* 124: 37–38.

———. 1959. *Iris Culture in the Deep South: Garden Irises.* Ed. L. E. Randolph, Amer. Iris Soc. Ithaca, New York: Cayuga Press. 63–66.

Dormon, C. 1943. The story of Louisiana irises. *Bull. Amer. Iris Soc.* 91: 3–9.

———. 1946. Species notes—Louisiana seedlings. *Bull. Amer. Iris Soc.* 103: 74–75.

———. 1947. Those fabulous Louisiana irises. In *The Iris—An Ideal Hardy Perennial.* Nashville: American Iris Society. 45–52.

———. 1948. By their fruits. *Bull. Amer. Iris Soc.* 108: 45–48.

———. 1949. Onward with Louisiana irises. *Bull. Amer. Iris Soc.* 113: 61–62.

———. 1949. Some can take it: Louisiana irises get cold test. *Bull. Amer. Iris Soc.* 113: 67–69.

———. 1951. A new race of garden irises. *Bull. Amer. Iris Soc.* 122: 62–66.

———. 1951. Plenty to see. *Bull. Amer. Iris Soc.* 121: 5–8.

———. 1958. *Flowers Native to the Deep South.* Baton Rouge, Louisiana: Claitor's Book Store. 25–28.

———. 1965. *Natives Preferred.* Baton Rouge, Louisiana: Claitor's Book Store. 175–181.

———. 1967. The discovery and collecting of Louisiana irises. *Bull. Amer. Iris Soc.* 186: 32–33.

Douglas, G. 1940. Observations on beardless iris. *Bull. Amer. Iris Soc.* 79: 27–28.

———. 1942. Beardless in Shreveport. *Bull. Amer. Iris Soc.* 84: 27–28.

———. 1944. The iris family. *Bull. Amer. Iris Soc.* 93: 16–17.

———. 1946. Cajan country. *Bull. Amer. Iris Soc.* 102: 3–5.

———. 1947. Postman's holiday—Texas and Louisiana. *Bull. Amer. Iris Soc.* 106: 45–49.

Dozier, H. L. 1950. A startling new break in Louisiana irises. *Bull. Amer. Iris Soc.* 118: 34–36.

Dunn, M. 1974. Louisianas in a California garden. *Bull. Amer. Iris Soc.* 215. 19–20.

———. 1988. Growing Louisianas. *Bull. Amer. Iris Soc.* 269: 34–36.

Dyer, P. 1995. Louisianas today. *Bull. Amer. Iris Soc.* (May, anniversary ed.): 119–122.

Dykes, W. R. 1913. *The Genus Iris.* Cambridge: Cambridge University Press. 81–85. Reprint 1974. New York: Dover Publications.

———. 1920. Iris families you ought to know. *Garden Magazine* 31: 321–324.

Foster, R. C. 1938. *Iridis Species Novae.* Cambridge, Massachusetts: Gray Herbarium.

Fritchie, C. Jr. 1982. *Louisiana Iris Cultivars.* Soc. for La. Irises Special Publication.

Ghio, J. 1973. Louisianas everywhere. *Bull. Amer. Iris Soc.* 209: 47–50.

Giridlian, J. N. 1944. The unusual iris in Southern California. *Bull. Amer. Iris Soc.* 92: 31.

Granger, M. 1995. Hybridizing for double Louisiana irises. *Bull. Amer. Iris Soc.* 298: 44–45.

Grosvenor, G. 1995. From sea to shining sea. *Bull. Amer. Iris Soc.* 298: 39–43.

———. 1997. *Iris, Flower of the Rainbow*. Kenthurst, Australia: Kangaroo Press. 140–163.

Ingram, V. L. 1988. With ruffles and flourishes. *Southern Accents* (May-June): 174–177.

Ker, J. B. (Ker-Gawler). 1812. *Iris fulva*—tawny or copper colored iris. *Curtis's Botanical Magazine* 36: 1496.

Lawton, B. P. 1998. *Magic of Irises*. Golden, Colorado: Fulcrum Publishing.

Leonard, J. 1997. At pond's edge. *Water Gardening* (August): 14–19.

Lowery, D. 1988–1989. Mississippi marvels. *Garden Design* (Winter): 56–59.

MacKenzie, A. W. A. 1941. A critique of notes on native American irises. *Bull. Amer. Iris Soc.* 82: 72–74.

MacKenzie, K. K., and B. F. Bush. 1902. New plants from Missouri—*Iris foliosa*. Academy of Science of St. Louis, *Transactions* 12: 80–81.

Mathews, L. 1950. Two distinct iris cultures for Louisiana iris. *Bull. Amer. Iris Soc.* 117: 56–58.

McEwen, C. 1966. Tetraploidy in Siberian irises. In *The Iris Year-book, 1966*. London: British Iris Society. 77–84.

———. 1968. Methods for inducing tetraploidy. *The Siberian Iris* 2: 286–290.

———. 1974. Further experiences with tetraploid Siberian irises. *Bull. Amer. Iris Soc.* 213: 52–56.

———. 1976. Methods for inducing tetraploidy in Siberian and Japanese irises. *Bull. Amer. Iris Soc.* 223: 20–23.

———. 1978. Tetraploidy and its induction. In *The World of Irises*. B. Warburton and M. Hamblen, eds. Witchita, Kansas: American Iris Society. 431–432.

———. 1996. Tetraploidy: methods and identification. In *The Siberian Iris*. Portland, Oregon: Timber Press. 171–176.

Mertzweiller, J. K. 1967. The quest for tetraploid Louisiana irises. *Bull. Amer. Iris Soc.* 186: 36–39.

———. 1968. Louisiana iris: rainbow spectacular. *The Floral Magazine* 67: 26–33.

———. 1972. Induction of tetraploidy in Louisiana irises. *Australian Iris Soc. Yearbook*.

———. 1984. Detecting and hybridizing with chimera and tetraploid Louisiana irises. *Bull. Amer. Iris Soc.* 255: 51–55.

———. 1988. Role of the Abbeville irises in development of the Louisianas. *Bull. Amer. Iris Soc.* 269: 25–30.

——. 1990. Follow-up on 'Ruth Holleyman'. *Bull. Amer. Iris Soc.* 279: 84–86.

——. 1992. Hybridizing Louisiana irises—tetraploid and interploidy hybridizing. *Bull. Amer. Iris Soc.* 284: 42–51.

——. 1995. Milestones in development of Louisiana irises. *Bull. Amer. Iris Soc.* (May, anniversary ed.): 122–124.

——. 1995. The rebirth of the blues—and the yellows and the reds. *American Nurseryman* (15 December): 47–50.

Morgan, D. L. 1993. The Louisiana iris: pretty profits in the pond. *Nursery Management Buyers Guide* (March): 40–44.

Nelson, B., and C. W. Arny Jr. 1978. Louisiana irises. In *The World of Irises*. B. Warburton and M. Hamblen, eds. Witchita, Kansas: American Iris Society. 205–216.

Nelson, I. S. 1944. A review of Louisiana irises. *The National Horticultural Magazine* (October): 183–192.

——. 1946. Abbeville giant irises. *Bull. Amer. Iris Soc.* 102: 11–16.

——. 1949. Significant variants in Louisiana irises. *Bull. Amer. Iris Soc.* 115: 71–74.

——. 1959. Louisiana iris. In *Garden Irises*. Ed. L. F. Randolph. Ithaca, New York: Cayuga Press. 226–235.

Norris, S. N., 1990. 'Ruth Holleyman'. *Bull. Amer. Iris Soc.* 277: 19–21.

Ogilvie, P. W. 1995. Louisiana iris: a literature review. In *Gardening with Iris Species: Proceedings of International Symposium*, Species Iris Group of North America. Ed. James W. Waddick. St. Louis: Missouri Botanical Garden. 81–113.

Ostheimer, R. 1995. Programmed for success. *American Nurseryman* (December): 51–54.

Peckham, E. A. S. 1932. Hunting for rarebits. *Bull. Amer. Iris Soc.* 43: 29–37.

Pope, T. E., J. F. Garofalo, and J. K. Mertzweiller. 1969. Louisiana iris. Louisiana State Univ. Extension Service Publication.

Raabe, B., ed. 1979. The world of Louisiana iris. International Committee of the Soc. for La. Irises, Sydney, Australia.

Randolph, L. F. 1934. Chromosome numbers in native and introduced species and cultivated varieties of iris. *Bull. Amer. Iris Soc.* 52: 61–66.

——. 1966. A new species of Louisiana iris of hybrid origin. *Baileya* 14: 143–169.

Randolph, L. F., ed. 1959. *Garden Irises*. Ithaca, New York: Cayuga Press.

Randolph, L. F., J. Mitra, and I. S. Nelson. 1961. Cytotaxonomic studies of Louisiana irises. *Bot. Gaz.* 123: 125–131.

Randolph, L. F., I. S. Nelson, and R. L. Plaisted. 1967. Negative evidence of introgression affecting the stability of Louisiana iris species. Cornell Agr. Exp. Station Memoir 398.

Reed, G. M. 1931. Hybrids of *Iris fulva* and *Iris foliosa*. *Brooklyn Bot. Garden Contrib.* 59: 243–253.

——. 1947. Southern United States irises—species and hybrids. *Bull. Amer. Iris Soc.* 106: 52–81.

Richard, J. G. 1950, 1966. Louisiana native iris. La. State Univ. Extension Service Publication.

Riley, H. P. 1938. Character analysis of *Iris fulva, Iris hexagona* var. *giganticaerulea* and natural hybrids. *Amer. Jour. Bot.* 25: 727–738.

——. 1939. Problems of species in the Louisiana irises. *Bull. Amer. Iris Soc.* 74: 3–7.

Robin, C. C., 1817. *Flora of the State of Louisiana*. Trans. and ed. C. S. Rafinesque. New York: C. Wiley and Co. 10.

Roland, H. C. 1988. My goals in hybridizing Louisiana Irises. *Bull. Amer. Iris Soc.* 269: 40–45.

Ryan, J. 1989. Louisiana iris—a flower for all seasons. *Neil Sperry's Gardens* (April): 8–11.

Schuster, E. 1990. Louisiana iris. *Gartenpraxis* (December): 8–12.

Segura, P. M. 1967. Mary Swords DeBaillon. *Bull. Amer. Iris Soc.* 186: 29–30.

Shepard, D. 1988. Growing Louisianas in Arizona. *Bull. Amer. Iris Soc.* 269: 31–32.

Simpson, D. 1988. Louisianas—a love story from Maryland. *Bull. Amer. Iris Soc.* 269: 52–54.

Slocum, P. D. 1996. Louisiana irises—the jewel of the pool. *Water Gardening* (July-August): 30–35.

Small, J. K. 1925. *Iris foliosa. Addisonia* 9: 53.

——. 1925. *Iris hexagona, Addisonia* 9: 51–52.

——. 1927. *Iris fulva, Addisonia* 12: 7–8.

——. 1929. *Iris giganticaerulea, Addisonia* 14: 56.

——. 1930. Harvesting iris seeds in the Gulf States. *Jour. of New York Bot. Garden* 31: 272–277.

——. 1931. *Manual of the southeastern flora*. New York: New York Bot. Garden.

——. 1931. Salvaging the native American irises. *Jour. of New York Bot. Garden* 32: 175–184.

——. 1931. Vanishing iris. *Jour. of New York Bot. Garden* 32: 277–278.

Small, J. K., and E. J. Alexander. 1931. Botanical interpretation of iridaceous plants of the Gulf Coast. *Contrib. New York Bot. Garden* 327.

Smith, B. 1988. Implications for Louisiana irises in northern Florida. *Bull. Amer. Iris Soc.* 269: 32–33.

Smith, L. J. 1991. Southern belles. *Country Home* (June): 115–118.

Starkey, M. 1982. Experimenting with irises in Florida. *Bull. Amer. Iris Soc.* 246: 49.

Sturtevant, G. 1933. The Washington hybrids. *Bull. Amer. Iris Soc.* 49: 38–40.

Traub, H. P. 1951. Colchicine induced *Hemerocallis* polyploids and their breeding behavior. *Plant Life—Herbertia*: 83–116.

Viosca, P. 1932. Irises of Louisiana. *Flower Grower* 19: 386–387.

———. 1935. The irises of southeastern Louisiana. *Bull. Amer. Iris Soc.* 57: 3–55.

———. 1946. The irises of the Abbeville, Louisiana, region. *Bull. Amer. Iris Soc.* 102: 18–23.

Warburton, B., and M. Hamblen, eds. 1978. *The World of Irises.* Witchita, Kansas: American Iris Society.

Westfall, L. 1988. Growing Louisianas in southeastern Pennsylvania. *Bull. Amer. Iris Soc.* 269: 46–48.

Wiesner, J. F. 1936. New American *Iris* species. *Garden Digest* 8: 30–31.

Wilder, Rh. 1995. Back to basics. *Bull. Amer. Iris Soc.* 299: 74–75.

Wilhoit, M. 1988. Growing Louisiana irises in the Midwest. *Bull. Amer. Iris Soc.* 269: 37–41.

Index of Plant Names

About the Contributing Editors

M arie Caillet is a charter member of the Society for Louisiana Irises and served as the secretary-treasurer for nine years and the newsletter editor for fourteen years. She was co-editor of the 1988 first edition of *The Louisiana Iris*. She has been a member of the American Iris Society for more than fifty years and received their Distinguished Service Medal. She lives and grows irises north of Dallas in Denton County, where she promotes Louisiana irises through giving tours of her garden and writing articles for gardening magazines.

J. Farron Campbell grew up in south-central Louisiana and attended the University of Louisiana, Lafayette, and Louisiana State University. He has worked for Southwestern Bell Telephone for twenty-two years. In 1986, he first attended the annual conventon of the Society for Louisiana Irises, shortly after which he began hybridizing. In 1997 he introduced his first Louisina irises. He was named co-editor of the *SLI Newsletter* in 1990 and later served on the board of directors, as vice president, and as president of SLI. He edited the society's 1989 Louisiana iris checklist and was part of the editorial staff that produced the *1995 Special Publication*. He received the Service Award from SLI in 1994. Campbell is a member of the American Iris Society, as well, serving as a director and awards chairman. Also a garden judge, he compiled the section on Louisiana irises in the *AIS Handbook for Judges and Show Officials*. He travels throughout the United States to give programs and conduct AIS-sanctioned judges' training schools. The Iris Society of Dallas and the Fort Worth Iris Society also count him among their membership.

Kevin C. Vaughn has been involved with plants since age ten, making his first crosses then and continuing unabated until today, with almost 200 varieties of plants on the market from his hybridizing. Many of these have won awards internationally. His current interests besides irises include daylilies, hostas, spiderworts, pentsemons, and hardy geraniums. He earned a Ph.D. in botany from Miami University in Ohio and is currently with the U.S. Department of Agriculture investigating herbicides and herbicide-resistant weeds. He has served as a board member, chaired the scientific committee, and is currently president of the Society for Louisiana Irises.

Dennis Vercher, a native of West Orange, Texas, studied communications at Lamar University, then briefly pursued master's studies while coaching the school's debating teams. He then turned his career to journalism, directing radio news and public information departments in southeastern Texas. Upon moving to Dallas, he became editor-in-chief of *Dallas Voice*, an award-winning weekly news and entertainment publication, a post he has held for nearly fifteen years. He joined the Society for Louisiana Irises in 1986 and was co-editor of the *SLI Newsletter* from 1990 to 1999. He was a member of the committee that produced the society's full-color *1995 Special Publication*. In 1996 he received the society's Service Award for his work on the organization's publications.